Why You Shou

MW00468531

Analyzing Documented Facts Not Speculations

* * *

The underlying premise of this book is that within official government reports there is abundant credible evidence to seriously question the accepted wisdom regarding Lee Harvey Oswald and the role of Oswald and others in the murder of President Kennedy. To underscore this assertion, whenever it is consistent with maintaining a readable flow, the text of this work consists of direct quotes from these reports.

At the end of the book is a chapter-by-chapter breakdown wherein the source(s) for the topics in that chapter reference entire sections so that reader can verify context.

Each and every fact set forth in in the following pages of this book – whether in quotes or not – is drawn directly and exclusively from the following five sources:

Report of the President's Commission of the Assassination of President John F. Kennedy, US Government Printing Office (1964) [Warren Report]

Alleged Assassination Plots Involving Foreign Leaders, Select Committee to Study Governmental Operations with respect to Intelligence Activities, United States Senate, US Government Printing Office (1975).

The Investigation of the Assassination of President John F. Kennedy, Senate Select Committee to study Governmental Operations, US Government Printing Office (1976).

Investigation of the Assassination of President John F. Kennedy, Select Committee on Assassinations of the US House of Representatives, US Government Printing Office (1979).

Final Report of the Assassination Records Review Board (1998) as mandated by the President John F. Kennedy Records Collection Act of 1992, 44 U.S.C. Section 2107 (Supp. V 1994)

*With a special chapter detailing the official
documented facts in the planning of the motorcade.*

A "Hit" Waiting to Happen

Santos Trafficante, Jimmy Hoffa, Carlos Marcello, David Ferrie,
anti-Castro Cubans & the "communist defector" Lee Harvey Oswald

The Intrigue Behind
The JFK Motorcade Murder

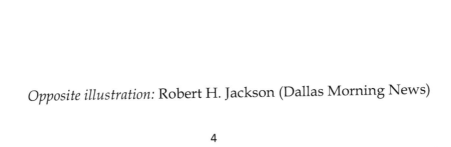
Opposite illustration: Robert H. Jackson (Dallas Morning News)

Ask Yourself...

If Oswald was the only shooter

does that mean that there was not a conspiracy?

Who was Lee Harvey Oswald?

Why did Jack Ruby shoot him?

Are these unrelated questions?

James R. Duffy
Full Court Press – New York
Copyright © James R. Duffy 2013

ISBN 1-59528-000-6

Only "Conspiracy Nuts" Question
The Warren Report?

"Doubts about the Warren Commissions' findings were not restricted to ordinary Americans. Well before 1978, President Johnson, Robert Kennedy, and four of the seven members of the Warren Commission all articulated, if sometimes off the record, some level of skepticism about the Commission's basic findings."

FINAL REPORT OF THE ASSASSINATION RECORDS REVIEW BOARD 1998, as mandated by the President John F. Kennedy Records Collection Act of 1992, 44 U.S.C. Section 2107 (Supp. V 1994)

* * *

"I'll tell you something about Kennedy's murder that will rock you ...Kennedy was trying to get Castro, but Castro got to him first."

President Lyndon B. Johnson *(from "How CIA Plot to Kill Castro Backfired" by Harry Altshuler, quoting Howard K. Smith interview of LBJ.)*

* * *

"One of your guys did it."

Robert Kennedy to **Cuban exile leader** Harry Ruiz Williams *(from "Brothers" by David Talbot p.10)*

* * *

"I'm as certain as one can be that there was no other gun shot. But it's not silliness to speculate that somebody was behind Oswald. I'd almost bet on the [anti-Castro] Cubans."

Nicholas Katzenbach, former Asst. Attorney General: *(from "Brothers" by David Talbot, p. 290)*

"If the CIA did find out what we were doing [talks toward normalizing relations with Cuba], this would have trickled down to the lower echelon of activists, and Cuban exiles, and the more gung-ho CIA people who had been involved since the Bay of Pigs ...

...I can understand why they would have reacted so violently. This was the end of their dreams of returning to Cuba, and they might have been impelled to take violent action. Such as assassinating the President."

William Attwood, former Ambassador to the UN *(from "Not in Your Lifetime", by Anthony Summers, p. 307)*

* * *

"We have not been told the truth about Oswald."

Senator Richard Russell, former <u>Warren Commissioner</u> *(from Whitewash IV, by Harold Weisberg, p. 21.)*

* * *

"Hoover lied his eyes out to the Commission on Oswald, on Ruby, on their friends, the bullets, the guns, you name it."

Hale Boggs, Majority Leader, <u>Warren Commissioner</u>

* * *

"He wished he had never been on it [the Commission] and wished he'd never signed it [the Report]."

Lindy Boggs, wife of Hale Boggs *(both Boggs quotes from Coincidence or Conspiracy?, by Bernard Fensterwald Jr. and Michael Ewing, p. 96)*

* * *

"What really happened?"

Nikita Khrushchev, Premier of the Soviet Union: Responding to the official account of the JFK assassination *(From interview with Drew Pearson, May 1964)*

"On what basis is it claimed that two shots caused all the wounds? It seemed to me that Governor Connally's statement negates such conclusion. I could not agree with this statement"

Senator John Sherman Cooper, <u>Warren Commissioner</u>
(from "The Zapruder Film" by David Wrone, p. 247)

* * *

"I told the FBI what I had heard [two shots from behind the grassy knoll fence], but they said it couldn't have happened that way and that I must have been imagining things. So I testified the way they wanted me to. I just didn't want to stir up any more pain and trouble for the family."

Ken O'Donnell, Special Assistant to President Kennedy
)from "Man of the House" by Thomas P. "Tip" O'Neill Jr., p. 178)

* * *

"After Kennedy was killed, the CIA launched a fantastic cover-up. Many of the facts about Oswald unavoidably pointed to a Cuban connection .....In a chilling parallel to their cover-up at Watergate, the CIA literally erased any connection between Kennedy's assassination and the CIA."

H.R. Haldeman, former Nixon chief of staff *(The Ends of Power, by H.R. Haldeman with Joseph DiMona, p. 39)*

* * *

"The fatal mistake the Warren Commission made was not to use its own investigators but instead to rely on the CIA and FBI personnel, which played directly into the hands of senior intelligence officials who directed the cover-up."

Senator Richard Schweiker, Church Committee member
(speaking on Face the Nation on 27 Jun 1976)

* * *

"I now no longer believe anything the Agency [CIA] told the committee any further than I can obtain substantial corroboration for it from outside the Agency for its veracity...We also now know that the Agency set up a process that could only have been designed to frustrate the ability of the committee in 1976-79 to obtain any information that might adversely affect the Agency.

G. Robert Blakey, former Chief Counsel, HSCA *from web page, Frontline episode "Who Was Lee Harvey Oswald?"*

* * *

"Perhaps there was only one assassin, but he did not act alone.....Dallas was the ideal location for such a crime."

William Walton, speaking on behalf of Robert and Jacqueline Kennedy *(from "Brothers" by David Talbot, p. 32)*

"First of all, nobody ever goes that way for a visa. Second, it costs money to go that distance. He (Oswald) stormed into the embassy, demanded the visa, and when it was refused to him, headed out saying 'I'm going to kill Kennedy for this.'.....What is your government doing to catch the other assassins? It took about three people."

Fidel Castro, Prime Minister of Cuba: *(Warren Commission Document 1359)*

* * *

**"Vous me blaguez! (*You're kidding me*)
Cowboys and Indians!"**
Charles DeGaulle, President of France Responding to the
"lone nut" theory (from "The Mother of All Cover-ups", Salon magazine, by David Talbot)

A MOST MYSTERIOUS MAN

On September 20, 1959 a man left the U.S bound for Moscow. At the height of the Cold War, he was defecting to Russia. The man was a just-discharged U.S. Marine. He had been a radar operator. His home base served the super-secret U-2 Spy Plane. In Moscow this man went to the U.S. Embassy and stated he was renouncing his American citizenship. He stated that he was an ex-Marine radar operator. He said he intended to give to the Soviets special information he possessed. The Soviets later claimed that they had no military interest in this ex-Marine radar operator from the U-2 Spy Plane base, and that they had never debriefed him.

On June 1, 1962, the man re-defected to the United States. The United States intelligence agencies claimed that they never debriefed this man when he returned from Russia, even though he had bragged that he was going to reveal to the Soviets special information learned in his role as a Marine radar operator.

The man had an IQ that placed him in the upper range of bright normal intelligence. Yet, those who later "defined" him to the American public and to the world, chose to portray him as dull-witted.

Following his return to the United States, he was to all outward appearances a vocal and dedicated follower of Fidel Castro. Yet, he never actually associated himself with any such group or individual.

Indeed, every single human contact this man had was not on the left, but on the right. Moreover, there is evidence connecting this man with organized crime leaders, with the FBI, and with anti-Castro Cubans.

On November 22, 1963, this mysterious man was arrested and charged with assassinating President Kennedy.

Within days and even before the Warren Commission had begun, the highest levels of the U.S. Government had declared him to be a loner, and an assassin who had acted without any other people being involved in any way.

There is evidence that contrary to the picture presented, he was not a loner, indeed he was engaged in numerous activities where he acted not alone but with others.

There is evidence that these "others" had the means, motive and opportunity to kill the President.

On November 24, 1963, this mysterious man was himself assassinated by Jack Ruby. Ruby later claimed he killed this man out of sorrow over the President's assassination and sympathy for the President's widow and children. It subsequently was learned that this alleged motive was a lie, having been spoon-fed to him by his lawyer. Though he was posing as "sympathetic" and "patriotic", Ruby was in fact a life-long mobster who may have had other motivations for rubbing out our mysterious man.

After Kennedy's assassination, the F.B.I. and the Warren Commission in effect took Oswald at his own word, describing him, without qualification or further meaningful investigation, as an avowed Marxist and a dedicated follower of Castro. They gave full credence to what Oswald said and did to so portray himself. They used that as the evidence for the conclusions they had already declared. In the process, they overlooked or ignored other information perhaps pointing in a different direction; information that one can find by carefully reading and analyzing material in the Warren Commission's own documents.

But who was Lee Harvey Oswald, really? Was he what he said he was? Was he what he presented himself to be? Was he what he seemed to be? One needs to answer these questions in order to determine whether the entire record, carefully analyzed and evaluated, supports the Warren Commission's portrait of Oswald.

The Warren Commission portrait of Oswald as a lone, crazed, isolated gunman effectively ended any inquiry into the possibility that others may have been involved in the killing of the President, even if those others were not the actual shooters.

Piercing the veil surrounding the true Oswald leads to the questions that demand satisfactory answers after all these years;

Was there any connection between Oswald and any of the following people; Santos Trafficante, Carlos Marcello, Jimmy Hoffa, David Ferrie, and members of the anti-Castro Cuban community?

Did Santos Trafficante, Carlos Marcello, Jimmy Hoffa, David Ferrie, and members of the anti-Castro Cuban community have a history of performing or arranging for numerous assassinations of their enemies?

Did Santos Trafficante, Carlos Marcello, Jimmy Hoffa, David Ferrie, and members of the anti-Castro Cuban community have many common interests including imperative motives to assassinate President Kennedy?

Was it known that Kennedy was an easy target by virtue of his penchant for riding in open-roofed motorcades in many cities throughout the world?

Was there any prior plan to shoot Kennedy in a motorcade in a city other than Dallas, a city not connected to Oswald, and if so, how does that square with labeling Oswald as the Lone Crazed Gunman?

Exploration of these crucial questions and much, much more are the subject of this book.

CONTENTS

PREFACE

"The enduring controversy of who Oswald really was, what he was, is an inherent part of the historical truth of this case...Oswald, as you know, is the most complex alleged or real political assassin in American history."

Philip H. Melanson, Chancellor Professor of Policy Studies at University of Massachusetts Dartmouth. *(Final Report of the Assassination Records Review Board 1998, p.84)*

As a trial lawyer who specializes in serious and complicated litigation, I have a natural interest in the analysis of complex fact patterns and the evaluation of intricate fact patterns. Most assuredly, the assassination of President John F. Kennedy has produced one of the most intricate, complex and complicated bodies of evidence in history.

In the decades since the Kennedy murder, there has been much debate in this country and indeed around the world, as to whether or not the Warren Commission Report should be accepted or rejected. On one side of this debate we find the establishment, including, for some strange reason, a rather trusting, compliant and unquestioning media, which uses its influential position to challenge the sanity and the emotional stability of anyone who points out defects in the Warren Report. On the other side are the critics, many of whom undermine their credibility by doing precisely what they criticize the Warren Commission for doing; i.e., selectively utilizing the evidence to prove their pre-determined theory.

THE BRANDING OF THE "LONE CRAZED GUNMAN"

For the most part, both sides of the above described dispute (who disagree about every thing else) have one thing in common: they seem to accept, with very little question, the Warren Commission's characterization of Lee Harvey Oswald. The Warren Commission hearings and their report are both grounded in and centered upon the characterization of Oswald as a Lone Crazed

Gunman. Even those who believe that Oswald was not the gunman have done little if anything to challenge the remaining part of the characterization, and so, for most of them, he remains a loner and a more-or-less crazy man. As a result of all this, a truly crucial aspect of the Kennedy Assassination has received little, if any, attention.

Instead of addressing that crucial issue, the debate has evolved as follows. The Warren Commission focused on "proving" their pre-ordained conclusion that Oswald was a Lone Crazed Gunman. Thereafter, many of the writers and other experts seem to have directed most of their analysis of Kennedy's murder solely to the question of Oswald's "guilt or innocence." While such inquiry is certainly not unimportant, it fails to deal with what might be an even more central issue. To put that issue in context, consider the following question:

If we assume that only Oswald shot at Kennedy,

does that mean that there was not a conspiracy?

Well, if you start off with the proposition that Oswald was a loner and a crazy man, maybe so.

On the other hand, even if he was the sole shooter, if he was not a crazed loner, what then? The proposition that Oswald was the only shooter is not necessarily the equivalent of the proposition that he acted alone. To be able to state that he acted alone would also require proving that he did it with no help, with no urging, with no encouragement, with no prodding, with no inducement, with no instructions, amongst other things.

Still other critics of the Warren Report have dealt with the question of whether someone else *in addition* to Oswald fired a weapon at the President (the Grassy Knoll controversy, for example). In great part, these inquiries address the physical evidence in Dealey Plaza, and they do little, if anything, to probe the Warren Commission's description of who and what Oswald was and had been.

If the Kennedy killing had been investigated by any decent local police department in the country, the statement that Oswald had committed the crime *acting alone* would be made not before the start but at the conclusion of a proper investigation. It would be a *finding* based upon all of the evidence, it would not be the unchallenged premise before even beginning.

However, with the Kennedy murder, from the very outset Oswald was not only identified as the murderer, he was also immediately declared and defined as a crazed loner. The so-called exhaustive investigation by the Warren Commission amounted to little more than an accumulation of evidence to support the Lone Crazed Gunman conclusion that had been declared before the Warren Commission ever even existed.

(see quoted material below in section: "Important Excerpts from Official Sources")

In trying to understand how this occurred, it is necessary to understand how the Warren Commission came about and how it operated. The Warren Commission came into existence to accomplish the goal of the person who created it, President Lyndon Baines Johnson.

It is impossible to truly understand what appears to have occurred without appreciating the important fact that President Johnson had a huge concern that perhaps overrode other considerations at the time he created the Warren Commission. Johnson, it appears, was sincerely worried that if the American public came to believe that President Kennedy had been assassinated by operatives from one of America's Cold War enemies, Russia or Cuba the United States would be inevitably drawn into a war where millions of Americans would be killed. Johnson believed that the good of the Country, the patriotic thing, demanded that the public quickly and convincingly be persuaded that there was no conspiracy in the assassination.

This view of what the good of the nation demanded was translated by President Johnson into a call to patriotism by him to members he appointed to the Commission, an example of which can be gleaned from this excerpt from a telephone conversation at 8:55PM on 11/29/63 from the President to Senator Richard Russell. Johnson, in discussing his just announced creation of the Commission to which Russell had been publicly named, states to Russell:

> "... this is a question that has a good many more ramifications than on the surface and we've got to take this out of the arena where they're testifying that Khruschchev and Castro did this and did that and check us into a war that can kill 40 million Americans in an hour..."

There is an even deeper problem that goes beyond the possibility that the members of the Commission saw their role as preventing the public from blaming our Cold War Enemies. Even if they had started with an absolutely clean slate, the outcome of the Commission's work would probably have come out the same way, since their report was necessarily dependent upon the evidence they had before them.

However, the Commission did not do their own investigation. All the investigation, and all the accumulation of the evidence upon which the Commission premised their report was done by the FBI.

As the next section demonstrates, before the Commission had done one ounce of work or evaluation, the conclusion that Lee Harvey Oswald was the Lone Crazed Gunman had been preordained by the FBI Director, J. Edgar Hoover, and other high-level administration officials, and efforts were underway to get that conclusion out to the public. To be more precise, as of the date on which the Warren Commission and its membership was being announced by President Johnson, Lee Harvey Oswald had already been declared the assassin, and had been defined and branded as a man essentially lacking sanity and with no friends: a Lone Crazed

Gunman, and the public relations maneuver known as "leaking" that information was taking place.

Thus, before the Warren Commission had even come into existence, Oswald had already been declared to have acted alone. Then, miraculously, the Warren Commission became the authority for the proposition that Oswald acted alone.

It seems at least worthy of consideration that this preemptive branding of Oswald as the Lone Crazed Gunman underlies everything the F.B.I and the Commission members did, how they did it, and the conclusions they drew.

Oswald having been officially branded as a crazed loner at the outset, this issue was really not a significant subject of the investigation, but rather it was more an unchallenged article of faith that underlay and colored every other aspect of the investigation. Indeed it was the prism through which all other evidence was viewed

It would then seem that the following question would also be at least worthy of consideration: If Oswald was not the person prematurely painted as the Lone Crazed Gunman, what validity can one give to the conclusion that Oswald *acting alone* killed the President?

IMPORTANT EXCERPTS
FROM
OFFICIAL SOURCES
(*all emphasis added*)

The material contained in this section provides a foundation for a fuller and more complete understanding of the subject matter of the book that follows

Excerpts From :

THE SENATE SELECT COMMITTEE TO STUDY GOVERNMENTAL OPERATIONS WITH RESPECT TO INTELLIGENCE ACTIVITIES

(United States Senate, April 23, 1976, Report No. 94-755)

* * *

III. THE UNITED STATES GOVERNMENT RESPONSE TO THE ASSASSINATION : **NOVEMBER 22, 1963 TO JANUARY 1, 1964**

"This section of the Report discusses the performance of the FBI and the CIA **during the weeks immediately following the assassination of President John F. Kennedy**. The performance of these agencies should not be evaluated in isolation. Senior government officials, both within the agencies and outside them, wanted the investigation completed promptly and all conspiracy rumors dispelled. For example, a mere **three days after the assassination,** Deputy Attorney General Nicholas Katzenbach wrote Presidential Assistant Bill Moyers:

'It is important that all the facts surrounding President Kennedy's assassination be made public in a way which will satisfy people in the United States and abroad that all the facts have been told and that a statement to this effect be made now.

1. **The public must be satisfied that Oswald was the assassin; that he did not have confederates who are still at large; and that the evidence was such that he would have been convicted at trial.**

2. **Speculation about Oswald's motivation ought to be cut off, and we should have some basis for rebutting thought that this was a Communist conspiracy or (as the Iron Curtain press is saying) a right-wing conspiracy to blame it on the Communists'"**

"On November 29, 1963, President Johnson told Director Hoover that, although he wanted to 'get by' on just the FBI report, the only way to stop the 'rash of investigations' was to appoint a high-level committee to evaluate that report. "

"On **December 9, 1963**, Deputy Attorney General Katzenbach wrote each member of the Warren Commission recommending that the Commission **immediately issue a press release stating that the FBI report clearly showed** there was no international conspiracy, and **that Oswald was a loner.**"

* * *

"Almost immediately after the assassination, Director Hoover, the Justice Department and the White House "exerted pressure" on senior Bureau officials to complete their investigation and issue a factual report supporting the conclusion that Oswald was the lone assassin."

* * *

"On **December 3, 1963**, the UPI wire carried a story reported in various newspapers under the following lead:

'An **exhaustive** FBI report now nearly ready for the White House will indicate that **Lee Harvey Oswald was the lone and unaided assassin of President Kennedy**, Government sources said today.'"

Excerpts from:

REPORT OF THE

SELECT COMMITTEE ON ASSASSINATIONS

(US House of Representatives)

* * *

"The Committee believes, on the basis of the evidence available to it, **that President John F. Kennedy was probably assassinated as a result of a conspiracy** . . .

"Supreme Court Justice Oliver Wendell Holmes once simply defined conspiracy as 'a partnership in criminal purposes'. That definition is adequate. Nevertheless, it may be helpful to set out a more precise definition. If two or more individuals agreed to take action to kill President Kennedy, and at least one of them took action in furtherance of the plan, and it resulted in President Kennedy's death, the President would have been assassinated as a result of a conspiracy . . .

"Even without physical evidence of conspiracy at the scene of the assassination, there would, of course, be a conspiracy if others assisted Oswald in his efforts. Accordingly, an examination of Oswald's associates is necessary . . .

"It is important to realize, too, that the term 'associate' may connote widely varying meaning to different people. A person's associate may be his next door neighbor and vacation companion, or it may be an individual he has met only once for the purpose of discussing a contract for a murder."

"I think the CIA deliberately deceived the Warren Commission, based on the evidence that I have seen. I think the answer that they have given that they didn't provide the information because nobody asked them is the kind of statement I get from criminal defendants time in and time out."

(*House Committee testimony by Judge Burt W. Griffin, formerly Assistant Counsel for the Warren Commission*)

Excerpt From:

THE REPORT OF THE PRESIDENT'S COMMISSION ON

THE ASSASSINATION OF PRESIDENT KENNEDY

(The Warren Commission)

* * *

"…to determine the motives for the assassination of President Kennedy, one must look to the assassin himself. Clues to Oswald's motives can be found in his family history, his education or lack of it, his acts, his writings, and the recollections of those who had close contacts with him throughout his life. The Commission has presented with this report all of the background information bearing on motivation which it could discover. **Thus others may study Lee Harvey Oswald's life and arrive at their own conclusions as to his possible motives.**"

INTRODUCTION

* * *

There have been many – perhaps too many – books purporting to solve the myriad of technical questions which have been raised regarding the tragic events in Dealey Plaza on November 22, 1963 (the number of shots, the angle of fire, the grassy knoll, the Zapruder film, the various wounds, the 'magic bullet', etc.), most of them having as their objective either proving or disproving that Lee Harvey Oswald was the assassin. This is *not* such a book.

There have been a number of books wherein the writers purport – on the basis of their own personal research and interviews – to reveal some new information about the assassination. Interesting, but in the end totally dependent upon accepting the credibility and impartiality of the authors, who may in fact be merely setting forth their own pet theories. This is not *that* type of book, either.

As the introductory quotes suggest, this is a book about Lee Harvey Oswald, his background and his "associates" – a word not ordinarily employed when discussing this man.

Oswald has, from the time of the assassination, been widely perceived as a somewhat one-dimensional, almost sub-human figure: non-conforming, anti-social, a malcontent, anti-American, an avowed Marxist and Communist, isolated, profoundly alienated, frustrated, resentful, hostile, presumably possessed of less than ordinary intelligence and – perhaps the most important of all – he has consistently been portrayed as a "loner." To be sure, there is evidence to suggest that he was all of these things.

Yet, scattered through various official US Government document, there are bits and pieces of information which, when brought together, constitute a substantial body of evidence that permits some rather strikingly different conclusions to be drawn about this notorious but "unknown" man.

WHO WAS LEE HARVEY OSWALD?

The Warren Commission defined Oswald's personality and attributed his motives, at least in part, to his urge to try to find a place in history, and despair at times over failures in his various undertakings. However, they were evaluating that part of Oswald's character in the pigeon-hole thinking of him as a loner, an island, with no outside human influence playing upon, or even taking advantage of his serious character defects in order to pursue their own goals.

This book, derived wholly and solely from United States Government investigations and reports, narrates all the relevant evidence about Lee Harvey Oswald, and about a vast array of individuals to whom he was connected; violent individuals who had the means, motive and opportunity to assassinate JFK.

It tells the story of a surprisingly intelligent young man, but one who bore significant personality disturbances and emotional scars emanating substantially from a whacky childhood defined predominantly by his self-involved and conflicted mother. A young man who fantasized doing patriotic things, such as becoming a United States Marine, such as emulating Herbert Philbrick, the TV hero who led an undercover life infiltrating the communist party.

It tells the arresting story of one of history's most bewildering characters, and the threads seemingly linking him to remarkably diverse groups of people: threads of a web which included intelligence agents and underworld bosses, communists and anti-communists, patriots and spies, big shots and bimbos – a web of bizarre, indeed shocking activities ranging from infiltration and subversion to assassination plots against the leaders of a number of countries. It proves once again the old adage that "Truth is stranger than fiction."

BOOK ONE

* * *

THE
FORMATIVE
YEARS

CHAPTER 1

THE FAMILY

* * *

"A vivid fantasy life turning around the topics of omnipotence and power through which he tries to compensate for his present shortcomings and frustrations."

Dr. Renatus Hartogs, Chief Psychiatrist, Youth House, NYC

Exchange Alley on the outskirts of the French Quarter was a rough area. It was the hub of some of the most notorious, openly conducted underworld joints in New Orleans. This narrow bleak street was the location of various gambling operations affiliated to the organization of Carlos Marcello, the city's crime boss. Sordid bars also operated there, including some in which aggressive homosexuals and prostitutes were frequenters.

At 126 Exchange Alley, over the pool hall which was a hangout for gamblers, was a dingy little apartment where, during 1955 and 1956, a teenager named Lee Harvey Oswald lived with his once-widowed, twice-divorced mother.

Marguerite Claverie, born in New Orleans in 1907, had first married one Edward John Pic, Jr. in August 1929. By the summer of 1931, she and Pic were separated, though she was then three months pregnant with a son who would be named John Edward Pic.

On July 20, 1933, having obtained a divorce from Pic, Marguerite married Robert Edward Lee Oswald, an insurance premium collector whom she had been seeing during her separation. Mr. Oswald's offer to adopt his wife's young son was objected to by Marguerite since that might cut off her support payments from Edward Pic.

A son born to the Oswalds on April 7, 1934 was named Robert Oswald, Jr.. On October 18, 1939, two months after her husband died suddenly of a heart attack, Marguerite gave birth to the second son of this marriage, naming him Lee after his father and Harvey which was his paternal grandmother's maiden name.

The two older boys, John Pic and Robert Oswald, were soon sent to a Catholic school in Algiers, Louisiana, where they remained for about a year. They then returned home for a while, but on January 3, 1942 their mother placed them in an orphan asylum, known as Bethlehem Children's Home. Marguerite had actually inquired about placing all three boys in the orphanage, but Lee was not accepted because at two years of age he was too young to be admitted.

Marguerite returned to work, leaving Lee for much of the next year with her sister, Mrs. Lillian Murret, and at other times with a sitter.

Then, on the day after Christmas, 1942, three-year-old Lee Harvey Oswald was sent to the orphanage.

During the year of 1943, Marguerite was dating Edwin A. Ekdahl, and by January 1944 they had decided to marry. Marguerite withdrew Lee from the orphanage and moved with him to Dallas, where Ekdahl expected to be working. John and Robert were thereafter withdrawn from the home and went to live with their mother in Dallas. Marguerite then decided she did not want to marry Ekdahl, though she continued to see him. Finally, however, she and Ekdahl were married in May 1945.

Several months before this, in February 1945, Marguerite had stated that she expected to travel a great deal, and tried to return the older boys to the home. Though she failed in that endeavor, in the fall of that year she succeeded in sending John and Robert away to a military academy where they would live until the summer of 1948.

Concurrent with sending the older boys off to the military academy, the Ekdahls moved to Benbrook, a suburb of Fort Worth, Texas. Lee was immediately entered into the first grade at the Benbrook Common School (whose records show his birth date as

July 9, 1939, an incorrect date presumably given by his mother to satisfy the age requirement).

Lee became quite attached to Ekdahl, finding in him the father he never had. But his father-son relationship was to be short-lived, for the marriage between his mother and Ekdahl soon became stormy. Marguerite separated from Ekdahl, and moved with Lee to Covington, Louisiana.

Since Lee had not completed the first grade at Benbrook, in September 1946 he was again entered into the first grade, this time at the Covington Elementary School. He was withdrawn from the Covington School on January 23, 1947 because the Ekdahls, having reconciled, were now moving to Fort Worth. He finally completed first grade in the Clayton Public School and entered second grade at that school the following September. However, relations between the Ekdahls having deteriorated again, Marguerite moved to another location in Fort Worth and Lee completed second grade at the Clark Elementary School.

The Ekdahls were finally divorced in June 1948, after a bitter trial in which the jury found that Marguerite was guilty of "excesses, cruel treatment, or outrages" unprovoked by Ekdahl's conduct. The divorce restored to Marguerite her former name, Marguerite C. Oswald.

Mrs. Oswald then purchased a small, one-bedroom house in Benbrook and moved in with her three sons. John and Robert slept on the porch, and Lee slept with his mother (a practice which continued until he was almost eleven years old). By the end of the summer, she had sold this house and moved once again into Fort Worth. Lee attended third grade at the Arlington Heights Elementary School, but the following year he was transferred to his sixth school, Ridglea West Elementary School, which he attended for the next three years.

After the divorce, Marguerite complained considerably about how unfairly she was treated, dwelling on the fact that she was a widow with three children. She overstated her financial problems, was unduly concerned about money, and Lee was brought up in an atmosphere of constant money problems.

Marguerite worked in miscellaneous jobs after her divorce from Ekdahl. When she worked during the school year, Lee not only left an empty house in the morning, but then returned to it at lunch and then again at night, his mother having trained him to do that rather than play with the other children. Lee seemed to enjoy being by himself and to resent discipline.

In 1950, John entered the Coast Guard, and in July 1952 Robert joined the Marines. In August 1952, Marguerite and Lee moved to New York City. They lived for a time with John (who was stationed there) and his wife and baby. Marguerite did not get along with John's wife, with whom she quarreled frequently. In late September, Marguerite and Lee moved to their own apartment.

Lee's truancy soon became a severe problem, and after several unsuccessful attempts were made to resolve the situation, on March 12, 1953 the attendance officer filed a petition in court which ultimately resulted in Lee being remanded to Youth House from April 16 to May 7 for psychiatric study.

The Chief Psychiatrist at Youth House, Dr. Renatus Hartogs, found Oswald to be "a tense, withdrawn and evasive boy who intensely disliked talking about himself and his feelings." He noted that Lee liked to give the impression that he did not care for other people but preferred to keep to himself so that he was not bothered and did not have to make the effort of communicating. Oswald's withdrawn tendencies and solitary habits were thought to be the result of "intense anxiety, shyness, feelings of awkwardness and insecurity." He was reported to have said, "I don't want a friend and I don't like to talk to people," and "I dislike everybody." He was also described as having a "vivid fantasy life turning around the topics of omnipotence and power through which he tries to compensate for his present shortcomings and frustrations."

Dr. Hartogs summarized his report on Lee by stating: "This 13-year-old well built boy has superior mental resources and functions only slightly below his capacity level in spite of chronic truancy from school which brought him into Youth House. No finding of neurological impairment or psychotic mental changes could be made. Lee has to be diagnosed as 'personality pattern disturbance with schizoid features and passive-aggressive tendencies'. Lee has to be seen as an emotionally, quite disturbed youngster who suffers under the impact of really existing emotional isolation and deprivation, lack of affection, absences of family life and rejection by a self-involved and conflicted mother."

Mrs. Evelyn Strickman Siegel, a social worker who interviewed both Lee and his mother while Lee was confined in Youth house, described him as a "seriously detached, withdrawn youngster." She also noted that there was 'a rather pleasant, appealing quality about this emotionally starved, affectionless youngster which grows as one speaks to him." She thought that he had detached himself from the world around him because "no one in it ever met any of his needs for love." She observed that since Lee's mother worked all day he made his own meals and spent all his time alone because he didn't make friends with the boys in the neighborhood. She thought that he "withdrew into a completely solitary and detached existence where he did as he wanted and he didn't have to live by any rules or come into contact with people." Mrs. Siegel concluded that "Lee just felt that his mother never gave a damn for him. He always felt like a burden that she simply had to tolerate." Lee confirmed some of those observations by saying that he felt almost as if there were a veil between him and other people through which they could not reach him but that he preferred the veil to remain intact. He admitted to fantasies about being powerful and sometimes hurting and killing people but refused to elaborate on them. He took the position that such matters were his own business.

Irving Sokolow, a Youth House psychologist, reported that: "The Human Figure Drawings are empty, poor characterizations of persons approximately the same age as the subject. They reflect a considerable amount of impoverishment in the social and emotional areas. He appears to be a somewhat insecure youngster exhibiting much inclination for warm and satisfying relationships to others. There is some indication that he may relate to men more easily than to women in the view of the more mature conceptualization. He appears slightly withdrawn and in view of the lack of detail within the drawings that may assume a more significant characteristic. He exhibits some difficulty in relationship to the maternal figure suggesting more anxiety in this area than in any other."

Lee scored an IQ of 118 on the Wechsler Intelligence Scale for Children. According to Sokolow, this indicated a "present intellectual functioning in the upper range of bright normal intelligence." Sokolow said that although Lee was "presumably disinterested in school subjects he operates on a much higher than average level." On the Monroe Silent Reading Test, Lee's score indicated no retardation in the reading speed or comprehension; he had better than average ability in arithmetical reasoning for his age group.

Lee's probation officer, John Carro, later testified that, "There was nothing that would lead me to believe when I saw him at the age of 12 that there would be seeds of destruction for somebody. I couldn't in all honesty sincerely say such a thing."

Mrs. Siegel concluded her report with the statement that, "Despite his withdrawal he gives the impression that he is not so difficult to reach as he appears and patient prolonged effort in a sustained relationship with one therapist might bring results. There are indications that he has suffered serious personality damage but if he can receive help quickly this might be repaired to some extent."

Dr. Hartogs recommended that Lee be placed on probation with a requirement that he be provided help and guidance during the probation. However, such help and guidance was never provided, the basic problem being that the few facilities which provided the necessary services already had full case-loads.

On 24 September, the day the probation had originally been scheduled to end, Mrs. Oswald phoned the probation officer and said that she could not appear in court, adding that there was no need to do so, as Lee was attending school regularly and was now well adjusted. The probation was extended until October 29, before which date the school was to submit a progress report. Mrs. Oswald's assurances to the contrary notwithstanding, the report, when it was submitted, was a highly unfavorable one.

On October 29, Mrs. Oswald again telephoned to say she would be unable to appear. The probation was continued until November 19, on which date Lee and his mother appeared. But, despite Mrs. Oswald's request that Lee be discharged, Justice Sicher stated his belief that Lee needed treatment, and he continued his probation until January 29, 1954. The probation officer was directed to contact the Big Brothers counseling service in the meantime. On January 4 a caseworker from Big Brothers visited the Oswald home, where he was cordially received, but was told by Mrs. Oswald that further counseling was unnecessary.

Mrs. Oswald informed the Big Brother caseworker that she intended to return to New Orleans. The caseworker advised her that she must obtain Lee's release from the court's jurisdiction before she left. The next day she called the probation officer. In his absence (he was away on vacation) his office advised Mrs. Oswald not to take Lee out of the jurisdiction without the court's consent. The same advice was repeated to her by the Big Brother caseworker on January 6. Without further communication to the court (and without him ever getting any of the help or treatment deemed necessary for him) Mrs. Oswald took Lee to New Orleans sometime before January 10.

CHAPTER 2

ANOTHER KIND OF "FAMILY"

* * *

"The DA's office was then under the corrupt influence of the gambling syndicate - Carlos Marcello and various others - to a very significant degree."

Aaron Kohn, Chairman, Metropolitan Crime Commission of New Orleans

Back in New Orleans, Lee and his mother stayed with her sister and brother-in-law, Mr. and Mrs. Charles Murret, until they got an apartment of their own. Lee had developed a close relationship with the Murrets during his numerous stays with them over the years. Now that he was back in New Orleans, he visited with them regularly, eating dinner with them on Friday evenings and spending his Saturdays there. His uncle, Charles Murret, was a father figure of sorts. The Murrets served as the closest thing to a real family he had been exposed to up to that point. This special relationship would continue throughout Oswald's life.

Years earlier, Charles Murret (commonly called 'Dutz') who had been involved in promoting several prize-fighters in New Orleans, had served as the manager of a boxer named Tony Sciambra. After his boxing days, Sciambra had gone on to become a lieutenant to a local organized crime leader named Sam Saia.

"Dutz" Murret later became involved with Saia in an underworld gambling syndicate affiliated to the Carlos Marcello crime family. Saia, who had made his money by dope peddling in the early years, was one of the largest bookmakers in New Orleans, and the financial backer of numerous underworld clubs throughout the New Orleans area. Saia was known to be "very close" to Carlos Marcello, and it was through the gambling wire service controlled by Marcello that Saia and his associates such as "Dutz" Murret conducted their betting operations.

Prior to her first marriage, Lee's mother had been working as a secretary for a New Orleans lawyer named Raoul Sere. They became friendly enough that when that marriage failed, Sere re-hired her and helped her pay some debts she had acquired for furniture and other items. This friendship continued into at least 1960, when Sere took her out to dinner on at least one occasion. In the interim Sere, who was politically active as an attorney, had for a period of time become an assistant district attorney for the city of New Orleans.

Aaron Kohn, chairman of the Metropolitan Crime Commission of New Orleans, has testified that "Sere played a key role in running the DA's office during the period in which that office was later proven to be highly corrupt" and, "The DA's office was then under the corrupt influence of the gambling syndicate – Carlos Marcello and various others – to a very significant degree."

Marguerite had been friends from childhood with another New Orleans attorney, Clem Sehrt, whose law partner counted Carlos Marcello among his clients. Sehrt, a former state banking official, had risen to prominence in Louisiana through his close relationship with Louis J. Rousell, a New Orleans banking executive who was an old and close associate of Carlos Marcello. During the 1950's, when Sehrt's relationship to him was the closest, Rousell had become involved in a political scandal concerning reported cash pay-offs to two Louisiana Supreme Court justices from an unreported corporate payroll of Rousell plus the provision of a new Cadillac each year to the Chief Judge of the Louisiana Supreme Court.

Another of Marguerite's friends (as well as of "Dutz" Murret and Sam Saia) was Sam Termine, who, according to the New Orleans Metropolitan Crime Commission, was a Louisiana crime figure involved in a number of illicit operations including syndicate gambling and prostitution, as well as in the operation of a motel used for underworld activities. Termine was particularly close to Carlos Marcello, whom he had once served as a chauffeur and bodyguard. - Of the ubiquitous Carlos Marcello, more later.

CHAPTER 3

SVENGALI

* * *

"Ferrie's tremendous influence and close association with these young men eventually became a controversial subject with many parents."

John Espenan, father of CAP cadet

Upon returning to New Orleans, Lee had been enrolled in the eighth grade at Beauregard Junior High School on January 12, 1954, and he continued there in the ninth grade that September. In September 1955 he entered the tenth grade at Warren Eastern High School.

Meanwhile, in the early summer of 1955, Lee Harvey Oswald had begun attending meeting of the Civil Air Patrol, a student aviation organization which met twice a week. The first unit he was involved with was located at the Lakefront Airport. The commander of that group, who also participated in the training of the recruits, was a man named David Ferrie. There was another CAP unit over at Moisant Airport, and by late summer both Lee Oswald and David Ferrie had become attached to that unit. For at least the next few months Lee Harvey Oswald had continued involvement at the Moisant Airport unit of the CAP with David Ferrie. The House Select Committee provides an extensive discussion on David Ferrie who was born in Cleveland, Ohio in 1918.

"Although there are no indications that his childhood was anything but normal, numerous acquaintances and associates of Ferrie reveal that he grew to be a complex, even bizarre individual One aptly stated, 'Not inappropriately, he (Ferrie) was described as a paradox.

"His unusual personal appearance was partially a result of the loss of his body hair induced by a rare disease. He wore a makeshift toupee and exaggerated fake eyebrows affixed crudely with glue as compensation. Persons who knew him considered him sloppy and unkempt, with a proclivity for foul language. Ferrie was often described as 'very aggressive' and 'obnoxious.' He resented authority, was opinionated, and often difficult to get along with. Yet he was able to exert tremendous influence over his close associates, including many young men in his Civil Air Patrol squadron.

"Several of Ferrie's associates indicate he was a homosexual and a misogynist. His sexual exploitation of younger men would eventually cause him numerous problems.

"Although his formal education was not extensive, Ferrie was considered highly intelligent, even brilliant. He had originally studied theology in the hope of becoming an ordained priest, but he left seminary school before graduation because of 'emotional instability.' Later, in 1941, he received a Bachelor of Arts degree from Baldwin-Wallace College, majoring in philosophy. He also received, through a correspondence course, a doctorate degree in psychology from an unaccredited school, Phoenix University, Bari, Italy...

"Ferrie spent considerable time studying medicine and psychology, especially the techniques of hypnosis which he frequently practiced on his young associates.

"He was rabidly anti-Communist... frequently critical of each Presidential administration for what he perceived to be sell-outs to communism.

"...... he often gave parties at his residence where liquor flowed freely; and he offered his home as a place for the boys to stay when they were unhappy at home. He urged several boys to join the armed forces, to begin their careers in aviation, or to join seminaries. Many of Ferrie's cadets became involved in Ferrie's wide spectrum of other activities. Ferrie's tremendous influence and close association with these young men eventually became a controversial subject with many parents."

The eccentric David Ferrie will reappear later in our story.

Meanwhile, in October 1955, Lee Harvey Oswald, who had just turned sixteen, dropped out of school and tried to enlist in the Marines, using a false affidavit from his mother stating that he was seventeen. Lee was by all accounts particularly susceptible to the thought of entering the service. His older brothers had both done so, perhaps as a way of escaping from their mother, and Lee himself had seen the service as a way to be on his own, according to Evelyn Strickman, the social worker who had seen him in New York.

The attempted enlistment failed, and according to his mother, Lee spent the next year reading and memorizing the Marine Manual, which he had obtained from Robert, and "living to when he is age 17 to join the Marines."

Anticipating that Lee would join the Marines as soon as he was seventeen, Mrs. Oswald moved in July 1956 to Fort Worth, where Lee was enrolled in the tenth grade at the Arlington Heights High School. Lee became seventeen on October 18 and enlisted in the Marines on October 24, 1956.

CHAPTER 4

THE CHAMELEON

* * *

"His study of Communist literature, which might appear to be inconsistent with his desire to join the Marines, could have been another manifestation of Oswald's rejection of his environment."

Warren Commission

The period of time, beginning in mid-1955, when he first came into contact with David Ferrie, until October, 1956 when he entered the Marines, marks the emergence of the first in a long series of what appear to be striking inconsistencies in the conduct of Lee Harvey Oswald. Careful evaluation of these seemingly incongruous actions is essential if we can ever hope to discern who or what that chameleonic figure really was like.

At some point during this period, Lee had begun – and had openly flaunted – the reading of Communist literature, surely a curious choice of reading material for one so intent on joining the United States Marine Corps.

The Warren Commission speculated that "his study of Communist literature, which might appear to be inconsistent with his desire to join the Marines, could have been another manifestation of Oswald's rejection of his environment." Perhaps so.

But that theory did not take into account that this was an even more curious, more inconsistent activity for someone who might have been involved with such a fanatical anti-Communist as David Ferrie. It is indisputable that it did not take this into account because the Warren Commission was not even aware of the "Ferrie connection," which only came to light many years later.

To be more precise, as the following material from the House Committee suggests, the FBI investigation and the Warren

Commission questioning on this issue was just plain incompetent. Either that, or, starting with the conclusion that Oswald was the Lone Crazed Gunman, they went out of their way to not pursue a possible Oswald connection to any other human being, including Ferrie.

The House Committee informs us that when questioned by the FBI in 1963, Ferrie denied ever knowing Lee Harvey Oswald, and the House Committee commented that, "The brief FBI and Secret Service investigations of Ferrie had not focused to any significant degree on Ferrie's background and working associations ...."

First, some background. As the House Committee material (discussed in subsequent chapters) discloses, David Ferrie became a person of interest after the Kennedy Assassination because of his personal associations and working relationships with Cuban exiles, purported links to the CIA, as well as his employment during 1963 with G. Wray Gill, the attorney for Carlos Marcello. Indeed, Ferrie's investigative work for Marcello had brought him into close personal association with the organized crime leader.

Thus, there was a clear requirement for a thorough investigation when information surfaced as to a possible relationship between Ferrie and Oswald, including any that might have existed since Oswald's teen years when he was for a brief period of time a member of the Civil Air Patrol ("CAP"). The material from the House Committee makes clear that there was no real investigation of this issue at all.

The House Committee informs us: "The committee undertook an extensive examination of Lee Harvey Oswald's involvement in the Civil Air Patrol and sought to determine whether Oswald did in fact have any contact with Ferrie during that period. The committee believed that the possibility that Oswald and Ferrie may have been in contact during that period presented significant questions that needed to be resolved. A number of areas of information regarding possible associations between Oswald and Ferrie in 1963 had been developed by the committee, information that the committee believed to be of important evidentiary value.

"Edward Voebel was a former classmate of Oswald's who had attended the CAP meetings with Oswald. Voebel, whom the Warren Commission had established was Oswald's closest friend during his teenage years in New Orleans, had attended Beauregard High School with Oswald and had actually been the friend who first accompanied Oswald to the CAP meetings. The Warren Commission itself used Voebel's Commission testimony as a primary source of information on Oswald's adolescent years. Speaking of Voebel, Mrs. Marguerite Oswald told the Warren Commission, 'This young man and Lee were very friendly * * he and Lee joined the Civil Air Patrol together * *. And he often came to the house.' Oswald's cousin, Marilyn Murret, further told the Commission that Voebel was 'the only one' of Oswald's classmates whom he was close to and that Voebel 'got him to join the Civil Air Patrol, in which he was very interested.'

"On November 25, 1963 .... Voebel was interviewed by the FBI. He stated that he had become a close friend of Oswald during the period 1954-55, and that they used to play pool together after school at a poolroom next to Oswald's home in Exchange Alley. Oswald seemed to be a typical teenage boy during the period of their friendship. Voebel said that reports that Oswald was already 'studying Communism' were a 'lot of baloney' - Oswald commonly read 'paperback trash.' During this first interview with FBI agents, Voebel spoke of his involvement in the CAP with Oswald. Voebel stated that he and Oswald were members of the Civil Air Patrol in New Orleans with Capt. Dave Ferrie during the time they were in school .

"Voebel at this time seemed to indicate clearly that there had probably been contact between Ferrie and Oswald in the CAP. He became uncertain about such contact during the course of a second interview with FBI agents later that same day, November 25, 1963. Then he stated that he had persuaded Oswald to attend the meetings of his CAP unit at Moisant Airport in 1955. Oswald had 'attended two or three drills and possibly four drills at the most.' Voebel further stated that it was difficult to recall how often Oswald was at the CAP meetings because 'Oswald had a knack for being there and not being noticed.' The CAP unit met once or twice a week and included 20 to 25 members, some of whom were girls.

"According to the FBI report of this second interview Voebel stated that he could not recall if Capt. Dave Ferrie was commander of the unit at the time Oswald attended meetings or whether Oswald attended meetings prior to Captain Ferrie taking command. Voebel stated that Ferrie was commander of his CAP unit during part of 1955, but that he could not recall precisely when or if it was during the same period that Oswald attended the meetings.

"Voebel recalled that Captain Ferrie was 'very intelligent,' reportedly held several degrees, and was then a pilot for Eastern Airlines. He said that Oswald quit attending the Moisant Airport CAP meetings sometime after being enrolled as a member because another CAP unit (at New Orleans Lakefront Airport) would be closer to home. Voebel further told the FBI that Ferrie had once taken his CAP unit on an overnight 'bivouac' in which Ferric had instructed the cadets to bring along rifles for shooting practice. Voebel did not believe Oswald had participated in this outing.

"The FBI report noted that Voebel received 'a crank-type telephone call' during the course of the interview, and had mentioned that he 'had also been frightened' by a person who came to his home earlier claiming to be a news reporter. This man disturbed him and had 'acted very suspicious.' An FBI teletype from the New Orleans office to Director J. Edgar Hoover on November 26, 1963, summarized that 'Voebel was unable to recall if Oswald attended meetings under command of Ferrie or with previous commander.'

"On November 27, 1963, 5 days after President Kennedy's murder, Voebel was also interviewed by New Orleans Police

Department officers. In a report of this interview, prepared for Maj. P. J. Trosclair, Jr., of the department, it was noted that Voebel believed Oswald had attended the Moisant CAP meetings for 'only about 1 month.' During the course of this police interview, however, Voebel also stated that while he could not be sure, he thought that Oswald may once have attended a party given by Ferrie during their involvement with the CAP. According to the report: 'Voebel stated that he believed Oswald attended a party (not sure) at the home of David Ferrie (captain) right after the members of the CAP received their stripes. Voebel did not elaborate on this event.

"Two days later, on November 29, 1963, in an internal FBI memorandum from Assistant Director Alex Rosen to Associate Director Alan Belmont, Voebel's account of his CAP involvement was again summarized: 'Edward Voebel, on interview, said he had been a member of the CAP, New Orleans, for approximately 1 year, 1955-56. David William Ferrie took over as commander of the CAP unit during this time. Voebel took Oswald to one of the meetings and stated Oswald attended several meetings, possibly four meetings at the most.

On April 7, 1964, the testimony of Edward Voebel was taken by Warren Commission senior counsel Albert Jenner in New Orleans. While the Warren Commission had not actively investigated the possibility of an association between Oswald and Ferrie, Ferrie's name came up briefly when Voebel was questioned about Oswald's activities with the CAP. Voebel recalled that he had first become a friend of Oswald's when he witnessed him being beaten up one day after high school. Two brothers who had earlier gotten into a fistfight with Oswald had sent a friend of theirs to beat him up. Voebel noted that their school 'seemed to draw a lot of bad characters' and that 'it was almost impossible to go to school without brushing against somebody or getting involved in a fight.' In his testimony, Voebel stated that Oswald had attended 'two or three meetings' of the CAP and 'bought a uniform and everything, and * * * seemed to be very interested at the outset.' Toward the end of his testimony, Voebel was asked if he could recall who had headed their CAP unit at that time:

Mr. JENNER. Who was the majordomo of the CAP unit that you attended?

Mr. VOEBEL. I think it was Captain Ferrie. I think he was there when Lee attended one of these meetings, but I'm not sure of that. Now that I think of it, I don't think Captain Ferrie was there at that time, but he might have been. That isn't too clear to me."

Let us pause a moment to consider what the Warren Commission knew or did not know about a possible David Ferrie connection to Lee Harvey Oswald, and any actions or conclusions such knowledge or lack of knowledge played in their findings.

Let us take as a given that Edward Voebel did not positively establish that Ferrie knew or had any relationship with Oswald.

But, would you say that Voegel clearly and affirmatively established that there was no possibility of any connection between Oswald and Ferrie? Or would your view be, maybe yes, maybe no?

Let's now add some additional considerations. We know that Ferrie told the FBI that Oswald never attended CAP meetings while Ferrie was in attendance. You are conducting a murder investigation - here's a guy that is a person of interest for a number of reasons including relationships with organized crime individuals – do you take his denial without checking it out? What was done to verify that allegation?

The House Committee states: "Interestingly, when Ferrie was interviewed by FBI agents on November 25, 1963, in the aftermath of President Kennedy's murder, he recommended [Jerry] Paradis as a CAP member who would be able to verify whether Oswald had ever been involved in the CAP unit headed by Ferrie. Ferrie told the FBI agents that he had never known Oswald and that other witnesses could confirm that Oswald had never attended CAP meetings during the period that Ferrie was active with the group. According to the report of his FBI interview, Ferrie stated that 'during the period he was commander of the squadron, Jerry C. Paradis was the recruit instructor and took all the squadron recruits through their training.' Ferrie supplied the Bureau with the home and business addresses of Paradis, so as to aid the agents in interviewing him."

Is this any different from a murder investigation where a suspect says, I was home in bed, my wife can attest to that? Would any responsible investigator close that case without speaking to the wife?"

Below is the House Committee's report on the questioning they did on this issue. As we shall see, amongst the witnesses interviewed by the House Committee is Jerry Paradis. The Warren Commission had the name and address of Jerry Paradis -given to them by David Ferrie. Unaccountably, the Warren Commission never contacted Paradis.

The House Committee provided the following information regarding a number of witnesses: "The committee sought to locate Edward Voebel to take his testimony, but learned from his father, Sidney Voebel of New Orleans, that his son had died in 1971. Sidney Voebel could not recall what his son had told him regarding his past contacts with Oswald and Ferrie.

"The committee found that the incomplete and disorderly state of the registration and membership records of the New Orleans Civil Air Patrol did not permit a clear determination of Oswald and Ferrie's respective periods of involvement with the organization. In an interview with the FBI on November 25,1963, Alvin Meister, a commander of the New Orleans CAP, stated that the CAP cadet files were kept for only 1 year after a cadet terminated his service. In an FBI interview that same day, a former executive officer of the CAP noted another difficulty in trying to reconstruct the membership records from the period of time in which Oswald had been involved.

"Harold Toole, then of the St. Bernard Parish Sheriff's Office, informed the FBI that 'most of the records of the squadron were stolen in late 1960.'

"In an FBI interview on November 27, 1963, another CAP executive was able to supply partial information regarding Oswald's involvement. Joseph Ehrlicker told FBI agents that while he was unable to find a CAP application by Oswald, he was able to locate a record indicating that 'Oswald was enrolled as a CAP cadet on July 27, 1955, at which time he was given Serial No. 084965.' Oswald was then enrolled in the cadet squadron at Moisant Airport. The records did not indicate when Oswald left the CAP unit.

"Also with regard to David Ferrie, Ehrlicker was able to determine that Ferrie's first period as Squadron Commander was terminated December 31, 1954. He was working at Moisant Airport at this time. It was later found out that Ferrie subsequent to this date was working with the squadron at Moisant without official connection with the CAP. As of late 1955 he was no longer with the squadron. As can be seen from the fragmented CAP membership documentation provided by Ehrlicker, Ferrie was involved with the Moisant CAP unit (in an apparently unofficial capacity) for an uncertain period of time between December 31, 1954, and 'late 1955.'

"The same CAP documentation indicated that Oswald had been involved in the same CAP unit in the summer of 1955, having officially enrolled on July 27, 1955. Thus, while the CAP documentation available in 1963 did not permit a conclusive determination, the records themselves lent substantial credence to the possibility that Oswald and Ferrie had been involved in the same CAP unit during the same period of time.

"While Ferrie stated during his November 25, 1963, FBI interview, that he had been a commander of the Lakefront Airport CAP unit, it was not until December 10, 1963, when he provided another statement to the Bureau, that he said he had also worked with the Moisant Airport CAP.

"During the course of its investigation of Oswald's involvement with the CAP and his possible contact with Ferrie, the committee interviewed [Fred] O'Sullivan, a former high school classmate and friend of Oswald who had also been involved with Oswald and Voebel in the CAP. Fred O'Sullivan had originally suggested to Oswald and Voebel that they might enjoy attending CAP meetings and asked them to participate in his squadron. O'Sullivan's past involvement with Oswald in the CAP unit first came to the attention of the FBI on November 25, 1963, when New Orleans Assistant District Attorney Herman Kohlman informed FBI Agent Regis Kennedy that 'An unknown police officer had told the Intelligence Division of the New Orleans Police Department that he was in the Civil Air Patrol with Lee Harvey Oswald and that Ferrie knew Oswald.' Later that day, the FBI was able to identify Fred O'Sullivan of the New Orleans Police Department Vice Squad as the classmate. In an interview with Bureau agents that day, O'Sullivan stated that he had persuaded his classmates, Lee Oswald and Ed Voebel, to attend his CAP squadron meetings at the New Orleans Lakefront Airport. Oswald and Voebel had come 'to one or two meetings, but did not join.' O'Sullivan stated that Oswald thought the Lakefront CAP location was too far away and decided to attend the Moisant Airport CAP squadron instead. O'Sullivan told the FBI that Ferrie 'was Squadron Commander' at the 'approximate time' that Oswald came to the Lakefront CAP meetings. He added, however, that he "could not say for certain that Oswald ever met Ferrie" at the time. He further stated that Ferrie himself also subsequently began working with the other CAP unit at Moisant Airport.

"In a second FBI interview, on November 26, 1963, O'Sullivan further advised that Ferrie might have had contact with Oswald at the Moisant Airport CAP. According to the FBI report of this interview, 'Ferrie * * * transferred and assumed command of the CAP at Moisant Airport at about the same time O'Sullivan thought Oswald might have joined.' O'Sullivan further informed the Bureau that he had only recently learned of Ferrie's homosexual background. He also noted that Ferrie 'had acquired a reputation for being able to hypnotize people,' and that he had once hypnotized a man following one of the CAP meetings.

"In an interview with the committee on October 17, 1978, O'Sullivan repeated the account of his contacts with Oswald and Ferrie that he had provided the FBI in 1963. Now a security director for Hilton Hotels, he stated that he could not say with certainty that he ever saw Oswald and Ferrie together, although he believed they probably did in fact attend the CAP meetings during the same period. In an interview on December 15, 1978, O'Sullivan again told the committee that while 'Ferrie ran the unit then, and Oswald came a couple, or a few times,' he could not recall any more specific information about the matter."

On December 9, 1978, Collin Hamer, an official of the New Orleans Public Library, testified before the House Committee as follows:

".... he had attended "about ten or twelve meetings" of the CAP unit during which Oswald was also present. Hamer knew both Oswald and Voebel and said that Oswald had begun attending the CAP meetings sometime around the summer of 1955. He stated that the 10 or 12 meetings that Oswald attended were held at the Eastern Airlines hangar at Moisant Airport. He further stated that Oswald had attended the meetings for roughly 2 months, during which the unit usually met twice a week, on Friday nights and Sunday afternoons. Hamer commented that he had never been interviewed by the FBI following the assassination of President Kennedy. According to Hamer, David Ferrie had been present during the CAP meetings that Oswald attended: 'Ferrie was at all the meetings during the time Lee and I were involved in CAP. He didn't always do the teaching, but he was always there.' Hamer told the committee that Oswald 'was a real quiet kid' and that Ferrie 'treated Oswald just like the rest of us. He was just the teacher so to speak.' Hamer further stated, 'I don't know anything about whether or not Ferrie and Oswald had any contact outside of the CAP. All I know is that Oswald was in our unit for about 2 months, and Ferrie ran it during that time.' Hamer further recalled that Ferrie was 'a tough commander' who became irritated if the cadets 'goofed around at all.' Hamer also recalled calling Oswald's home on one occasion to make sure that Oswald was going to attend a CAP meeting. Hamer did not know why Oswald left the CAP unit. Hamer also told the committee that he was aware that some CAP cadets had 'hung around' at Ferrie's house and engaged in outside activities with him. He did not know if Oswald ever had such contact with Ferrie

"The committee also interviewed a former commander of the Moisant Airport CAP squadron, Mrs. Gladys Durr. Mrs. Durr had been interviewed by the FBI on November 25, 1963. In that interview, she advised that she had assumed command of the CAP unit in October or December 1955, which would have been several months after the CAP records indicated Oswald left. Mrs. Durr stated that she did not recall knowing Lee Oswald, but that David Ferrie had been 'expelled' from the CAP squadron 'at about the time' she joined it. While Mrs. Durr became commander of the squadron subsequent to the time when Oswald was a member, her recollection that Ferrie was still active in the unit until late 1955 would indicate that he probably was in fact with the unit during the period that Lee Oswald was in it. The available records indicate that Oswald was enrolled as a cadet on July 27, 1955, and his CAP colleagues generally recalled him being active in the unit for a couple of months. Thus, with Ferrie's lengthy involvement in the CAP ending (temporarily) in late 1955, according to Commander Durr, the likelihood of Ferrie's service with the CAP unit during Oswald's membership in the summer of 1955 seems logical.

"In her committee interview, Mrs. Durr stated that while she did not know Oswald, she could recall other cadets remembering that he attended the meetings. She further recalled that Ferrie had originally conducted CAP classes at New Orleans Lakefront Airport, but had then begun teaching at Moisant Airport where she was commander. She said Ferrie was a magnetic and intelligent man who had a strong following among the cadets. He also had a reputation for having bad moral character, and on one occasion some CAP cadets had become drunk at his home and engaged in various activities in the nude. Mrs. Durr stated that such incidents were what led to Ferrie being expelled from that particular CAP unit.

"The committee interviewed another former commander of the New Orleans CAP, John Irion, active with the group from 1955 to 1959. Irion, a management and public relations consultant, worked closely with Ferrie during their years with the CAP. The two were personal friends for over 10 years, and Irion once testified on Ferrie's behalf during a legal proceeding against him. Irion, Ferrie, and the mayor of New Orleans were once photographed together, a CAP photograph later published by the New Orleans Times Picayune. Irion recalled that Ferrie was a 'dynamic' leader known for his intelligence. He recalled being introduced by Ferrie to Carlos Marcello's attorney, G. Wray Gill, on more than one occasion. Irion told the committee that he recalled Lee Oswald going through 'basic training' with the CAP during the period in which he and Ferrie were with the New Orleans squadron, but he could not recall any specific personal contact between Oswald and Ferrie. He believed that contact was highly probable during that period. Irion stated that he did not recall Oswald continuing with the CAP for a significant length of time following his participation in the unit's 'basic training.' Irion said he was never questioned by the FBI during the investigation of President Kennedy's death.

"The committee was able to locate and interview Anthony Atzenhoffer, who had served as the platoon sergeant for the Moisant Airport CAP squadron in late 1954 and 1955. Atzenhoffer recalled helping coordinate the small CAP unit at Moisant and noted that his duties had included calling the roll at meetings and handling registration matters. He told the committee that Ferrie was an instructor at the Moisant CAP meetings during this period. Ferrie had taken him on his first airplane flight and kept his small private plane in a hangar at the Moisant Airport. Atzenhoffer recalled attending a party with Ferrie and other CAP cadets during that period; the party may have been at Ferrie's house. He also recalled that Ferrie once tried to recruit his CAP cadets in the squadron to participate in some kind of medical experiment. Additionally, Atzenhoffer told the committee that Oswald was active in the CAP unit during the period. He recalled Oswald's membership in the squadron and described him as being a quiet young man.

"He could not, however, remember any specific details regarding Oswald's participation in the unit or specific contact between Oswald and Ferrie, although he believed both were involved in the CAP unit at the same time. Atzenhoffer stated: 'I can't recall seeing the two of them together. I don't have that detailed of a memory. But I'm sure they were there together at the same time.' Atzenhoffer said that he could not recall any more specific information and added: 'I can't say that I know anything about Ferrie and Oswald being together anywhere else, except at the CAP meetings."

"The committee also interviewed George Boesch, another former CAP member in New Orleans who worked with Ferrie during that period. Boesch, now a member of the New Orleans Fire Department, had worked with Ferrie in the New Orleans Lakefront Airport squadron of the CAP. He once accompanied Ferrie to a national competition match of the CAP and had traveled with him elsewhere. He, too, recalled Ferrie as highly intelligent and of good moral character, a man devoted to teaching flying to young men. Boesch told the committee that he accompanied Ferrie when Ferrie left the Lakefront squadron and began teaching the CAP squadron at Moisant Airport. He and Ferrie helped reorganize the Moisant CAP program, which by then also included female cadets. Boesch also remembered Lee Oswald attending the CAP meetings at Moisant during the period when he and Ferrie were there. He could recall Oswald being there for 2 to 3 months while Ferrie was the instructor. Boesch stated that there were usually not more than 15 cadets at these CAP meetings and that Oswald was relatively quiet. Boesch did not recall anything in particular about the relationship between

Oswald and Ferrie, anything unusual; he did not know of any other contact between them. Boesch stated that he was not familiar with Ferrie's personal life and was unaware of his activities outside the CAP.

"The committee also interviewed Jerry Paradis, the former recruit instructor of the New Orleans Lakefront CAP unit. In confirming that Oswald had attended the Lakefront squadron meetings (in addition to the Moisant CAP meetings), Paradis corroborated the accounts of other Oswald colleagues in the CAP. Paradis, now a corporate attorney, told the committee that Oswald attended the Lakefront CAP meetings for several weeks or several months. During the period that he had served as recruit instructor, Paradis could recall that Oswald came to 'at least 10 or 15 meetings,' attending the CAP sessions 'quite a few times.' Oswald was a quiet person and rarely discussed anything with him other than CAP business and instructions."

"In his interview with the committee on December 15, 1978, Paradis stated that he had never been contacted or interviewed by the FBI about his past involvement in the CAP with Oswald and Ferrie. He also stated that no other investigators had ever interviewed him.

"Paradis told the committee that Oswald had attended numerous CAP meetings at which Ferrie had been the instructor. Ferrie 'was always there' during the period in which Oswald attended the Lakefront squadron. Paradis repeated that he believed there were 'at least 10 or 15 meetings' during which Oswald and Ferrie were present. He told the committee, 'Oswald and Ferrie were in the unit together. I know they were there because I was there.' Further, 'I specifically remember Oswald. I can remember him clearly, and Ferrie was heading the unit then. I'm not saying that they may have been there together, I'm saying it is a certainty.'

"Paradis noted that he and Ferrie were good friends and he had always respected Ferrie, even though Ferris was somewhat 'unusual.' Paradis stated that he had no knowledge of any relationship between Oswald and Ferrie outside of the CAP meetings and did not recall anything unusual about their contact at the meetings. He recalled that Ferrie was a 'fairly stern, but generally likable' instructor.

"Paradis also stated that Ferrie and others from the Lakefront CAP unit sometimes participated in the Moisant CAP squadron meetings and that Ferrie later left the Lakefront unit to instruct at Moisant full-time.

"Paradis recalled that he had been surprised that he was not interviewed by the FBI following the President's assassination, stating, 'I sure could have told them when Oswald and Ferrie were in the CAP. I could have given them what they wanted.'

"Paradis further told the committee that he did not believe the personal contact between Ferrie and Oswald 'mean[t] anything really,' and that he never believed that Ferrie 'was a bad guy or anything like that."

* * *

David Ferrie categorically denied not only that he had a relationship with Oswald, but that Oswald was even in the CAP while Ferrie was there. The material quoted above does not directly establish that there was a personal relationship between the two. However, the same material is rather clear that Oswald attended CAP at two different locations, both at the same time that Ferrie is established to have been there.

Given the description of every witness interviewed by the House Committee as to the personality of Ferrie, the type of commander he was, is it likely that he would not have known who Oswald was and that Oswald had been in two of his units?

If it is fair for the Warren Commission to conjecture that the inconsistency of Oswald's actions "could have been another manifestation of Oswald's rejection of his environment" - is it equally fair to conjecture that if there was a Ferrie connection, such connections should not be so easily dismissed?

While the Warren Commission's conjecture may be spot-on, shouldn't any rational analysis of this incongruity at the very least consider the relationship between the emotionally-starved, fatherless, young Lee Harvey Oswald, and the Svengali-like David Ferrie?

Though perhaps somewhat more extreme than others, Ferrie's anti-Communism was not unique for the time. Since the end of World War II, the fear of Godless Communism had been a major concern of many Americans. It was the era of the House Un-American Activities Committee, Senator Joseph McCarthy, the Smith Act, the Internal Security Act of 1950, and the Communist Control Act of 1954.

It was also the era of covert action programs run by the FBI. While the FBI by no means had a monopoly on such anti-Communist covert action programs, they did initiate a new one in 1956, an operation called COINTELPRO, which was their acronym for 'counter-intelligence program'.

Counter-intelligence, an art-form practiced as well by the CIA and the various military intelligence groups, can be defined as those actions by an intelligence agency intended to protect its own security including affirmative action taken to undermine or neutralize hostile intelligence operation.

One contemporaneous example of counter-intelligence (and of the public obsession with Communism) was the highly-popular television series, *I Led Three Lives*, a program which purported to relate the clandestine adventures and triumphs of Herb Philbrick, an FBI undercover agent who had been surreptitiously infiltrated into the Communist Party. According to the Warren Commission testimony of Lee's mother, Marguerite Oswald, *I Led Three Lives* was a steady part of the TV viewing diet of Lee Harvey Oswald.

Reading and flaunting Communist literature, while at the same time avidly studying the Marine Manual, and wishing his life way until he could join the Marines, was not his only contradictory trait during this time.

On October 3, 1956, just two weeks before the birthday on which he had long planned to leave the Fort Worth area in order to enter the Marines Corps, Lee wrote the following letter to the Socialist Party of America:

Dear Sirs:

I am sixteen years of age and would like more information about your youth League, I would like to know if there is a branch in my area, how to join, etc., I am a Marxist, and have been studying socialist principles for well over fifteen months I am very interested in your Y.P.S.L.

Sincerely

Lee Oswald

What are we to make of this letter? Was Oswald simply delusional when he wrote it? He is asking for information to be sent to the home he is leaving? He is asking about how to join a branch in the geographical area where he will no longer reside? Or, when viewed in the light of other activities we will be discussing, was this "window dressing?"

CHAPTER 5

THE UNIQUE MARINE

* * *

The U.S. Marine Corps in 1958 was not exactly a bastion of liberal tolerance and freethinking.

Philip H. Melanson Chancellor Professor of Policy Studies University of Massachusetts, Dartmouth

On October 26, 1956, Lee Harvey Oswald reported for duty at the Marine Corps Recruit Depot in San Diego, California. His preference of duty was recorded as Aircraft Maintenance and Repair, the duty assignment for which he was recommended.

Following basic training at San Diego and then at Camp Pendelton, California, Oswald was assigned for additional training, first to the Naval Air Technical Training Center at the Naval Air Station in Jacksonville, Florida, then to Kessler Air Force Base in Biloxi, Mississippi, and then to the Marine Corps Air Station at El Toro, California.

While at San Diego, Oswald was trained in the use of the M-1 rifle. His practice scores were not very good, but somehow when his company fired for record on December 21, he scored 212, two points above the score necessary to qualify as a 'sharpshooter' on a marksman/sharpshooter/expert scale. (He did not do nearly as well when he fired for record again shortly before he left the Marines.)

It may just have been another case of the service assigning an Eskimo to the tropics, but it has been perhaps too facilely passed over that the additional training Oswald received at these military locations was as a radar operator; and it was in that capacity that he ultimately came to be assigned to the Marine Air Control Squadron at Atsugi Air Base, 20 miles west of Tokyo, Japan.

Radar, by definition, is "a method of detecting distant objects and determining their position, velocity, or other characteristics by analysis of very high frequency radio waves reflected from their surfaces." The training, in addition to radar theory and use, included aircraft surveillance, map reading and air traffic control procedures.

On his aptitude tests, taken on October 30 – which are presumably what would have prompted someone to assign Oswald to this particular specialty – although Oswald scored significantly above the Marine Corps averages in reading and vocabulary, yet he scored significantly *below* the average in arithmetic and pattern analysis, and near the bottom of the lowest group in the radio code test, and his composite general score was 105, two points below the Corps average.

At the Naval Air Station, Jacksonville, Oswald finished 46th in a class of 54 students in Aviation Fundamental School, in which he received basic instruction in his specialty, including such subjects as basic radar theory, map reading, and air traffic control procedures.

Then a most surprising thing happened at Kessler, following a six-week course during which none of his fellow Marines knew where he spent his free time, except that it was thought to be away from the base. At Kessler, he attended the Aircraft Control and Warning Operator Course, which included instruction in aircraft surveillance and the use of radar. In this more advanced course, Lee placed 7th in a class of 30.

We shall in a subsequent chapter consider whether there could have been some purpose in taking Oswald, despite his *non*-aptitude test scores, and qualifying him to be a radar operator

The specialty of radar operator, even from the training stage, required dealing with confidential material. On May 3, 1957, this young man who had been flaunting an apparent interest in Communist literature was granted a "confidential" clearance.

Oswald retained his "confidential" clearance throughout his enlistment despite the fact that he became more and more blatant in overtly showcasing his interest in Russia – a fact which is rather curious considering that Atsugi Air Base was a home to the super-secret U-2 spy plane which took off and landed there.

Most of those who knew him in the Marines, at Atsugi and at the other bases, were able to recount anecdotes which suggested to the Warren Commission that Oswald was anxious to publicize his liking for things Russian, sometimes in good humor and sometimes seriously. Some of his colleagues called him "Oswaldskovich." apparently to his pleasure. He was said to have had his name written in Russian on one of his jackets; to have played records of Russian songs "so loud that one could hear them outside the barracks;" frequently to have made remarks in Russian or used expressions like "da" or "nyet" or addressed others (and been addressed) as "Comrade;" to have come over and said jokingly, "You called?" when one of the marines played a particular record of Russian music. When he played chess, according to one of his opponents he chose the red pieces, expressing a preference for the "Red Army." He regularly and openly read a Russian language newspaper; Lieutenant John Donovan though it was a Communist newspaper and believed Oswald had a subscription to it.

It appeared to most observers that connected with the Russophilia was an interest in and acceptance of Russian political views and Communist ideology. Indeed, Kerry Thornley, a marine who described himself as a close acquaintance but not a good friend of Oswald, thought he definitely believed that "the Marxist morality was the most rational morality to follow." And Communism "the best system in the world."

Oswald the political heretic received even more endorsement as a malcontent with his two court martials in 1957, one for possession of an unauthorized .22 caliber derringer pistol, and the other for verbally assaulting and pouring a drink on a non-commissioned officer. For these offenses his combined punishments cost him $105, a reduction in rank to the grade of private and confinement to hard labor for 48 days.

Most of the marines who knew Lee Oswald were aware that he was studying the Russian language. By February 25, 1959 his studying had progressing to the point that he attempted a foreign language qualification test; his rating of "poor" on this exam must be evaluated in light of the fact that he was apparently studying on his own. One observer with some knowledge of Russian, Rosaleen Quinn, thought that he spoke the language well in view of his lack of formal training.

Oswald's fellow marines at his various units can provide little if any information as to his activities when not actually on the base and in the unit. Throughout his tour of duty, Oswald invariably tended to disappear from the view of his fellow marines during off-hours, weekends and leaves.

In November 1958 Oswald finished his overseas tour of duty, and was shipped back to California; after travel time and thirty-day leave, he was assigned to a Marine Air Control Squadron at the Marine Corps Air Station at El Toro, where he had been based briefly before he went overseas.

In March 1959, Oswald applied to Albert Schweitzer College in Churwalden. Switzerland, for admission to the spring term in 1960. This application was approved by the college, and by letter dated June 19 Oswald sent his registration fee of $25.

Lee was obligated to serve on active duty until December 7, 1959 (the date having been adjusted to compensate for the period of confinement). But then, in August, he made a voluntary allotment of $40 to his mother, applied for a dependent's quarters ("Q") allotment on her behalf, and on August 17 he submitted a request for dependency discharge on the ground that his mother needed his support due to an injury she had sustained at work (there had been an injury, but it was the previous December). Within two weeks, the application had been approved.

This is one of a number of occasions when Lee Harvey Oswald appeared to be remarkably expeditious in cutting through red tape, ostensibly because this unintelligent non-conformist somehow seemed to always have his papers complete and in order.

But it so happens that this particular application was not truly complete. Although the requisite preconditions of a voluntary allotment and request for "Q" allotment had been made, and although the application was accompanied by an affidavit of Mrs. Oswald and corroborating affidavits from an attorney, a doctor, and two friends, all the supporting affidavits for the quarters allotment had not been submitted at the time the hardship discharge application was filed. Nonetheless, the application was quickly forwarded, with merely an endorsement that the reviewing officers were aware that both the requisite voluntary contribution and the application for a quarter's allotment had been made.

However, under the applicable procedures, Oswald's requisite application for a quarters allowance for his mother should have been disallowed because he had not contributed any money to her during the preceding year. Moreover, the reviewing officer in his endorsement, dated August 19 (only two days after it was submitted), stated "A genuine hardship exists in this case, and in my opinion approval of the 'Q' allotment will not sufficiently alleviate this situation."

This is a puzzling statement in light of the fact that the Fort Worth Red Cross office indicated that only a quarters allotment was necessary for Marguerite Oswald, rather than a hardship discharge for Lee. On August 28, the Wing Hardship or Dependency Discharge Board recommended that Oswald's request for a discharge be approved, which was done shortly thereafter.

On September 4, pending his hardship discharge so he could go home and support his injured mother, Oswald applied for a passport. His application stated that he planned to leave the United States on September 21 to attend Albert Schweitzer College and the University of Turku in Finland, as well as to travel in Cuba, the

Dominican Republic, England, France, Germany, and Russia. The passport was issued six days later.

Oswald received his hardship discharge on September 11. He arrived in Fort Worth by September 14, gave his mother $100, and departed three days later for New Orleans.

BOOK TWO

* * *

DEFECTOR?

CHAPTER 6

DESTINATION GOLUB

* * *

Louis Hopkins, the travel agent who arranged for Oswald's passage from the United States, was not aware of Oswald's ultimate destination and so had nothing to do with the London-Helsinki trip. Moreover, Hopkins has testified, had he known Oswald's ultimate destination, his advice would have been to sail not on the Marion Lykes, but on a different ship to a port more convenient for Russia. Golub disclosed during a luncheon conversation that Moscow had given him authority to give Americans visas without prior approval from Moscow....

House Select Committee

The Warren Commission, utilizing Oswald's own "Historic Diary" together with various documents and testimony from Russian and American sources, reconstructed a rather detailed account of his defection to, and life in, the Soviet Union. In summary, according to this account Lee Harvey Oswald sought to defect to Russia; was rejected; became despondent, and attempted suicide, which resulted in the Russians accepting him; was sent to an obscure job in an obscure city; grew dissatisfied with Russian life; and thereupon re-defected to the United States, having in the meantime acquired a Russian wife.

Information has subsequently emerged which demonstrates that there are significant problems with each of the sources for this account, and which therefore suggests that the above scenario may be totally untrue. Indeed, one of the questions that arises is: Could it be that Lee Harvey Oswald was actually an agent of the United States, and that his defection to Russia was for some mission of the US?

What follows below is the Warren Commission reconstruction supplemented by the more recent evidence and observations. According to the Warren Report:

"On September 17. Oswald spoke with a representative of Travel Consultants, Inc., a New Orleans travel bureau; he filled out a 'Passenger Immigration Questionnaire' on which he gave his occupation as "shipping export agent", and said that he would be abroad for 2 months on a pleasure trip. He booked passage from New Orleans to Le Havre, France, on a freighter, the SS *Marion Lykes*, scheduled to sail on September 18, for which he paid $220.75. On the evening of September 17, he registered at the Liberty Hotel.

"The *Marion Lykes* did not sail until the early morning of September 20... [It] carried only four passengers. Oswald shared his cabin with Billy Joe Lord, a young man who had just graduated from high school and was going to France to continue his education... The other two passengers were Lieutenant Colonel and Mrs. George B. Church....

"Oswald disembarked at Le Havre on October 8. He left for England that same day, and arrived on October 9. He told English customs officials in Southampton that he had $700 and planned to remain in the United Kingdom for 1 week before proceeding to a school in Switzerland. But on the same day he flew to Helsinki, Finland, where he registered at the Torni Hotel; on the following day, he moved to the Klaus Kurki Hotel. Oswald probably applied for a visa at the Russian Consulate on October 12, his first business day in Helsinki. The visa was issued on October 14... He left Helsinki by train on the following day, crossed the Finnish-Russian border at Vainikkala, and arrived in Moscow on October 16... He was met at the Moscow railroad station by a representative of 'Intourist', the state tourist agency, and taken to the Hotel Berlin, where he registered as a student."

* * *

There are noteworthy difficulties with the above scenario. To begin with, the report is incorrectly stating what its own evidence demonstrates. Commission Exhibit 946 is Oswald's passport. It unequivocally shows that Oswald left London on the 10th, not the 9th as the Warren Commission reconstruction asserts. Further, both Commission Exhibits 2676 & 2677 demonstrate that it was late on the night of the 10th, not the 9th, on which Oswald checked into the Torni Hotel in Helsinki. So, without question, Oswald left England and arrived in Helsinki on the 10th, not the 9th. Was it merely carelessness that led to such a misstatement in the Report? Perhaps so, but that should provide little comfort to those who place such reliance on the much advertised comprehensiveness and great accuracy of the Report.

On the other hand, there are disturbing questions that arise from this misstatement of the Warren Report. First, picture in your mind the Warren Commission writer having before him the evidence showing that Oswald arrived in England on the 9th and departed on the 10th. How can that writer make the mistake of writing that Oswald arrived on the 9th and left the same day? Then, consider the fact that this Report is purporting to account for every step of Oswald's trip. If the Commission writes in its report that Oswald arrived in England on the 9th but did not depart until the 10th, how do they account for the time he spent in England?

Putting aside the issue of the appropriate dates, the circumstances surrounding Oswald's trip from London to Helsinki are most suspicious and mysterious. Again, Oswald's passport indicates he arrived in Finland on October 10, 1959, and the Torni Hotel in Helsinki has him registered as a guest on that same date. However, unless Oswald received some well-placed help, there was no way that he could have been registered at the Torni on the same day he arrived in Finland. That is true because of two immutable facts, which no investigation has found to be in error or dispute:

1- the only direct flight from London to Helsinki landed at 11.33 p.m. on that date; and,

2- as documented in Commission Exhibit 2677, a memorandum by the then CIA Deputy Director, Richard M. Helms, "[I]f Oswald had taken this flight, he could not normally have cleared customs and landing formalities and reached the Torni Hotel downtown by 2400 (midnight) on the same day."

In Commission Exhibit 2677, dated July 1, 1964, almost three months before the issuance of the Warren Report, Richard Helms on behalf of the CIA wrote the following to J. Lee Rankin, Chief Counsel to the Warren Commission: "We are presently attempting to determine if Oswald could have taken a more circuitous flight from London, with a stop in Stockholm, Copenhagen, or some other city. Any additional information received will be forwarded to you promptly." It seems clear that no such flight was taken by Oswald since there is no additional information by the CIA documenting such.

As noted above, Louis Hopkins, the travel agent who arranged for Oswald's passage from the United States, was not aware of Oswald's ultimate destination and so had nothing to do with the London-Helsinki trip. Moreover, Hopkins has testified, had he known Oswald's ultimate destination, his advice would have been to sail not on the *Marion Lykes*, but on a different ship to a port more convenient for Russia. The mystery is enhanced by Louis Hopkins' observations that Oswald did not appear to be particularly well-informed about travel in Europe.

Further questions arise from Oswald's obtaining a Soviet entry visa within only two days of having applied for it on October 12, 1959 (October 10, the date of arrival, having been Saturday, the first opportunity to apply for a visa would have been on Monday, October 12).

Normally at least a week would elapse between the time of a tourist's application and the issuance of a visa. This minimum time was, if anything, all the more necessary if, in addition to the processing of the visa application, lodgings were to be arranged through Soviet Intourist, as appears to have been the case with Oswald, inasmuch as he was met at Moscow railroad station by an Intourist representative and taken to the Hotel Berlin.

However, the Soviet Consul in Helsinki, Gregory Golub, was suspected by American intelligence of also being an officer in the Soviet KGB. Golub had once disclosed in a luncheon conversation that Moscow had given him authority to give Americans visas without prior approval from Moscow, and that "as long as he was convinced the American was 'all right.' he could give him a visa in a matter of minutes."

An American Embassy dispatch, dated October 9, 1959, the day before Oswald arrived in Helsinki, illustrates that Golub indeed had such authority (while at the same time, it prompts some intriguing questions). The dispatch, which had been referring to an earlier telephone contact between Golub and the American Embassy in Helsinki, goes on to state, "… Since that evening [September 4, 1959] Golub has only phoned [the US consul] once and this was on a business matter. Two Americans were in the Soviet Consulate at the time and were applying for Soviet visas thru Golub. They had previously been in the American consulate inquiring about the possibility of obtaining a Soviet visa in 1 or 2 days. [The US Consul] advised them to go directly to Golub and make their request, which they did. Golub phoned [the US Consul] to state that he would give them their visas as soon as they made advance Intourist reservations. When they did this, Golub immediately gave them their visas…"

The House Select Committee, which developed this evidence about Golub, concluded: "Thus based upon these two factors, (1) Golub's authority to issue visas to Americans without prior approval from Moscow, and (2) a demonstration of this authority, as reported in an embassy dispatch approximately 1 month prior to Oswald's appearance at the Soviet Embassy, the Committee found that the available evidence tends to support the conclusion that the issuance of Oswald's tourist visa within 2 days after his appearance at the Soviet Consulate was not indicative on an American intelligence agency connection." And, in a footnote, they observed: "If anything, Oswald's ability to receive a Soviet entry visa so quickly was more indicative of a Soviet interest in him."

This footnote is puzzling in the extreme, since it appears to be inconsistent with the very conclusion it footnotes. That conclusion makes crystal clear that Oswald's ability to receive a Soviet entry visa so quickly had absolutely nothing to do with a Soviet interest in him; that, in fact, its speedy issuance would indicate that it was not cleared in Moscow (a presumption which the reader might find even more compelling when we discuss the less-than-enthusiastic reception Oswald received in Moscow).

However, the conclusion itself is, if anything, more puzzling than the footnote. What the conclusion really amounts to is a statement that there is no American intelligence agency connection, since we have evidence that the expedited visa was issued by Golub.

But the premise does not support the conclusion. The probable involvement of Golub in the issuance of Oswald's expedited – and uninvestigated – visa does not eliminate the possibility of American intelligence agency involvement; it may, in fact, make such involvement more likely.

Logically, it should be the beginning of a line of inquiry that asks the simple question: Why Golub?

The above cited evidence would seem to justify the following speculative queries on that score:

1. If the United States wished to infiltrate someone into the Soviet Union, would it be helpful if the necessity of prior clearance from Moscow for his visa could be circumvented?

2. Did the United States know that the necessity of prior visa clearance from Moscow could be circumvented via Gregory Golub?

3. If (hypothetically) the United States wished to infiltrate a Lee Harvey Oswald into the Soviet Union, would it make sense to steer him to Gregory Golub?

4. Might 'Destination Golub' explain Oswald's odyssey from New Orleans to Le Havre to London to Helsinki, instead of proceeding to a port more convenient for Russia?

5. If the answers to the last four questions appear to be in the affirmative, may it be that the Committee has actually proven the exact opposite of the conclusion it has stated?

In other words, might "Destination Golub" point to involvement of U.S. intelligence in Oswald's defection?

CHAPTER 7

RUSSIA

* * *

"At the time it seemed to me that LHO was reciting propaganda formulas, as well as phrases used in connection with his demand for citizenship renunciation, that he perhaps did not fully understand himself, and that he may have been coached by persons unknown."

John A McVickar, Consul, American Embassy, Moscow

The Warren Commission set forth a reconstruction of the two years eight months of Oswald's time in Russia. The following is a summary of the Warren Commission reconstruction.

On the day after his arrival in Moscow, Oswald was met by a representative of "Intourist," the state tourist agency, and taken to the Hotel Berlin where he registered as a student. On the same day he met Rima Shirokova, the young woman assigned by Intourist as his guide during his stay in Russia. Almost immediately he told her that he wanted to leave the United States and become a citizen of a Soviet Union. He then sent a letter to the Supreme Soviet requesting that he be granted citizenship.

On October 21, an official of the Passport and Visa Department notified Oswald that his visa had expired and that he had to leave Moscow within two hours. Oswald responded to this unfavorable decision by cutting himself above the left wrist in an apparent suicide attempt, which resulted in his being taken to the Botkinskaya Hospital where he was confined for three days in the psychiatric ward before being transferred to the "somatic" ward. He was released from the hospital on October 28.

Oswald now checked out of the Hotel Berlin and registered at the Metropole. His visa had expired while he was in the hospital, and his presence in Russia was technically illegal; he had received no word that the decision that he must leave had been reversed. Later that day, however, an official at the Pass and Registration Office sent for him, and asked whether he still wanted to become a Soviet citizen. Oswald replied in the affirmative, and provided his Marine Corps discharge papers for identification. He was told that he could not expect a decision soon, and was dismissed. For the next three days, he remained in his room, near the phone, fully dressed and ready to leave immediately if summoned.

Then, on the afternoon of October 31 (a Saturday), he apparently decided to act. He took a taxi to the American Embassy, where he asked to see the consul. When the receptionist asked him first to sign the tourist register, he laid his passport on the desk and said that he had come to "dissolve his American citizenship."

Richard E. Snyder, the second secretary and senior consular official, was summoned, and he invited Oswald into his office. There, with Snyder's assistant, John A. McVickar, also present, Oswald declared that he wanted to renounce his American citizenship; he denounced the United States and praised the government of the Soviet Union. Over Oswald's objections, Snyder sought to learn something of Oswald's motives and background and to forestall immediate action. Oswald stated his admiration for the system and policies of the Soviet Union and his desire to serve the Soviet State; and at one point alluded to hardships endured by his mother as a "worker," saying he did not intend to let this happen to him.

Oswald informed Snyder that he had been a radar operator in the Marine Corps, intimating that he might know something of special interest, and that he had informed a Soviet official that he would give the Soviets any information he possessed.

Oswald handed to Snyder a note which suggests that he had studied and sought to comply with section 349 of the Immigration and Nationality Act (which provides for the loss of American citizenship) since the note attempts to cast off citizenship in three of the ways specified by the statute.

The interview ended when Snyder told Oswald that he could renounce his citizenship on the following Monday, two days later, if he would appear personally.

Oswald returned to the hotel angry about the delay, but "elated" by the "showdown" and sure that he would be permitted to remain after his "sign of faith" in the Russians.

Snyder has testified that in telling Oswald to come back on Monday, he was attempting to delay Oswald's decision so as to give him a chance to reconsider before making such a step. However, no sooner had Oswald left these closed offices than the Embassy sought out and notified the press of the defection.

Soon after he returned to the hotel, he was approached by A. I. Goldberg, a reporter for the Associated Press, and later that day by two other reporters, R. J. Korengold and Aline Mosby. He answered a few questions for the latter two, but refused to be interviewed at that time (though a few weeks later he did give an interview to Miss Mosby of United Press International in which among other things he referred again to his mother's poverty).

A few days after his Saturday visit, the Embassy received a letter from Oswald dated November 3, which requested that his citizenship be revoked. The Embassy replied on November 9 that he could renounce his citizenship by appearing at the Embassy and executing the necessary papers.

Both on November 8 in a letter to his brother Robert, and on November 13 in the interview with Aline Mosby, Oswald stated that he had been told that he could remain in the Soviet Union. This conflicts with his diary which states that he was not told until later that he could even remain temporarily. Indeed, according to his diary it was this "comforting news" that prompted him to grant a second interview on November 16, this time with Priscilla Johnson of the North American Newspaper Alliance.

When, during this November 16 interview, Miss Johnson suggested that if Oswald really wished to renounce his American citizenship he could do so by returning to the Embassy, he said he would "never set foot in the Embassy again," since he was sure he would be given the "same run-around" as before. Miss Johnson impression was that Oswald "may have purposely not carried through his original intent to renounce in order to leave a crack open." The Warren Commission related that "reporters noticed Oswald's apparent ambivalence in regard to renouncing his citizenship – stormily demanding that he be permitted to renounce while failing to follow through by completing the necessary papers. [...] He seemed to be avoiding effective renunciation, consciously or unconsciously, in order to preserve his right to re-enter the United States. [...] ... if he had expatriated himself his eventual return to the United States would have been much more difficult and perhaps impossible."

On January 4, Oswald was summoned to the Soviet Passport Office and issued Identity Document for Stateless Persons No. 311479. He was told that he was being sent to Minsk, an industrial city located about 450 miles southwest of Moscow, with a population at the time of about 510,000. On the following day, he went to a Government agency, which the Russians call the "Red Cross;" it gave him 5,000 rubles (about $500). He used 2,200 rubles to pay his hotel bill and 150 rubles to purchase a railroad ticket to Minsk, where he arrived on January 7. On the following day he met the "Mayor," who welcomed him to Minsk and promised him a rent-free apartment.

Oswald reported for work at the Belorussian Radio and Television Factory on January 13. The factory, a major producer of electronic parts and systems, employed about 5,000 persons. His salary varied from 700 to perhaps as high as 900 rubles per month ($70 - $90), a salary which was normal for his type of work. It was supplemented, however, by 700 rubles per month, which he received from the 'Red Cross', and, according to Oswald, his total income was about equal to that of the director of the factory. In August he applied for membership in the union; he became a dues-paying member in September.

Undoubtedly more noteworthy to most Russians than his extra income was the attractive apartment which Oswald was given in March 1960. It was a small flat with a balcony overlooking the river, for which he paid only 60 rubles a month. Oswald describes it in his diary as "a Russian dream." Had Oswald been a Russian worker, he would probably have had to wait for several years for a comparable apartment, and would have been given one then only if he had a family. The "Red Cross" subsidy and the apartment were typical of the favorable treatment which the Soviet Union has given defectors.

Oswald's diary records that he enjoyed his first months in Minsk. His work at the factory was easy and his co-workers were friendly and curious about life in the United States. He dated frequently, attending the theater, a movie, or an opera almost every night. He wrote in his diary "I'm living big and am very satisfied."

The spring and summer passed easily and uneventfully. There were picnics and drives in the country, which Oswald described as "green beauty." On June 18, he obtained a hunting license and soon afterwards he purchased a 16 gauge single-barrel shotgun. He joined a local chapter of the Belorussian Society of Hunters and Fishermen, a hunting club sponsored by his factory, and hunted for small game in the farm regions around Minsk about half a dozen times in the summer and fall, spending the night in small villages. (Parenthetically, Russian records contain statements from fellow hunters that Oswald was an extremely poor shot and it was necessary for persons who accompanied him on hunts to provide him with game.) According to his diary, at about this period of time he felt "uneasy inside" after a friend took him aside at a party and advised him to return to the United States. In another entry he writes, "I have become habituated to a small café which is where I dine in the evening. The food is generally poor and always exactly the same menu in any café at any point in the city. The food is cheap and I don't really care about quality after three years of the USMC." *(Note: Oswald's numerous spelling errors are omitted throughout this book.)*

According to Russian records, on January 4, 1961, one year after he had been issued his "stateless" residence permit, Oswald was summoned to the passport office in Minsk; was asked if he still wanted to become a Soviet citizen; he replied that he did not, but asked that his residence permit be extended for another year.

The entry in his diary for January 4-31 reads, "I am starting to reconsider my desire about staying. The work is drab. The money I get has nowhere to be spent. No nightclubs or bowling alleys, no places of recreation except the trade-union dances. I have had enough."

Moving chronologically, we next reach a series of incidents that occurred in January, 1961. First, some background. There was a report that on or about January 26, 1961, Marguerite Oswald appeared at the U.S. Department of State in Washington, D.C. where she spoke with D. E. Boster and Edward J. Hickey. Warren Commission exhibit CE 2748, Vol. XXV1, page 124 states in relevant part the State Department's "Memorandum of Conversation" of this meeting.

"Mrs. Oswald said she had come to Washington to see what further could be done to help her son, indicating that she did not feel that the Department had done as much as it should in his case. She also said she thought there was some possibility that her son had in fact gone to the Soviet Union as a United States secret agent, and if this were true she wished the appropriate authorities to know that she was destitute and should receive some compensation. Mrs. Oswald was assured that there was no evidence to suggest that her son had gone to the Soviet Union as an agent, and that she should dismiss any such idea."

The Warren Report relates that five days later, on February 1, 1961, the Department of State in Washington forwarded to the

Moscow Embassy a request informing the Embassy that Oswald's mother was worried about him, and asking that he get in touch with her, if possible. Then, few weeks later, on February 13, 1961, the American Embassy in Moscow received a letter from Oswald postmarked Minsk on February 5, asking that he be readmitted to the United States.

In Appendix XV of the Warren Report, we are told that the message from the State Department to the Moscow Embassy read, "The Embassy is requested to inform the [Soviet] Ministry of Foreign Affairs that Mr. Oswald's mother is worried as to his present safety, and is anxious to hear from him." In this Appendix, it is asserted that this request had not been acted upon by the 13th because the diplomatic pouch which left Washington for Moscow on the 1st did not reach Moscow until the 10th or 11th.

Considering the timing of the State Department message and Oswald's letter, the Warren Commission opined that "the simultaneity of the two events was apparently coincidental." The basis for this conclusion is stated to be that, "The request from Marguerite Oswald went from Washington to Moscow by sealed diplomatic pouch and there was no evidence that the seal had been tampered with. The officer of the Department of State who carried the responsibility for such matters has testified that the message was not forwarded to the Russians after it arrived in Moscow."

This statement and reasoning by the Warren Commission gives rise to a few questions. To begin with, the unopened message from Washington to Moscow is reported to be "that Oswald's mother was worried about him, and asking that he get in touch with her, if possible."

But that is not exactly what was said to have been communicated to the State Department by the ever-avaricious Marguerite. She was not expressing concern for Lee's safety. She was not stating that she was anxious to hear from him. She was not asking to have Lee contact her. She began by complaining that the

Department had not done as much as it should in his case. That opening salvo is the hook for her making the "pitch" she is actually there for. What does she mean by "as much as it should in his case"? Well, they should be doing more because she says her son went to the Soviet Union as a United States secret agent. And what does she propose the Department should be doing to help her son? Why, help his mother, of course! - "If this were true she wished the appropriate authorities to know that she was destitute and should receive some compensation."

What was it that the Warren Commission is disproving? Are they disproving the proposition that Marguerite's message prompted Lee to send his letter indicating he wanted to re-defect? Are they disproving the proposition that this was a subterfuge by the American Government to alert Oswald that it was time to come home? Are they disproving the proposition that the message prompted the Russians to have Oswald write his letter?

The picture regarding communications involving Oswald's decision to re-defect and its timing becomes murkier when one turns to the letter mentioned above, sent by Oswald dated February 5. Oswald complains in that letter that he had written an earlier letter which had not been answered. However, the Warren Commission found that there is evidence that such a letter was never sent – specifically, the Warren Commission states that the entry in Oswald's letter that there had been an earlier letter is false based upon the fact that Oswald's diary refers to this February letter as his "first request." As we shall see in the next chapter, there is no more reason to believe that the Diary is accurate than to believe that the letter is accurate.

Oswald's letter noted that he did not appear personally because he could not leave Minsk without permission. The Second Secretary, Richard Snyder, answered on February 28 that Oswald would have to appear at the Embassy personally to discuss his return to the United States. A second letter from Oswald, posted on March 5 reached the Embassy on March 20; it reiterated that he was unable to leave Minsk without permission, and asked that preliminary inquiries be put in the form of a questionnaire and sent to him.

The Warren Commission noted that, "The Soviet authorities had undoubtedly intercepted and read the correspondence between Oswald and the Embassy and knew of his plans. Soon after the correspondence began, his monthly payments from the 'Red Cross' were cut off."

Sometime in the second week of March, Miss Katherine Mallory, who was on tour in Minsk with the University on Michigan Symphonic Band, found herself surrounded by curious Russian citizens. A young man who identified himself as a Texan and former Marine stepped out of the crowd and asked if she needed an interpreter; he interpreted for her for the next 15 or 20 minutes. Later he told her that he despised the United States and hoped to stay in Minsk for the rest of his life. Miss Mallory was unable to swear that her interpreter was Oswald, but was personally convinced that it was he.

A few days later, probably on March 17, Oswald attended a dance at the Palace of Culture from Professional Workers in Minsk, where he met 19-year-old Marina Nikolayevna Prusakova. They met again at another dance a week later, danced together most of the evening, and when he walked her home they arranged to meet again the following week.

However, on Thursday, March 30, Oswald was admitted to the Clinical Hospital, where Marina worked as a pharmacist. By the time he left the hospital on April 11, he had asked her to be his fiancée, and she had agreed to consider it. After his discharge from the hospital he visited Marina regularly at her aunt and uncle's apartment, where she had lived since the previous fall (she never knew her father; her mother died in 1957, and she subsequently left her stepfather with whom she did not get along). By April 20, they had filed notice with the registrar of their intent to marry, and had obtained the special consent necessary for an alien to marry a citizen. After waiting the usual ten days, they were married on April 30. Marina testified that when she agreed to marry Oswald, she believed – based upon his statements to her – that he did not intend to, and indeed could not, return to the United States. Oddly enough, this would also have to mean that nothing was said to Marina when she applied for permission to marry this alien who the authorities knew was intending to leave the country.

But of greater curiosity is the fact that this would have to mean that her intended's plans to leave the country were kept from her by the beloved uncle with whom she lived, for that uncle was not some ordinary, uninformed Soviet citizen – on the contrary, her uncle, Colonel Ilya Vasilyevich Prusakov, was a high-ranking official in the Minsk MVD.

Oswald's diary says that he told Marina "in the last days of June" that he was anxious to return to the United States. If true, it would mean that Oswald had been making official inquiries into arranging for Marina to leave Russia prior to her knowing about it. On May 25 the Moscow Embassy had received a letter mailed in Minsk about ten days earlier, in which Oswald asked for assurances that he would not be prosecuted if he returned, and informing the Embassy that he had married a Russian woman who would seek to accompany him to the United States.

It is interesting to note Oswald's social activities at this time. Among his stated reasons for wanting to leave the Soviet Union were complaints about the sameness of the food, and the complaint that there were no places of recreation. Yet, the Warren Commission relates that, "While these preparations were being made, the Oswalds apparently enjoyed their new life. They ate most of their meals in cafes or at restaurants where they worked. For amusement they went boating, attended the opera, concerts, the circus, and films; occasionally, they gathered with a group of friends for a cooperative meal at someone's apartment."

Weeks went by, but Lee received no response to his letter informing the Embassy of his desire to bring his new bride with him to the United States. Then, on July 8, he appeared at the Embassy in Moscow. It being Saturday, the offices were closed. He used the house telephone to reach Snyder, who came to the office, talked with him briefly, and suggested that he return on the following Monday. Oswald called Marina and asked her to join him in Moscow, which she did, arriving on Sunday. At the Embassy on Monday, Marina waited outside during Oswald's interview with Snyder, who asked to see his Soviet papers and questioned him closely about his life in Russia and possible expatriating acts. Oswald stated that he was not a citizen of the Soviet Union and had never formally applied for citizenship, that he had never taken and oath of allegiance to the Soviet Union, and that he was not a member of the factory trade union organization. He said that he had never given Soviet officials any confidential information that he had learned in the Marines, had never been asked to give such information, and "doubted" that he would have done so had he been asked.

The Warren Commission concluded that, "Some of Oswald's statements during his interview were undoubtedly false. He had almost certainly applied for citizenship in the Soviet Union and, at least for a time, been disappointed when it was denied. He possessed a membership card in the union organization. In addition, his assertion to Snyder that he had never been questioned by Soviet authorities concerning his life in the United States is simply unbelievable."

Snyder concluded that Oswald had not expatriated himself and returned to him his passport, stamped valid only for direct travel to the United States. Accompanied by his wife, Lee came to the Embassy again on the following day to initiate procedures for her admission to the United States as an immigrant

Marina had testified that when the news of her visit to the American Embassy reached Minsk, she was dropped from membership in "Komsomol," the Communist Youth Organization, and that "meetings were arranged" at which "members of the various organizations attempted to dissuade her from leaving the Soviet Union." She also says that her aunt and uncle did not speak to her for "a long time." Indeed, Lee wrote to the Embassy on October 4 to request that the US Government officially intervene to facilitate his and his wife's applications for exit visas. He stated that there had been systematic and concerted attempts to intimidate Marina into withdrawing her application for a visa, which had resulted in her being hospitalized for a five-day period on September 22 for nervous exhaustion. There is no record of such hospitalization and Marina agrees there was no such hospitalization. As to the rest of the harassment and outrage, if it was sincere and not for show, it makes even more incomprehensible the apparently blasé approach of the authorities and her uncle to her courtship by and marriage to Oswald after he had applied for readmission to the United States.

The Embassy replied to Oswald's letter on October 12, saying that it had no way of influencing Soviet conduct on such matters and that its experience had been that action on applications for exit visas was "seldom taken rapidly." On December 25, 1961, Marina was called to the local passport office in Minsk, where she was told that authority had been received to issue exit visas to her and her husband. The Oswalds did not pick up their exit visas immediately, one reason probably being the fact that Marina was pregnant with their first child, June, who was born on February 15. In the meantime, the American Embassy in a letter dated January 5 suggested that since there might be difficulties in obtaining an American visa for Marina, Oswald should consider returning alone and bringing her over later. He replied on the 16th that he would not leave Russia without her. There was apparently less urgency about the departure for the United States after June was born, as Oswald wrote to his mother and brother that he would probably not arrive for several months. On June 1, Oswald signed a promissory note at the Embassy for a repatriation loan of $435.71. He and his family boarded a train for Holland, passing through Minsk that night. They crossed the Soviet frontier at Brest on June 2. Two days later they departed from Holland on the SS *Maasdam*, which landed at Hoboken, New Jersey, on June 13, where they were met by Spas Y. Raikin, a representative of the Travelers Aid Society, which had been contracted by the Department of State. The society referred the Oswalds to the New York City Department of Welfare, which helped them find a room at the Times Square Hotel. On the afternoon of June 14, the Oswalds left New York by plane for Fort Worth.

Some additional observations are in order at this point. Our knowledge of what transpired regarding Oswald while in the Soviet Union is essentially the Warren Commission reconstruction based substantially on Oswald's diary. As we shall discuss in the next chapter, that diary is in all likelihood a total and complete sham.

In the Final Report of the Assassinations Records Review Board September, 1998, we learn that in 1996 three members of the Board reviewed the extensive KGB surveillance file kept in Minsk by the Belarusian KGB. The file details over two years of extensive surveillance and analysis by the KGB of Lee Harvey Oswald during the time that he resided in the Belarusian capital. We are not told what was in any of those records. We are told that "the Board was unable to obtain a copy of the file, in part due to the deteriorating relationship between the United States and Belarus." However, we are told that "some of these records were utilized by Norman Mailer in his book, *Oswald's Tale*," and that Mailer's collaborator in *Oswald's Tale*, Lawrence Schiller, agreed in response to the Board's request, to donate copies of documents from the Minsk files...." The Board goes on to state that that material, for some reason, will not be released in the JFK Collection until a later date. Thus, we not only do not have the records that were provided by Schiller, but we have no idea what is in them.

Presumably the records, whether from Belarus or from Schiller, will become available at some point. When they become available, what validity or significance should be attributed to them? One caution suggests itself. When one looks at *Oswald's Tale*, it appears Mailer was authenticating the Russian records by finding that they corresponded to Oswald's diary, or in the alternative, authenticating Oswald's diary by finding it corresponded to the Russian records. Thus, if the reader has reason to suspect that Oswald's diary was creating fiction, how much faith can one place in Russian records if they mimic that fiction?

CHAPTER 8
THE DIARY THAT WASN'T

* * *

The writing has a continuity from page to page and line to line that is indicative of being written about, or at, the same time. It does not give the impression of being "random", as would be expected of a diary extended over a period of time. It appears that this diary has been written within a short period of time and not over any extensive period.

Joseph P. McNally, Fellow, American Academy of Forensic Sciences

It has been pointed out that there are significant problems with each of the sources utilized to reconstruct Oswald's thoughts and activities while in the Soviet Union.

For many years Oswald's "Historic Diary" was the virtually unchallenged primary source of information on this period of his life, purporting, as it does, to be his contemporaneous documentation of events. However, some skeptics pointed to certain entries in the diary which they said reflected information which could only have become known after the supposed time of the entries.

The House Select Committee on Assassinations had a number of documents about which there were various questions; inevitably, Oswald's diary came to be amongst them. In order to resolve these questions, the Committee first asked the President on the American Society of Questioned Document Examiners for his recommendations on the leading experts in the field of questioned document examination, specifically hand-written documents. The Committee then asked each of the people he recommended for their suggestions as to whom the Committee might retain for these purposes. Three names appeared consistently. After ascertaining that none had had a connection with the FBI or the Kennedy case, the Committee requested that this impartial panel undertake an examination of various documents. The panel members, all of whom belonged to the American Society of Questioned Document Examiners, were Joseph P. McNally, David J. Purtell and Charles C. Scott. The Committee provided the following material extracted from their qualifications:

"McNally received a BS and an MPA in police science from the John Jay College of Criminal Justice, University of New York City in 1967 and 1975 respectively. He started in the field of questioned document identification in 1942 with the New York Police laboratory. He has been supervisor of the document identification section of the police laboratory, training officer in the police academy, commanding officer of the police laboratory and handwriting expert in he district attorney's office on New York County. He retired from the police department with the rank of captain in 1972 and entered private practice. He serves as a consultant to New York's Human Resources Administration. McNally is a fellow of the American Academy of Forensic Sciences, and a member of the International Association for Identification, and the American Society for Testing and Materials. He has lectured at the University of New York City, Rockland College, and the New York Police Academy."

"Purtell receiver a Ph.B, with a major in mathematics and chemistry, from Northwestern University in 1949. He began his career in questioned document identification in 1942 with the Chicago Police Department, where he served as a document examiner in the scientific crime detection laboratory. He retired in 1974 as chief document examiner and captain of police, and entered private practice in 1973. He is a fellow of the American Academy of Forensic Sciences and served as chairman of the questioned document section and chairman of the program committee. He is past vice president and president of the American Society of Questioned Document Examiners. Purtell has lectured at Northwestern University, the University of Illinois, the University of

Indiana and St Joseph's College, among other schools. He has presented and published numerous scientific papers."

"Scott received an AA degree from Kansas City Junior College in 1930 and a JD from the University of Missouri School of Law in 1935, whereupon he became a member of the Missouri bar. While attending law school, he founded the *University of Missouri at Kansas City Law Review* and was its first editor-in-chief. He began his career as a questioned document examiner with the Federal Reserve Bank in 1935 and has been in private practice since 1946. The first edition of his three-volume-book, *Photographic Evidence*, was published in 1942. Now in its second edition, it has become the standard textbook on the subject. He served on the first board of directors of the American Board of Forensic Document Examiners. He has conducted seminars on scientific document examination for more than 20 State bar associations, written numerous professional articles, and, since 1954, has been an adjunct professor of law at the University of Missouri School of Law."

The panel followed standard procedures and techniques in its examinations. The writings and signatures were looked at individually and in juxtaposition with each other, taking into consideration the gross characteristics of the writing process, writing skill, slant, speed, proportions of the letters, ratio of small to capital letters; height ratio, lateral spacing, and overall writing pattern. Significant differences were looked for. A stereoscope microscope was used for minute examination and comparison of individual letters and characteristics.

One of the issues addressed to these experts queried, "Was the 'historic diary' written in one sitting?' As to this, the panel concluded that, "Because of the poor condition of the historical diary, they are unable to conclude firmly whether it was written at one or more than one sitting. On balance, it appears to have been written at one or a few sittings." The problem referred to regarding the condition of the diary can best be understood from the comments of David J. Purtell: "With respect to timespan of the historical diary, an answer cannot be provided because of the present condition of the paper. The documents had been processed by the silver nitrate method in an attempt to develop latent fingerprints. While a recognized method, the drawback is that it soils the paper: the silver nitrate which remains on the paper causes it to turn black in time. Today, the pages are in very poor condition, and though the message can be read in part, it is a very difficult task. One observation that can be reported is that one sheet of paper is of a different weight (thickness) than the other sheets."

However, although scientifically dating the age of the writing might have proven helpful, inability to do so did not prevent addressing the truly crucial issue, which might be stated in the question: *Was this document an accumulation of random entries each entry having been made on the date indicated contemporaneous with the events being recorded?*

As to that very important question, the answer is most unsettling, for it appears to be rather clear that this document, upon which so much reliance has been placed in the reconstructing the defection, is a phony. In other words, Lee Harvey Oswald's "diary" was not a diary at all.

As Joseph P. McNally reported, "A check was made of the historical diary. The 12 pages were written with the same type of writing instrument. The paper used for 11 of the 12 pages is similar; only the last page differs – it is appreciably thinner. The writing has a continuity from page to page and line to line that is indicative of being written about, or at, the same time. It does not give the impression of being 'random,' as would be expected of a diary extended over a period of time. It appears that this diary has been written within a short period of time and not over any extensive period."

This determination not only calls into question the entire reconstruction of Oswald's life in Russia, but also gives rise to a most disturbing new question: Why?

CHAPTER 9

YURI NOSENKO, KGB DEFECTOR

* * *

"From the time of his defection, some U.S. intelligence officers suspected Nosenko was on a disinformation mission to mislead the American Government."

House Select Committee

Some CIA agents, including a Chief of Counter-Intelligence in the Agency's Soviet Branch, told the House Select Committee on Assassinations in 1978 that they believed it was possible that Lee Harvey Oswald had been recruited by the Soviet KGB during his military tour at Atsugi Air Base in Japan, as the CIA had identified a KGB program aimed at recruiting US military personnel during the period Oswald was stationed there. This was not a new concern. From the time of his arrest for the killing of President Kennedy, a primary concern was the question: Had Oswald been enlisted by the Soviet secret police, the dreaded KGB?

Then, in February 1964, only three months after the assassination, a most fortuitous event occurred: a Russian named Yuri Nosenko sought political asylum in the United States. According to CIA records, Nosenko declared that he had been a KGB agent; that in 1959 and again in 1963 he had been assigned to the KGB's American Tourist Section; that in that assignment he had reviewed Oswald's KGB file; and that he could categorically deny that Oswald had in any way been connected with the KGB. Norsenko's assertions did not end the inquiry into whether Oswald had a KGB connection. In fact, they only tended to complicate it.

This complication arose because, from the time of his defection, some U.S. intelligence officers suspected Nosenko was on a disinformation mission to mislead the American Government. In other words, they expressed doubt that Nosenko was a bona fide defector.

According to CIA records, back in 1962, while a security escort to a Soviet disarmament delegation in Geneva, Switzerland, Nosenko had offered to sell information to the CIA for 900 Swiss francs, claiming he needed the money to replace KGB funds he had spent on a drinking spree. After his defection he admitted that he had not really needed the money but had felt that an offer to merely give the information away for nothing would be rejected, as had been the case with similar offers by other Soviet agents. (This admission has not received all the study it deserves. For example, how would Nosenko have known of those prior offers, and why was Nosenko supposedly so anxious to pass information to the US as to make up such a story in order to be able to do so?).

Nonetheless, the CIA had made that 1962 deal with Nosenko. According to the records, at that time he asserted that he would never defect because he could never leave his family, and he told the CIA never to contact him in the Soviet Union. However, he assured them that he would make contact the next time he came abroad.

On January 23, 1964, eight weeks after the Kennedy assassination, Nosenko was once again in Geneva as escort to a disarmament delegation. Claiming that he was now disillusioned with his Government, and insisting that he would soon not be able to leave the Soviet Union again, Nosenko declared that he wished to immediately defect. The CIA stalled, but Nosenko was adamant. Then, "On February 4, Nosenko revealed he had received a telegram ordering him to return to Moscow directly. He said he feared the KGB was aware he was working with the West, and his life depended on his being permitted to defect immediately." Persuaded by his plea, the CIA accepted Nosenko as a defector. Nosenko would later admit that the recall telegram was a fake, and that he had made up the story in order to get the CIA to agree to his defection without further delay.

The FBI, having been informed by the CIA that Nosenko had information about Oswald, interviewed him upon his arrival in the United States. He reiterated what he had told the CIA regarding his knowledge of Oswald, including the reassuring fact that the KGB had never had any contact with President Kennedy's assassin. The conclusion of the report of this FBI interview reads: "On March 4, 1964, Nosenko stated that he did not want any publicity in connection with this information but stated he would be willing to testify to this information before the Presidential Commission provided such testimony is given in secret and absolutely no publicity is given either to his appearance before the Commission or to the information itself." The report also notes that two days later Nosenko inquired if his offer had been given to the appropriate authorities, and he was assured that this had been done.

By April 1964, officials of both the Soviet Russia and the Counter-Intelligence sections of the CIA were raising serious doubts as to whether Nosenko was a bona fide defector. The bases for their misgivings were stated to be:

(1) "Many leads provided by Nosenko had been of the 'givaway variety, that is, information that is no longer of significant value to the KGB, or information which in the probable judgment of the KGB is already being probed by Western intelligence, so that there is more to be gained from having a dispatched agent 'give it away' and thereby gain credibility.

(2) "A background check of Nosenko - of his schooling, military career and his activities as an intelligence officer - had led US officials to suspect Nosenko was telling them a 'legend.' that is, supplying them with a fabricated identity. Certain aspects of Nosenko's background did not check out, and certain events he described seemed highly unlikely.

(3) "Two defectors who had preceded Nosenko were skeptical of him. One was convinced Nosenko was on a KGB mission, the

purpose of which was to neutralize information one of the defectors had provided.

(4) "Information Nosenko had given about Oswald aroused their suspicions. The chief of the Soviet Russia section had difficulty accepting the statements about Oswald, characterizing them as seeming 'almost to have been tacked on or to have been added, as though it didn't seem to be part of the real body of the other things he had to say, many of which were true.'"

On April 4, 1964, the CIA placed Nosenko in isolation and commenced "hostile interrogations." The atmosphere was set by conducting a polygraph test wherein the CIA polygrapher was to accuse Nosenko of lying no matter what the test really showed. Presumably that did not require any great acting ability in this case, for in his report - in which he was to state his true conclusions- the polygrapher declared that Nosenko had indeed lied.

During 1964, Nosenko was interviewed on five occasions wherein at least some questions dealt with Lee Harvey Oswald. His story as it related to Oswald has been summarized as follows: "Nosenko related that he was assigned to the Seventh Department of the Second Chief Directorate when Oswald arrived in the Soviet Union in 1959, at which time Nosenko's section had responsibility for counter-intelligence operations against American tourists.

"At the time Oswald asked to remain in Russia, Nosenko reviewed information the KGB had on the American. Soon after Oswald went to Minsk, Nosenko was transferred and lost contact with him. However, he became re-involved in the case right after the assassination.

"Nosenko said that as soon as President Kennedy's assassin was identified as a man who had lived in the Soviet Union, the KGB ordered that Oswald's file be flown to Moscow and reviewed to determine whether there had been any contact between him and Soviet intelligence. Nosenko said further he was assigned to the review of Oswald's file. Based on that review, as well as his earlier contact with the case, he was able to report positively that Oswald had neither been recruited nor contacted by the KGB."

In October 1966, Nosenko was given his second polygraph test, during which he was again asked about Oswald. The CIA examiner was the same one who had administered the first test and he once again concluded that Nosenko was lying.

The Soviet Russia Section of the CIA wrote a 900-page report based on its interrogations of Nosenko, which was trimmed to 447 pages by the time it was submitted in February 1968. It came to the conclusion that Nosenko:

(1) "Did not serve in the naval reserve as he had claimed.

(2) Did not join the KGB at the time or in the manner he described.

(3) Did not serve in the American Embassy section of the KGB at the time he claimed, and was not a senior case officer or deputy chief of the seventh department, as he stated he had been.

(4) Was not chief of the American Embassy section.

(5) Was not a deputy chief of the seventh department in 1962, as he had claimed.'

From the time this report was first being drafted, the thrust of its conclusions was known by, and seemed to create quite a dilemma for, the leadership of the CIA. As a result, in mid-1967 a career security officer was assigned to write a critique of the handling of Nosenko. His conclusion - that Nosenko was who he claimed to be and that he was supplying valid information - led to the official CIA position that Nosenko was a bona fide defector.

On August 8, 1968, Nosenko was given a third polygraph test. Only two of the questions on this test related to information he had supplied about Oswald. This time Nosenko was deemed to have passed the test.

The official position of the CIA relative to the various polygraphs thereupon was stated to be that the third test – the one Nosenko passed – was considered to be a valid test. As to the first two tests - both of which Nosenko had failed - the official CIA position became that both of those tests were invalid or inconclusive.

In October 1968, the security officer who had been selected by the CIA brass issued a report, which disputed each and every conclusion of the report of the Soviet Russia Section written eight months earlier. However, neither of these reports paid very much attention to the Oswald aspect of the Nosenko case, and neither even attempted to affirmatively analyze Nosenko's statements about Oswald. The combined total for both reports amounts to 730 pages, only fifteen of which deal in any respect with Oswald. The security officer's report did, nonetheless, reach the conclusion that Nosenko was not dispatched by the Soviet Government to give false information to the US officials about Oswald. He listed the reasons for this conclusion thus:

(1) "Nosenko's first contact with the CIA was in June 1962, 17 months prior to the assassination.

(2) Information provided by Nosenko was not sufficient in 'nature, scope and content' to convince US authorities of no Soviet involvement in the assassination.

(3) Even if the KGB were involved in the assassination, the Soviets would assume that US authorities would, in turn, believe only a few senior officers would be aware of it, and Nosenko would not be one of them."

Amongst the documents obtained by the House Committee is information of finances, in which we learn that: "Prior to Nosenko's defection on February 4 1964, he was promised $50,000 for previous cooperation, $10,000 for his identification in 1962 of a particular espionage agent, and $25,000 a year compensation for future services."

These were not exactly pauper's wages. The average annual earnings of fulltime employees in the US in the year 1964 were $5,503. (*Historical Statistics of the United States, UD Department of Commerce, Bureau of the Census, 1975, page 164, Series D 722-727*).

CHAPTER 10

PICK YOUR POLYGRAPH

* * *

The second test - in which the examiner determined Nosenko was lying - was the most valid and reliable of the three examinations administered to Yuri Nosenko.

Richard O. Arther, American Academy of Certified Polygraphists

The House Select Committee undertook its own investigation of the Nosenko case, which involved both the review of existing documentation and the eliciting of new evidence. As part of its investigation, the Committee retained Richard O. Arther to conduct an independent analysis of Yuri Nosenko's three polygraph tests. The House Committee provides the following information at to this important topic:

"Arther received a BS with honors in police science from Michigan State University in 1951, and an MA in psychology from Columbia University in 1960. Arther has been in private practice in New York City since 1963. He founded Scientific Lie Detection, Inc. and co-founded the National Training Center of Polygraph Science. He has taught at Brooklyn College, Seton Hall University, the John Jay College of Criminal Justice and the Graduate School of Public Administration of New York University. Arther has authored over 200 professional articles and two books. He is a member of the Academy of Certified Polygraphists and the American Polygraph Association."

"A polygraph examination records physiological responses to questions asked. The polygraphist attempts to design the examination in such a way that the truthful person will react to the control question and the lying person to the relevant questions. The test structure must be constructed so that it poses a threat to both the truthful and untruthful person.

"The polygraphist attempts to determine the 'psychological set' of the examinee. He tries to determine, by reading the physiological activity of the examinee in the polygraph charts, what questions or question areas pose the greatest threat to the examinee's well-being. A 'psychological set' is a person's fears, anxieties, and apprehension, [which] are channeled toward that situation causing the greatest threat to the individual's well-being. He will tune in on that which is of a greater threat, and tune out that of a lesser threat

"Responses to questions are recorded on a polygraph chart, which consists of tracings produced by three different types of psychological reaction associated with the circulatory, nervous, and respiratory systems:

(1) The breathing pattern is recorded by means of a rubber tube placed around the person's chest.

(2) The Galvanic skin response is measured by placing the attachments on either the fingers or the palms.

(3) Changes in blood pressure, heart beat, and pulse rate are obtained by a standard blood pressure cuff placed around the upper arm.

"Questions are broken down into three categories:

(1) Relevant - those pertinent to the investigation.

(2) Irrelevant - hopefully, meaningless, non-emotion producing ones to get the person used to being questioned and giving answers.

(3) Control - non-relevant, to which it can be assumed the person will lie during the test. These provide a standard for comparing the responses to relevant questions.

"If a person reacts more to a proper control question than to the relevant questions, then he is considered to be truthful to the relevants. On the other hand, if he reacts more to the relevants than to the proper control question, he is considered to be lying to the relevants.

"Relevant, irrelevant and control questions are interspersed throughout the polygraph chart. The examination may consist of various series covering various relevant issues. Each relevant issue must be asked a minimum of two times in a series, but as many times as necessary to conclude that relevant issue successfully. Each series should have a minimum of two charts, but as many charts as necessary to conclude the relevant issues in that series successfully.

"The procedure for a polygraph examination is as follows: The polygraphist first conducts a pre-test interview, during which the test questions are read to the person exactly as they are going to be asked. It is vital that all questions be properly worded and discussed with the person. Then the actual test is conducted."

Having conducted his independent analysis, Richard O. Arther concluded that the second test - in which the examiner determined Nosenko was lying - was the most valid and reliable of the three examinations administered to Yuri Nosenko.

As for the third test - where the examiner found Nosenko to be telling the truth - Mr. Arther, in addressing the only two questions on that exam which related to the information Nosenko had supplied about Oswald, characterized the first such question as "atrocious" and the second such question as "very poor" for use in assessing the validity of Nosenko's responses.

The fact is that this third examiner had even found Nosenko to be truthful when he answered "No" to the question, "Is there any possibility that the KGB would dispatch an officer to defect to the Americans?"

CHAPTER 11

NOT WORTHY OF BELIEF

* * *

"Here was this young American, Lee Harvey Oswald, just out of the Marine Corps, already inside the USSR,... The KGB never bothered to talk to him, not even once, not even to get an idea whether he might be a CIA plant...Can this be true?"

Mr. "D.C.," Deputy Chief, Soviet Bloc Division, CIA

The House Select Committee, in considering whether Nosenko was a bona fide defector, was interested to know why the CIA had apparently failed (or refused) to ascertain that there were inconsistencies within Nosenko's various statements, as well as between some of Nosenko's statements and knowledge from other sources. As part of its investigation on these points, the Committee took the deposition of the CIA employee who interviewed Nosenko on July 3 & 27, 1964. It turned out that this person who the CIA had detailed to question Nosenko was in no position to challenge Nosenko either on general knowledge or specifically on Oswald. In his deposition this CIA employee told the Committee he was not an expert on the KGB, nor had he any previous experience with KGB defectors. When asked about his knowledge of Oswald, since it was in his interviews that the most detailed questions about Oswald were asked, he replied, "I cannot specifically recall having read any files pertaining to Lee Harvey Oswald. Certainly I had read and heard a lot about him in the newspapers, television and radio. I may have had the opportunity to read some previous debriefings of Nosenko concerning Oswald, but I am not sure of that."

As to the security officer who wrote the 1968 report, when he was asked if he ever spoke to Nosenko about Oswald, he said, "No. Well, all I have you have there (Nosenko's three page statement). I did a write-up on it. I didn't see that it seriously conflicted with what we had." He was then asked, "And did you ever question him about what he wrote?" to which he responded, "No, because I had no reason to disbelieve him."

Questioned further as to why he did not compare all of Nosenko's statements on Oswald, he replied, "I did not have all the information on the Oswald investigation. That was an FBI investigation." The follow-up inquiry was, "Well, was it available to you if you had asked the FBI for their reports of what Oswald had said to them?" The answer was, "It might, under certain circumstances, but in this case here, as far as our office was concerned, the Oswald matter was an FBI matter."

Given the apparent failure of the CIA to critically evaluate the credibility of Nosenko's statements about Oswald, the Committee undertook to do this job, and, in review of all the evidence, the Committee noted that there had been significant inconsistencies over the years in Nosenko's story. A few of these will now be discussed.

In his interviews in 1964, among the points Nosenko stressed was that there had been no physical or technical surveillance on Oswald (in fact, he had even claimed that the KGB did not know that Marina was a friend of Oswald until they applied for marriage because there was no surveillance on Oswald to show that he know her). He claimed that he could unequivocally state this because he had thoroughly reviewed Oswald's KGB file. Yet, when being pressed on a slightly different tack in 1978, Nosenko claimed that he had been unable to read the entire Oswald file because it consisted of seven or eight thick volumes of documents due to all the surveillance reports.

Nosenko insisted that the KGB never had any contact whatsoever with Oswald, not even an interview. They not only did not question Oswald when he asked to defect, but they also did not interview him later when it was decided he would be permitted to remain in Russia. At no time did the KGB talk to Oswald. Yet, when the Committee asked Nosenko, "Would the KGB have any interest in an American student?" he replied, "As I told you yesterday, the

KGB is interested in students, but particularly those students who are studying the Russian language, Russian history, Russian economy." A subsequent question began, "Is it your testimony that Lee Harvey Oswald, who was a student, who was a professed Marxist, who had . . . " At this point Nosenko interrupted. "Students. I never heard that he was a student."

This is a fascinating statement by a man who claimed to know all there was to know about Oswald in the Soviet Union. Russian documents supplied to the United Stated presumably from the files Nosenko claimed to have reviewed show that upon his arrival in Moscow Oswald registered at the Hotel Berlin as a "student;" and in his application for an identity card at the Visa and Registration Office at the Moscow City Council, Oswald had filled out item 13 (occupation) with the word "student."

When asked, "And exactly why did no KGB officer ever speak to Oswald before they made the decision about whether to let him defect?" Nosenko answered, 'We didn't consider him an interesting target." But, when asked if he knew of any other defector who was turned away because he was uninteresting, Nosenko answered "No."

The head of the CIA Soviet Russia Section from 1963 to 1968 was asked by the Committee if he knew of comparable situations in which someone was not questioned, was just left alone, as Nosenko said Oswald was. He replied that he did not know of any former Soviet intelligence officer or other knowledgeable source to whom he had spoken who felt that this would have been possible. "If someone did," he said, "I never heard of it."

Nosenko was forced to admit that the KGB would have been "very interested" in the fact that Oswald worked as a radar operator at an air base form which the super secret U-2 spy planes took off and landed. But, Nosenko maintained, the KGB never spoke with Oswald and so it didn't know that he had any connection with the U -2 flights.

As the Committee summarized this tale, "In short, Nosenko's Oswald story is as follows: The KGB, although very interested in the U-2, never learned anything about it from Oswald because it didn't know he had any knowledge of the aircraft. Why? Because Oswald was never questioned by the KGB because the decision was made that Oswald was of no interest to Soviet intelligence."

Even John Hart, who appeared before the Committee to support the CIA's assessment that Nosenko was a bona fide defector, had to concede as follows: "I find it very hard to believe that the KGB has so little interest in this individual. Therefore, if I were in the position of deciding whether to use the testimony of Mr. Nosenko on this case or not, I would not use it." Mr. Hart was asked, ".... here you have someone in the Soviet Union who announces he wants to stay, that he wants to live there, that he wants to become a Soviet citizen, and the KGB according to Mr. Nosenko decides that on the basis of his application to come to the country he is uninteresting. Now, does that strike you as plausible, based on your information and your knowledge of intelligence and counter-intelligence activities, that the KGB would dismiss that kind of request merely by looking at the entrance applications, and not make an effort to talk to the person, to see what information they might be able to impart?" The answer to that question by this Nosenko apologist was:

"Congressman, I find it implausible. I might say that if this had ever been the case within the expertise of any of us who had anything to do with Soviet operations, it would have greatly facilitated our tasks in connection with **putting people into the Soviet Union . . . "**] *emphasis added]*

Hart's enthusiastic support for Nosenko's bona fides as a defector was rebutted at length by the Deputy Chief, SB Division (a man referred to only as Mr. D.C.) who, at the time of Nosenko's first contact with the CIA in Geneva, had served as head of the CIA's section responsible for counter-intelligence against the Soviet intelligence services, and later, as the deputy chief of the Soviet Bloc Division of the CIA, had assisted in further interrogations of

Nosenko. As related to Oswald, the testimony of this witness is dramatic and informative:

"Here was this young American, Lee Harvey Oswald, just out of the Marine Corps, already inside the USSR and going to great lengths to stay there and become a citizen. The KGB never bothered to talk to him, not even once, not even to get an idea whether he might be a CIA plant (and although even Nosenko once said, I think that the KGB feared he might be).

"Can this be true?

"Could we all be wrong in what we've heard about rigid Soviet security precautions and about their strict procedures and disciplines, and about how dangerous it is in the USSR for someone to take a risky decision (like failing to screen an applicant for permanent residence in the USSR)?

"Of course not."

CHAPTER 12

A DISINFORMATION MISSION?

* * *

If Nosenko was indeed on a disinformation mission, a mission to deflect attention away from an Oswald connection, and it was not the KGB that sent him, then who sent Nosenko and why?

Having evaluated all of the evidence, the Committee declared, not surprisingly, that they were "certain Nosenko lied about Oswald." However, that still left a question, which the Committee could not answer: *Why* did Nosenko lie about Oswald?

As for that issue, all they could do was to observe: "The reasons he would lie about Oswald range from the possibility that he merely wanted to exaggerate his own importance to the disinformation hypotheses with its sinister implications."

To this they appended a footnote: "Beyond those reasons for falsification that can be attributed to Nosenko himself, there has been speculation that the Soviet Government, while not involved in the assassination, sent Nosenko on a mission to allay American fears. Hence, while his story about no connection between Oswald and the KGB might be false, his claim of no Soviet involvement would be truthful."

The Committee's comments as to the question: "Why did Nosenko lie about Oswald?" appear to imply that there is absolutely nothing in the evidence that might prove helpful in trying to answer that question. Perhaps so.

The Committee also appears to be indicating that they have at least set the outer bounds - the range - of the possible answer to that perplexing question. Again, perhaps, so.

Yet, careful analysis of the available evidence seems to hint that there may be a very different and perhaps more logical explanation to the Nosenko enigma.

Let us re-examine the known facts and consider if there are reasonable inferences that such facts may warrant.

We are told that Nosenko sold information to the CIA in 1962. We are later told that Nosenko "said he feared the KGB was aware he was working with the West, and his life depended on his being permitted to defect immediately."

Suppose we reword these facts into language more meaningful to our inquiry: As of 1962, the CIA had compromised Nosenko, and thereby, as of 1962 the CIA "owned" Nosenko – they could at any time force him to do their bidding because they held over his head the ever-present threat of leaking to the Soviets the facts about Nosenko's sale of information to the CIA.

The language ascribed to Nosenko is also informative: "He said he feared the KGB was aware he *was working* with the West ..." The tense used hints at something quite to the contrary of the implication in the summary that there had been merely a single contact sometime in the distant past.

But we need not depend on semantics to show that there had been an ongoing relationship between Nosenko and the CIA. The information in another part of this body of work relative to finances would seem to rather clearly demonstrate that there in fact had been such a relationship: "Prior to Nosenko's defection on February 4, 1964, he was promised $50,000 for previous cooperation, $10,000 for his identification in 1962 of a particular espionage agent, and $25,000 a year for future services."

In the narrative we are told of only one contact, that being in 1962, and the nature of that contact is said to be the sale of information for the sum of 900 Swiss francs. So, as for that one stated contact, the CIA already had its information and Nosenko already had his money.

For what, then, was the sum of $60,000 being promised, if not for services provided during an ongoing relationship prior to the defection? Indeed, the very language tells us that is just what this $60,000 was for: "$50,000 for previous cooperation, and $10,000 for his identification, in 1962, of a particular espionage agent."

So, the evidence would seem to be conclusive that for some period of time preceding his defection, Yuri Nosenko had been a CIA asset – an undercover agent in place – who had been providing valuable services and information to the CIA. Can there by any question that under normal circumstances Nosenko's most valuable role to the CIA would be to remain as an agent in place? Logically, should the CIA want to encourage him to defect, thereby losing a well-placed spy?

Yet, if they were not encouraging him to defect, how else does one explain the statement: "*Prior* to *Nosenko's defection* on February 4, 1964, *he was promised* $50,000 for previous cooperation, $10,000 for his identification, in 1962, of a particular espionage agent, and $25,000 a year compensation for future services?"

Here was a KGB officer the CIA had "turned," and over whom they had permanent blackmail privileges. Are we to believe that the soft-hearted CIA let him off the hook just because he wanted out? No, we are told that he was permitted to defect because he reported that he had received a telegram recalling him immediately to Moscow, and that he feared the Soviets knew he was working with the West, so that his life was in danger if not allowed to defect.

But, let's look a bit more closely at this rationalization. Is there any believable explanation as to why – before allowing this compromised KGB officer - this valuable in-place asset -to defect, that no one demanded that he produce the alleged telegram supposedly ordering him back to his death in Moscow? Here, supposedly, was the proof Nosenko needed to persuade the CIA to permit him to defect. Would anyone have been believed it had he said he had destroyed this crucial life-saving evidence? What would he have said: That he destroyed it to keep it a secret? - keep it a secret from whom? We can conclude they never asked for the telegram, since:

(1) We know that no such telegram was sent and so could not have been produced; and

(2) Had the telegram been called for, there is no credible excuse Nosenko could have offered for failing to produce it.

It would appear, therefore, that in order to accept the alleged story of Nosenko's defection, we must first accept the premise that in utter dereliction of their duties, the responsible CIA officials permitted a valuable spy, a turned KGB officer, to hornswoggle them into accepting the story of a phantom recall telegram which they never even asked to see, and, in addition, that before permitting him the pleasure of bamboozling them, they first promised him amounts of money which were by 1964 standards most substantial indeed.

The alternative would seem to be that we have not been told a complete and accurate story about Nosenko's defection, which would certainly raise the question as to why we were misled. All of this leads inexorably to the following questions:

(1) Did the CIA (or elements there) order the defection of the CIA's longtime agent, Yuri Nosenko?

(2) Was it merely a coincidence that Nosenko's defection happened to come at a time when intense scrutiny was being addressed to the background of Lee Harvey Oswald?

(3) By insisting that he would be willing to testify regarding his knowledge of Oswald, *"provided such testimony is given in secret and absolutely no publicity is given either to his appearance before the Commission or to the information itself,"* was Nosenko participating in an endeavor to keep the Russians from knowing that false information would be provided in a charade to make it appear that the information originated from Russia?

LET'S FOLLOW THAT LAST THOUGHT FOR A MOMENT.

Who controlled the input of information if Nosenko's testimony about Oswald had been kept secret from all except those for whose ears it was intended?

What might the investigators be anticipated to suspect when elements of the CIA advise them that Nosenko might be a false defector?

Was Nosenko's Oswald story intentionally designed so that absolutely no one could possibly believe it?

When this possibly false defector relates his blatantly untrue Oswald story, are the listeners expected to conclude that the untrue Oswald story provides the final proof that he was, indeed, a false defector?

When the listeners conclude that this false defector has told an untrue Oswald story, are they to suspect that someone might have sent the false defector?

Are the listeners to suspect that whoever sent the false defector with the untrue Oswald story might have had a reason to want to deflect attention away from some connection they had with Oswald?

Does this mean that it was intended that the investigators should be led to believe that the KGB was trying to deflect attention way from its Oswald connection?

And, finally, if Nosenko was indeed on a disinformation mission, a mission to deflect attention away from an Oswald connection, and it was not the KGB that sent him, then who sent Nosenko and why?

CHAPTER 13

WHO SENT NOSENKO?

* * *

If Nosenko was lying about Oswald, then, by implication, Oswald would be left as being the agent of whoever sent Nosenko.

As if there were not already enough twists and turns to the Nosenko story, there is *possibly* yet another explanation to this increasingly bizarre puzzle. The word "possibly" is emphasized here because the evidence upon which this chapter is based was not authenticated by any of the official investigations we have been relying upon – at least not directly.

A writer named Edward Jay Epstein, utilizing the Freedom of Information Act, obtained documents detailing the differing CIA perceptions of Yuri Nosenko, which might be best described as: the "official" CIA position that he was a bona fide defector; and the "contrarian" unofficial view that he was a false defector. Mr. Epstein's book, *Legend*, was published in 1978, and it provided to the general public its first real knowledge of Nosenko. *Legend*, based in good part on adopting the contrarian view of Nosenko, made out a strong case that the Russians were seeking to deflect attention away from some relationship they had with Lee Harvey Oswald.

As it turns out, during his preparation for his book, Mr. Epstein spoke with the CIA official previously identified (in our chapter 11 above) as "Mr. D. C." In his testimony to the House Select Committee, Mr. D.C. acknowledged talking with Epstein in that regard, indicating that the primary help he provided to Mr. Epstein was to insure that there were no errors in the Nosenko story now being disseminated to the public. Specifically, Mr. D. C. stated in his sworn testimony that while he may not agree with some of the emphasis, "the facts that Mr. Epstein has in the book are generally accurate."

This leads us into yet another labyrinth, for in *Legend* Mr. Epstein relates certain facts relating to Yuri Nosenko for which we have no official verification except for this blanket "Amen" sworn to by Mr. D. C. However, these are facts about which Mr. D.C. would have firsthand knowledge, and so his endorsement under oath of the accuracy of the facts in Mr. Epstein's book is uniquely meaningful. It will be remembered that Mr. D.C. has previously been identified as having been in 1962 the head of the CIA's section responsible for counter-intelligence against the Soviet intelligence services. As such, he would have had more than a passing interest in a KGB officer who first contacted the Agency in 1962 offering information. More to the point, he testified that he was directly responsible for the case of Yuri Nosenko from 1962 to 1967.

Mr. Epstein in his book discloses that at the time of his first meeting with the CIA in 1962, Nosenko had related a story as to how the KGB had come to uncover and execute a CIA "mole," Pytor Semyonovick Popov. Popov, a lieutenant colonel in Soviet military intelligence, had for some time been perhaps the highest placed and most valuable CIA spy in Russia. The Agency had an understandable interest in how Popov had come to be discovered, since one obvious possibility that existed was that he had been betrayed by someone on the US side. Nosenko said that Popov had been detected through a new Soviet surveillance technique, which would indicate – comfortingly – that there had been no breach of security within the CIA.

Mr. Epstein also discloses that in what would have been late 1958 or early 1959, Richard Bissell, the father of the U-2 spy plane program, told the CIA deputy director of plans, Richard Helms, that Popov had been sending out information that the Russians now had ascertained some specific information about the super secret U-2. This was shocking news, since if they had discovered many of the flight characteristics of the U-2, this could accelerate their ability design a control system which would permit their high-altitude rockets to knock the planes from the sky. Helms and Bissell wondered how the Soviets could be gaining such knowledge.

Sometime later in 1959, at a meeting in Moscow with his CIA case officer, Popov revealed that the KGB had caught on to him indicating with hand gestures that he had been wired for sound and passing a note scribbled out on six pages of toilet paper. In September 1959, Popov was arrested and subsequently executed by Soviet counter-intelligence.

Obviously, Nosenko's information that Popov had been caught through a new Soviet surveillance technology would be comforting only if Nosenko were believed. If there were reason to doubt him, it would follow that he might have been sent to deflect attention away from the truth: to wit, that Popov had been identified by a Soviet mole within the American intelligence committee.

It is a tribute to their usual tight-mouthed discipline that we laymen tend to view the CIA as a monolithic organization of single-minded people. Spy novels aside, the testimony of and about Yuri Nosenko provides us with a rare glimpse into the real and very human world of the intelligence agent. We learn, for example, that at the time Nosenko presented himself in 1962, there was an internal struggle within the CIA as to the bona fides of a Russian defector identified as "X". Six months earlier, "X" had defected bringing information that there was a Russian mole highly placed in the American intelligence community. The question arose: Was "X" sent to sow dissent and distrust in the Agency, or did the intelligence community have the very serious problem of a mole?

The problem becomes more complex. Mr. D. C. told the House Select Committee that at the time of Nosenko's initial contact in 1962, he was suspicious of Nosenko because he believed Nosenko was deflecting information which had been given in the previous months by "X." In other words, Mr. D. C. says that from the word go he believed Nosenko was providing false information in order to deflect American attention away from the information which "X" had given.

Yet John Hart testified that "the first important communication which went back from Geneva after the two Americans emissaries had met with Mr. Nosenko was sent by a man who... I am going to call... the deputy chief of the SB Division, Soviet Bloc Division, throughout my testimony." [Elsewhere Hart makes clear that he is referring to the man as to the deputy chief of the Soviet Bloc Division although he did not as yet hold that rank]. "The deputy chief, who is the chief interrogator over there, sent back a telegram to Washington on June 11, 1962, in which he said 'Subject,' meaning Nosenko, 'has conclusively proved his bona fides. He has provided info of importance and sensitivity. Subject now completely cooperative. Willing to meet when abroad and will meet as often and as long as possible in his departure in Geneva from June 15. 'On June 15 both Nosenko and the Deputy Chief SB departed from Geneva, Mr. Nosenko to return to Moscow and his KGB duties, the Deputy Chief SB to return to Washington.

"In the course of my investigation, I asked the gentleman, who was for many years chief of the CIA counter-intelligence staff, to describe to me what ensued after the arrival in Washington of DCSB, and I shall give you a brief quote which was recorded and transcribed and which is held in our files. This is the chief of the counter-intelligence staff of the CIA speaking: 'We got the first message from Deputy Chief SB – that is the one I have just previously quoted to you – on Nosenko from Geneva, and Deputy Chief SB was ordered back to Washington, and we had a big meeting here on Saturday morning, and Deputy Chief SB thought he had the biggest fish of his life. I mean he really did. And everything I heard from him, however, was in direct contrast from what we had heard from Mr. 'X.'"

In 1978 Mr. D. C. told the House Committee, "In 1962 he made it absolutely clear to us that he would never defect, under no circumstances... He not only said he wouldn't defect but he wouldn't accept contact with us inside the Soviet Union. However, he would see us whenever he came out on official duty on Soviet delegations abroad. In January of 1964 he came out and stupefied us with this statement that he now wants to defect." We know from previous chapters that this rendition would appear to be incomplete, since the records indicate that there was an ongoing relationship after Nosenko's return to Russia during which he acted as an American agent in place.

In a 1976 internal CIA memorandum, the Chief of the Soviet Russia Division (SR Division) is quoted as stating in a memo dated February 10, 1964, "First I assured Subject [Mr. Nosenko] that I was satisfied that he was genuine. Based on this, and assuming his continued 'cooperation,' I said we would proceed to make arrangements to bring him to the States. Second, I confirmed our agreement to pay him $25,000 for each year in place ($50,000) plus $10,000 for [*a sensitive case*] and our readiness to contract for his services at $25,000 per year. Third, I explained the polygraph he would be expected to take as final proof of his bona fides."

In a memo dated February 17, 1964, the Chief of the SR Division writes, "None of the events of the past few days including the way the Soviets played the pre-confrontation publicity or the confrontation itself changes the substances of the conclusions contained in my February 10, memorandum. However, there is greater evidence now I believe for the view that this operation is designed for long-range goals of utmost importance to the Soviets. One of these is probably a massive propaganda assault on CIA in which Subject, most probably as a 're-defected CIA agent,' will play a major but not necessarily the sole role."

We know from previous chapters that from the time of Nosenko's defection, a long and bitter internal battle ensued as to Nosenko's bona fides. And from the material discussed immediately above we can understand that the perceptions of the various CIA factions as to Nosenko were shaped to a great extent by their perception of "X".

But what has all this to do with Oswald? A rather interesting fact is glossed over in the Nosenko/Oswald summaries of the House Committee. Mr. D.C., who was the man on the scene, testified that, "Nosenko *before* his defection, ...was meeting us under clandestine circumstances in Geneva. He was telling us about Lee Harvey Oswald. We, of course, took that and got it as straight and as thoroughly as we could under the circumstances. After he defected and came to the United States, it was made clear... that the FBI, as the primary investigative agency on the President's assassination, would manage the further and detailed questioning of Mr. Nosenko in the United States on his knowledge of Lee Harvey Oswald."

There is nothing in that rendition to indicate the FBI was warned at this time that Nosenko's bona fides were in question. Indeed the conclusion of the FBI report of their interview with Nosenko makes no such reference. Instead, it relates the famous offer by Nosenko to testify before the Warren Commission and the statement that the offer had been passed on to the appropriate authorities. [The records show that at a later date J. Edgar Hoover expressed himself as believing that Nosenko was a valid defector but that Mr. "X" was a provocateur].

It would appear from the official summaries that it was not until after the Warren Commission had been briefed on Nosenko's story that Oswald had never been contacted by the KGB that the CIA met informally with Commission member Allen Dulles to inform him that Nosenko's bona fides were in doubt. The official summaries imply that this was so because the doubts did not begin until after the Commission had been told Nosenko's Oswald story. However, the testimony of Mr. D.C. contradicts that, and indeed, indicates that the doubts went back to the time of the 1962 contact. Whatever the truth on these matters, the result is the same: The Warren Commission received information which could only lead them to suspect an Oswald/KGB connection, thereby deflecting them from considering other possible connections.

For a period of time after his defection, the monies promised to Nosenko before his defection were not paid. Obviously, whether the challenges to his bona fides were sincere or a sham, it wouldn't do to be paying him monies at that time. By the late 60s, the money had been worked out, and by the time of the House hearings in 1978, Nosenko was receiving in excess of $35,000 per year as a "consultant."

In a memorandum to the Director of Central Intelligence dated October 5, 1972, Harold J. Osborn, Director of Security, states: "An analysis of this case clearly indicates that Mr. Nosenko had been an extremely valuable source, one who has identified many hundreds of Soviet Intelligence Officers, and he has otherwise provided a considerable quantity of useful information on the organization of the KGB, its operational doctrine, and methods. [*Sensitive info*] has been forwarded to the Federal Bureau of Investigation based on data from Mr. Nosenko. He has conducted numerous special security reviews on Soviet subjects of specific intelligence interest, and he has proven himself to be invaluable in exploring counter-intelligence leads. He recently authored a book which is of interest to the Agency. In effect, Mr. Nosenko has shown himself to be a productive and hardworking defector, who is 'rehabilitated' and favorably disposed towards the Agency."

Then, as we have seen, in 1978, the House Committee received testimony by and about Nosenko which could only cause them to suspect an Oswald/KGB connection, thus –as with the Warren Commission - deflecting them from considering other possible connections. The question arises: How is it that this "extremely valuable" CIA employee delivers testimony about Oswald which the CIA then disowns as implausible and incredible?

After Nosenko again asserted he could state positively that Soviet intelligence had had no interest in ex-Marine Oswald because they didn't think he was interesting, a CIA official named David Murphy made sure everyone understood that nonsense could not be believed: "They will talk to a marine about close order drill. You follow me? It doesn't require that he be known to have been a radar operator or a... they would talk to him about his military affiliations just as we would... We in Germany will talk to a private in the East German Border Guards, period. The GRU would be interested in talking to a private. He was a corporal in the Marine Corps, who had stated to a consult in a consular office, which is manned by the Soviets, Soviet locals and what have you, fully accessible to the Soviets, unlike the higher floors of the Embassy, that he wanted to talk about his experiences, that he wanted to tell all. I guess I found it difficult to believe; this is one of the things that made (or one of the things that created) an atmosphere of disbelief: that there must be something to this case that is important, vitally important to the Soviet Union, and we can't understand it."

CIA Director Richard Helms, while on the one hand supporting Nosenko's bona fides as a defector, left no room for doubt in his testimony that the Committee should disbelieve Nosenko on Oswald. Helms was asked the following question:

"Given your work in the whole field of intelligence, is it reasonable for this Committee to assume that with Oswald's background and his attempt to defect, that he would be an 'uninteresting target' to the KBG?"

In response, Richard Helms testified:

"I simply do not understand that assertion. I would have thought, to begin with, that any American who went to the Russian Government and said 'I want to defect to the Soviet Union' would have immediately been take over by the KGB to find out what his game was because, after all, the KGB's charter is to protect the Soviet state against infiltration. How would they know that he was serious about this? How would they know that the CIA had not sent him to make a fake defection and to try to get into Soviet society through this device? So for that reason, if not for many others, I find it quite incredible, the assertion by Nosenko that Oswald was never interrogated or was never in touch with the KGB while he was in the

Soviet Union. This really stretches one's credulity. It goes back to the testimony this morning that this is the hardest thing about the whole Nosenko case to swallow, and I have not been able to swallow it in all these years."

The morning testimony to which Helms was referring began with a question by Chairman Stokes: "If it were clearly proven that Nosenko's statement concerning Oswald were untrue, what significance would you attach to such a finding insofar as the broader question of his overall bona fides are concerned?"

To that question Helms replied:

"I think, Mr. Stokes, that is just the point. This is the issue which remains, as I understand it, to this very day, that no person familiar with the facts, of whom I am aware, finds Mr. Nosenko's comments about Lee Harvey Oswald and the KGB to be credible. That still hangs in the air like an incubus. I think, therefore, this tends to sour a great deal of one's opinion of all the other things he may have contributed to the knowledge of the intelligence community about Soviet affairs and Soviet agents and so forth. I do not know how one resolves this bone in the throat. And therefore, if I sit here before you and say, Mr. Stokes, I believe that Mr. Nosenko is a bona fide defector and you can rely on everything he says, I am in effect saying now, Mr. Stokes, you can rely on what he says about Lee Harvey Oswald. And I would not like to make that recommendation to you. That is where this thing lies and it is a most difficult question even at this late date."

The true culmination of all this came a little further on when Chairman Stokes asked: "So it leaves you with the conclusion, then, that if Nosenko was lying about Oswald, that Oswald would in fact be left as being an agent of the KGB?"

Helms responded: "By implication."

Thus, the scenario painted by the various CIA witnesses apparently led the Committee to the following conclusions:

(1) Nosenko lied

(2) Nosenko was a false defector

(3) The Soviet Union sent this false defector,

(4) It was the Soviets who had the motive to lead the Committee to these conclusions.

Perhaps these conclusions are correct.

However, taking as a given that Nosenko was lying, does the above material support the proposition that it was the Soviets and could only have been the Soviets that caused Nosenko's defection?

The only action by the Soviets that the material supports is that they were said to have sent a telegram calling Nosenko back to Moscow, thereby precipitating the defection.

If such telegram had been sent in order for Nosenko to use as proof to facilitate his false defection, why would he tear it up? Then, when we learn that Nosenko admitted making up the story and that there never was such a telegram, where is there anything pointing to the Soviets as the moving force behind the defection? Are we to assume that the Soviets came up with some bizarre plot to have Nosenko make believe he got a telegram? Why wouldn't they just send one so that Nosenko could show it to the CIA?

Instead of the Stokes/Helms conclusion, would it be more logical to state: If Nosenko was lying about Oswald, then, by implication, Oswald would be left as being the agent of whoever sent Nosenko?

CHAPTER 14

THE AGENCY

* * *

"The nature of Oswald's employment while in Minsk has been examined by the Commission. The factory in which he worked was a large plant manufacturing electronic parts and radio and television sets."

Warren Commission

"The CIA maintained a large volume of information on the Minsk radio factory in which Oswald had worked. This information was stored in the Office of Research and Reports."

House Select Committee

In 1964, the CIA advised the Warren Committee that the Agency had never had a relationship of any kind with Lee Harvey Oswald. CIA Director John A. McCone testified not only that Oswald was not an agent, employee, informant of the CIA, and was never associated or connected directly or indirectly in any way whatsoever with the Agency, but, further, he swore that: "The Agency never contacted him, interviewed him, talked with him, or solicited any reports or information from him, or communicated with him directly or in any other manner." Does this sound strikingly like what Nosenko said as regards the KGB and Oswald? Is it any more believable? Is it believable that the CIA, which routinely attempts to solicit information from just regular Americans traveling to Russia, would not even contact and attempt to debrief a returning defector who had lived in Russia for some two and a half years? Let us accept that, for whatever reason, it is believable.

Is it believable if we consider the interest the CIA would clearly have – if not in this particular defector, as such – in adding to their information as to how the Russians handle defectors, should they want to "plant" a defector, as we know was done? (see, for example, the testimony of John Hart discussed above: ".. would have greatly facilitated our tasks in connection with putting people into the Soviet Union . . ")

Is it still believable if we now add the following additional facts?

(1) The returning defector had been a Marine radar operator carrying a security clearance of "confidential"

(2) He had worked at an air base where the super secret U-2 spy plane took off and landed

(3) Since his defection, Francis Gary Powers had been shot down over Russia in the first ever successful downing of a U-2.

Let us now add another little-known, but vital fact to the inquiry we have just begun. There are few people who do not know that during his years in Minsk, Oswald worked in the Belorussian Radio and Television Factory. On the other hand, few people know that the CIA had a very great interest in this particular radio factory. One of the unheralded pieces of information that comes to us from the work of the House Select Committee is that the CIA actively collected & carefully accumulated reams of information on the plant. The House Select Committee report informs us that "the CIA maintained a large volume of information on the Minsk radio factory in which Oswald had worked. This information was stored in the Office of Research and Reports."

Given the CIA's interest in this particular "radio factory", is it believable that the CIA would not even attempt to debrief Oswald when he re-defected? What are we to make of this categorical denial by the CIA that they ever had even the slightest contact with Oswald?

Let us look more carefully at this new piece of information, and see if it might tie in with any knowledge we learned earlier. To do that, let's explore two seemingly unrelated questions and see if there may be some point of convergence between them:

(1) Why was the CIA so interested in the Minsk radio factory?

(2) How did the Russians come to assign Oswald to this facility?

Are these unrelated questions? Since neither the CIA nor the Russians have been forthcoming with answers to these questions, we must approach the issue from a somewhat different tack. Are we to assume that the CIA's interest in this plant was because they were concerned that the Russians were about to swamp American markets with Russian radios or TV, at a time when there were not enough of either to satisfy Russian domestic consumption? Or, is it more logical to ask if there might have been some military implications to some of the activities at the Minsk radio plant? What type of activities might take place at a radio plant that might have military implications?

Let's return to a topic we discussed much earlier. Radio waves are used in a very important system which has significant military implications. By definition, radar is "a method of detecting distant objects and determining their position, velocity, or other characteristics by analysis of very high frequency radio waves reflected from their surfaces."

Surely, if the Russians were doing some radar work at this plant, that fact would seem to provide an answer to both of the questions we are currently exploring. It would certainly explain the CIA's interest in the plant, and it could explain why the Russians decided to send Oswald there. But where does that lead us?

We know from the testimony of John Hart that the CIA had, as part of its operations, the task of "putting people into the Soviet Union." Why would they want to infiltrate people into the Soviet Union? Is it reasonable to assume that the CIA did not on mere whim expose people to the great physical risk of "putting them into the Soviet Union?" Is it reasonable to assume that such risks were undertaken only in order to procure specific information which second-hand reports could not adequately provide?

Let us take as a given the great interest the CIA had in this plant, together with the presumptions that they must have had a good reason for that interest – for example, radar. Let us then assume hypothetically that the CIA desired to put their own man into that plant. How might they go about infiltrating this spy into the plant? Well, if the reason for the CIA interest was Russian radar work at that plant, it may seem a good bet that if the Russians had an American defector who was a radar operator, they might wish to utilize his knowledge at the Minsk plant. Of course, for that to happen, the CIA's man must be a radar operator – regardless of whether he really has the aptitude for that specialty or not. If, for example, the man selected had on his aptitude tests scored significantly below the average in arithmetic and pattern code analysis, that would not deter from his being assigned to radar, since the radar assignment would be not because of his aptitude, but because of his future mission. And if he finished his first six-week radar course forty-sixth in a class of fifty-four, that was no reason to drop him from the specialty. All that was needed was to help him place seventh in the class of thirty who went on to the second six-week radar course.

So in our hypothesis, we now have ourselves Lee Harvey Oswald, radar operator. But we need more. We need a radar operator who will be accepted as a bona fide defector. There happens to be an interesting thing about this Oswald. Within the recent past, preceding his entry to the Marines, he has been demonstrating an interest in socialism and communism. And, since entering the service, this Oswald has become more and more blatant in overtly showcasing his interest in things Russian, to the point where his fellow Marines call him "Oswaldskovich," apparently to his pleasure. He has his name written in Russian on one of his jackets; he plays records of Russian songs "so loud that one could hear them outside the barracks;" he frequently makes remarks in Russian, and uses expressions like "da" and "nyet" and addresses others and is addressed as "Comrade;" he has been known to have come over and said jokingly, "you called?" when one of his fellow Marines plays a particular record of Russian music; he makes a point of expressing a preference for the red pieces in chess, forming the "Red Army;" he regularly and openly reads a Russian language newspaper; and he is openly studying the Russian language.

Certainly, the last place one would wish to station such a Marine with this great vulnerability to things Russian would be at Atsugi Air Base in Japan, near which there is known to be operating a KGB program aimed at recruiting US military personnel. However, contact with this KGB program, together with a reputation of being a Russophile and a communist sympathizer together with being a malcontent as evidenced by two court martials, might be persuasive items on his resume at a later point.

CIA officials claimed that it was possible Oswald had been recruited by the KBG during his military tour of duty overseas. But would it more logical to presume that had he truly been recruited there, the Russians would *not* have wanted him to defect. Wouldn't they, as assuredly as the CIA, want a new asset to remain in place as an undercover agent – a spy?

However, if the Russians did want him to defect, they surely would not have needed to send him halfway around the world to Gregory Golub in Helsinki, Finland – only a narrow body of water separates Japan from Russia. Nor would Oswald or the Russians have been much concerned with the niceties of his finishing his enlistment if he were a true defector.

Is there any more logical explanation for Oswald's trek from New Orleans to Le Havre to London to Helsinki than that someone directed him to Gregory Golub, who could get him an entry visa without prior approval of Moscow? If so, who was that? It surely wasn't the Russians. If they wanted Oswald in Russia, they did not need to send him to someone who could get him in without prior approval. Moreover, we know that Oswald was neither expected or welcomed in Moscow, as evidenced by his reception – or lack thereof – when he arrived.

On the other hand, if the CIA had their radar operator whom they wished to clandestinely infiltrate into the Soviet Union, how better could they attempt to "put him into the Soviet Union" than by directing him to Gregory Golub, who was not only known to have authority to issue entry visas without prior Moscow approval, but also was known to have exercised that right without prior investigation?

Let us analyze a composite of one quote from chapter 13 and two from chapter 7:

> "He was a corporal in the Marine Corps, who had stated to a consult in a consular office, which is manned by the Soviets, Soviet locals and what have you, fully accessible to the Soviets, unlike the higher floors of the Embassy, that he wanted to talk about his experiences, that he wanted to tell all."

> "Oswald informed Snyder that he had been a radar operator in the Marine Corps, intimating that he might know something of special interest, and that he had informed a Soviet official that he would give the Soviets any information he possessed."

> "Oswald returned to the hotel ...sure that he would be permitted to remain after his "sign of faith" in the Russians."

Are these unrelated statements? Let's start at the end.

(1) What was Oswald's "sign of faith" in the Russians?

(2) How did Oswald think the Russians would know about this sign of faith?

(3) Did the Russians have the consular offices bugged?

(4) Did American Intelligence operatives know that the Russians had the consular offices bugged?

(5) Might this have been a staged event designed to entice the Russians to want to accept Oswald?

(6) Might the CIA's desire to obtain information about the Belorussian Radio and Television Factory be a reason to undertake this staged event?

(7) Might there have been any other reason for such an endeavor?

Since the writing of the House Report, the following fascinating information appears at page 113 in the Final Report of the Assassination Records Review Board (1998):

"Many researchers have wondered whether Lee Harvey Oswald learned enough about the U-2 airplane during his U.S. Marine Corp service in Japan to provide useful information to the Soviets as to its airspeed and altitude or whether he might have played a different role regarding Soviet knowledge of the airplane.

"In his 1994 personal memoir, Ben Rich, the former director of Lockheed's research and design 'Skunk Works,' states that Lockheed flight engineers produced four false test flight manuals at Richard Bissell's request. The false test flight manuals contained incorrect information on the plane's weight, speed, altitude, and load factor limits.

"Rich claims that Lockheed produced the four manuals but only Bissell knew how or if the CIA got them to the Soviets.

"Did Oswald, or others like him, carry these fake manuals into Soviet hands?

"......Lockheed, when queried, reported that records of that age, if they still existed, were neither indexed not archived ...... With Rich and Bissell both deceased, the existence or plans for four fake U -2 manuals remains a mystery."

The above makes clear that the American Intelligence community had grave concerns that the Soviets appeared to be acquiring sufficient information as to the airspeed and altitude and other important information about the U-2 that they sought to put false information about the U-2 into the hands of the Soviets. Sadly, they obviously had good reason for such fears, as evidenced by the fact that on May 1, 1960 the Soviets shot down the U-2 that was being piloted by Francis Gary Powers.

That was the very first U-2 they were able to shoot down, an event that the Americans had feared and tried to avert. The material above does not tell us how long American Intelligence was concerned that the Soviets might be getting too close. But given the ultra-secrecy surrounding all details of the U-2 from its inception, would it seem logical that for many years American intelligence was working to keep the Soviets from learning the accurate information? If so, would it seem logical that for years American intelligence engaged in many programs to keep the Soviets from learning the correct information by getting them to believe false information as to the specifics of the U-2?

We know that American intelligence in at least this one endeavor to mislead the Soviets had Lockheed produce four false test manuals. Presumably they intended to get at least one of those manuals into the hands of the Soviets in a manner that would lead the Soviets to believe the phony material. How might they go about trying to get such a manual into the hands of the Soviets in a manner designed to have the Soviets accept that it is legit material?

Assuming for the moment that American Intelligence utilized Oswald for this purpose, does that necessarily mean that the Soviets would have believed whatever Oswald provided by way of written or spoken information? In other words, would it make sense if the Russians suspected Oswald was there to give them false information on the U-2, for them to play along and see what it was that he would provide?

A former CIA finance officer named James Wilcott provided the House Select Committee on Assassinations with information that Lee Harvey Oswald had been a CIA agent who had received financial disbursements under an assigned cryptonym (a code designation for an agency project) and that he himself had disbursed payments for Oswald's project. In the face of categorical denials by every other CIA witness and the absence of any documentation to the contrary, the Committee concluded that Wilcott's allegation was not worthy of belief.

The Committee also had testimony from CIA personnel that a review of Agency files would not always indicate whether an individual was affiliated with the Agency in any capacity. And they recognized that there was not always an independent means of verifying that all materials requested from the Agency had, in fact, been provided. The Committee acknowledged that the very institutional characteristics that are designed to prevent penetration by foreign powers (such as the Agency's strict compartmentalization and the complexity of its enormous filing system) have the simultaneous effect of making congressional inquiry difficult.

Accordingly, the Committee specifically pointed out that, "Any finding that is essentially negative in nature – such as that Lee Harvey Oswald was neither associated with the CIA in any way, nor ever in contact with that institution – should explicitly acknowledge the possibility of oversight."

There are certain things that must be analyzed which are relevant to the question of whether Oswald was a true defector or an American agent. As of October 1959, the State Department had information which should have caused it to prepare a "lookout card" for Lee Harvey Oswald. A lookout card was filed in the lookout file in the Passport Office, and whenever anyone applied for a passport from any city in the world, his application was immediately forwarded to this office and his name and date of birth checked against the lookout file and if a lookout card was filed, appropriate action, including the possible refusal of a passport, was taken. No such lookout card pertaining to Lee Harvey Oswald was ever located and the Warren Commission reported that "certain file entries indicated that such card was never prepared." In itself, the absence of a lookout card may prove little. However, as part of a mosaic of oddities, it may take on some meaning.

Since long before the time we are discussing, the CIA has maintained what are known as 201 files. "201 files are opened when a person is considered to be of potential intelligence or counter-intelligence significance. The opening of such a file is designed to serve the purpose of placing certain CIA information pertaining to that individual in one centralized records system. The 201 file is maintained in a folder belonging to the Directorate for Operations, the Agency component responsible for clandestine activities."

A confidential State Department telegram dated October 31, 1959, sent from Moscow to Washington and forwarded to the CIA, reported that Oswald, a recently discharged Marine, had appeared at the U.S. Embassy in Moscow to renounce his American citizenship and "has offered Soviets any information he has acquired as [an] enlisted radar operator." At least three other communications of a confidential nature that gave more detail on the Oswald case were sent to the CIA in about the same time period. Agency officials questioned by the Committee testified that the substance of the October 31, 1959 cable was sufficiently important to warrant the opening of a 201 file. Oswald's file, however, was not opened until December 9, 1960.

An Agency memorandum dated September 18, 1975 indicates that Oswald's file was opened on December 9, 1960 in response to the receipt of five documents: two from the FBI, two from the State Department and one from the Navy. This explanation, however, is inconsistent with the presence in Oswald's file of four State Department documents dated in 1959 and a fifth dated May 25, 1960.

The September 18, 1975 memo also states that Oswald's file was opened on December 9, 1960 as a result of his "defection" to the USSR on October 31, 1959 and renewed interest in Oswald brought about by his queries concerning possible re-entry into the United States. There is no official indication, however, that Oswald expressed to any U.S. Government official an intention to return to the United States until mid-February 1961 (although there is the statement in Oswald's letter – inconsistent with his diary – stating it was a "second request"). The Committee interviewed a number of Agency people who attempted to explain away the above situation. The Committee, even after accepting their analysis of what had happened, declared, "Even so, this analysis only explained why a file on Oswald was finally opened; it did not explain the seemingly long delay in the opening of the file."

The form used to initiate the opening of a 201 file contains a box entitled "Other Identification." Lee Harvey Oswald's form had in that box the designation "AG." The Agency's explanation of this designation was that AG was a code meaning "actual or potential defectors to the East or the Sino/Soviet block including Cuba." Perhaps the Committee just assumed that this was another example of government agencies and certainly the intelligence community being in love with the use of code words and symbols. But it is unfortunate that no one on the Committee asked why the CIA would need a secret code on their own *internal* records to denote that the subject had defected or might defect: why not just enter "defector" or "potential defector?" Confusingly, another CIA witness said the "A" represented Communism while the "G" would represent some category within the Communist structure. In any event, all the Agency witnesses were most adamant that most certainly, the one thing that AG did not stand for was something like agent or agency.

The form used to initiate the opening of Oswald's 201 file contains a notation that this file was to be "restricted." The CIA admittedly had a practice of restricting access to agents' files to persons on a "need-to-know" basis. This restriction meant that any person seeking access to the file would first have to notify the restricting officer. The explanation offered by the CIA on this restriction was that the restricting officer had done so simply to allow her to remain aware of any developments that might have occurred with regard to the file. However, no explanation was offered as to why this was necessary.

At the time Oswald was in the Soviet Union, the CIA had a program known as "HT-Lingual," the purpose of which was to obtain intelligence and counter-intelligence information from letters sent between the United States and Russia. Intercepted letters and envelopes would be photographed and then returned to the mails. Despite the fact that Oswald is known to have sent or received more than fifty communications during his stay in the Soviet Union, the CIA represented that they had only one letter in their possession directly related to Oswald, a letter dated July 6, 1961 sent by Marguerite Oswald. The Committee, having questioned why the Agency ostensibly had just this one Oswald letter, stated, "In essence, the Agency's response suggested that HT-Lingual only operated 4 days a week, and, even then, proceeded on a sampling basis."

The Committee's review of HT-Lingual files pertaining to the Oswald case resulted in the discovery amongst other things of a reproduction of an index card regarding Lee Harvey Oswald dated November 9, 1959, which stated that Oswald was a recent defector to the USSR and a former Marine. It also bears the notation "CI/ Project/RE" and some handwritten notes. The Committee questioned former employees of the CIA who may have had some knowledge pertaining to the HT-Lingual project in general and this card in particular. Some of these employees recognized the card as relating to the HT-Lingual project, but were unable to identify the meaning of the notation "CI/Project/RE." However, one employee testified that the "CI/Project" was "simply a name of convenience that was used to describe the HT-Language project." Another testified that "CI/Project" was the name of the component that ran the HT-Language project, and that "RE" represented the initials of a person who had been a translator of foreign language documents.

The Agency's explanation for the term "CI/Project/RE" was that there existed an office within the counter-intelligence staff that was known as "CI/Project," a cover title that had been used to hide the true nature of the office's function of *exploiting* the material produced by the HT-Lingual project, and the RE represented the initials of a former employee. Thus, the Agency said, the full meaning of the notation was that on November 9, 1959, an employee whose initials were RE placed Oswald's name on the "watch list" for the HT-Language project for the reason stated on the card: that Oswald was a recent defector of the USSR and a former Marine.

The Agency's response also offered explanations for the handwritten material on the card, which was the number "7-305," and the notation "N/R-RI, 20 Nov. 59." The number 7-305, they said, was a reference to the communication from the CI staff to the Office of Security expressing the CI staff's interest in seeing any mail to or from Oswald in the Soviet Union. The notation "N/R-RI, 20 Nov. 59," according to the Agency, signified that a name trace run through the central records indicated that there was no record for Lee Oswald as of that date. How do these explanations of the Agency stand up to examination? Let's start at the end.

They claim that "N/R-RI, 20 Nov. 59" signifies that a name trace run through the central records register indicated that there was no record for Lee Oswald as of that date. Yet, that is in direct conflict with other Agency records which indicate the receipt of a telegram concerning Oswald on October 31,1959, and of two telegrams from the Navy concerning him on November 3 & 4, 1959.

They claim that the handwritten number 7-305 is a reference to the communication from the CI staff to the Office of Security expressing the CI staff's interest in seeing *any* mail to or from Oswald in the Soviet Union. Is this supposed to mean that the picking up of Oswald's letters is not to be left to chance (sampling)? But how does this square with the Agency's position that they have only one of the more than fifty communications to or from Oswald? Does it mean that the Office of Security is being advised that any Oswald communications which just happen to be picked up should be forwarded to the CI staff? Wouldn't that then make it rather superfluous for RE to also note that Oswald's name be placed on a watch list for the HT-Lingual Project, which is the Agency's explanation for the entry CI/Project/RE?

One aspect of that explanation which deserves more thought is the Agency's interpretation of "CI/Project." They say there was an office within the counter-intelligence staff that was known as CI/Project, a cover title that had been used to hide the true nature of the office's functions; and further they say that in fact this office was responsible for the exploitation of the material produced by the HT-Lingual project. That sounds good if you say it fast. But when you say it slow and consider what you are saying, certain questions emerge. For example, what would be the purpose of having the HT-Lingual project at all unless you were going to exploit the material it produced? If we take as a given that all the material is being gathered in the expectation of being exploited, doesn't it follow that all the material being produced would be of interest to the office responsible for exploiting the material? So, why would this particular card have on it a notation "CI/Project," supposedly identifying the exploitation unit?

Two Agency employees gave slightly different explanations for CI/Project, one stating that this was a name of convenience to describe the HT-Lingual project, and the other that it was the name of the component that ran the HT-Lingual project. To these explanations, the comments in the preceding paragraph might with equal force be made, and, in addition, it may well be asked why the code name HT-Lingual had been invented if it was going to need yet another code name, CI/Project, to refer to it?

Richard E. Snyder, it will be remembered, was the consular official in the US Embassy in Moscow who had handled the Oswald case both in 1959 at the time of the defection, and in 1961 at the time of the re-defection was initiated. It so happens that during 1949-50 while awaiting his foreign service appointment with the State Department, Snyder had worked for the CIA. However, Snyder swore to the Committee, he had had no contact with the CIA since resigning from the Agency in March 1950, other than a letter written in 1970 or 1971 inquiring about employment on a contractual basis. The Committee found that Snyder's CIA file revealed that at one time prior to 1974 it had been red flagged and maintained on a segregated basis. The file contained a routing indicator that stated that the file had been red flagged because of a "DCI (Director of Central Intelligence) statement and a matter of cover" concerning Snyder. In response to a Committee inquiry, the CIA indicated that the DCI statement presumably referred to comments from former Director Richard Helms had made in 1964 concerning the Oswald case (which was then under intense study) when Helms was Deputy Director for Plans. The CIA also stated that Snyder's file had been flagged at the request of DDO/CI (Directorate of Operations/ Central Intelligence) to insure that all inquiries concerning Snyder would be referred to that office. The Agency was unable to explain the reference to "cover" because according to its records Snyder had never been assigned any cover while employed. Further, the Agency stated that "There is no record in Snyder's official personnel file that he ever worked, directly or indirectly, in any capacity for the CIA after his resignation on September 26,1950." (he had said it was in March) The Committee did not regard this explanation as satisfactory, especially since Snyder's 201 file indicated that for approximately one year during 1956-7 he had been used by an Agency case officer as a spotter at a university campus because of his access to others who might be going to the Soviet Union, nor was the Agency able to explain specifically why someone considered it necessary to red flag the Snyder file. Knowing that Snyder may have had a CIA role while in Moscow, when combined with the fact that it was common knowledge that the Russians had hundreds of bugs in the Embassy, gives rise to the intriguing possibility discussed above that Snyder and Oswald were engaging in a charade for the benefit of eavesdropping Russian ears, when Oswald went to the Embassy to announce that he had important information he was going to give to the Russians.

Shortly after Lee Oswald had married Marina at the end of April 1961, a Dr. Alexis H. Davidson began a tour of duty as the US Embassy physician in Moscow. Davidson stated to the Committee that in connection with this assignment, he had received some "superficial" intelligence training. This training, he said, mainly involved lectures on Soviet life and instructions on remembering and reporting Soviet names and military activities. For reasons which will be immediately made clear, Davidson could not have attempted to claim total naiveté with respect to intelligence matters. And perhaps his training was not quite so "superficial" as he claimed. The fact is that for at least a year during his Moscow tour of duty, Davidson served as part of the signal system for a CIA agent who was a highly placed GRU officer, Colonel Oleg Penkovsky. When the Soviets finally broke the Penkovsky case in 1963, Davidson was publicly declared *persona non grata*. There is nothing in any of the official reconstructions of Oswald's time in Russia to indicate that there had ever been any contact whatsoever between Oswald and Davidson, or if any, the nature and extent of such. Interestingly, after the assassination of President Kennedy, it was determined that the flight that the returning Oswalds took from New York to Dallas on June 14, 1962 had stopped in Atlanta, and it was discovered that, for whatever reason, the name of Dr. Davidson's mother and her address in Atlanta, Georgia were in Oswald's address book under the heading "Mother of US Embassy Doctor."

Lee Harvey Oswald (center) with his brothers

Oswald — The Marine

David Ferrie (2nd from left) and Lee Harvey Oswald (far right)

Lee Harvey Oswald and David Ferrie
Civil Air Patrol

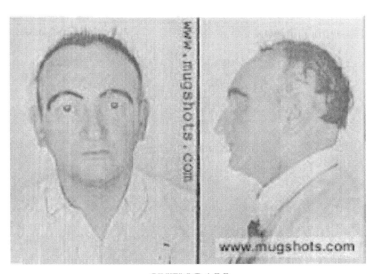

SVENGALI
David Ferrie — Rabid Anti-Communist, Intimate of Carlos Marcello,
Collaborator with Anti-Castro Cuban, friend to Lee Harvey Oswald

Oswald's passport showing his arrival in England on 9 October, 1959
and departure on 10 October, 1959

Photograph published at page 409 of the Warren Report
showing the loner Oswald distributing
"Fair Play for Cuba" literature

The "Loner" Oswald distributing literature with non-existent
members of his non-existent Fair Play for Cuba chapter.
Where did all of these guys in white shirts come from?

Marcello at the height of his power

Jack Ruby owner of the Carousel Club, Dallas;
regular briber of law enforcement officers and underworld intimate

The same man failed with the first assassination attempt
but succeeded with the second?

Level shot across this back year, stationary target
— missed General Walker?

This height and distance, vehicle emerging from trees
and moving away from him —hit President Kennedy at least twice.?

154

Ruby Kills Oswald

Credit: Robert H. Jackson (Dallas Morning News)

BOOK THREE

* * *

THE INTELLIGENCE CONNECTION

CHAPTER 15

THE ARISTOCRATIC SPY

* * *

"De Mohrenschildt was described as sophisticated and well educated, moving easily in the social and professional circles of oilmen and the so-called 'White Russian' community in Dallas, many of whom were avowed right-wingers."

"Oswald's 'lowly' background did not include much education or influence, and he was in fact shunned by the same Dallas Russian community that embraced de Mohrenschildt."

House Select Committee

Upon his return from Russia in June 1962, Oswald and his family lived for several months in Fort Worth, Texas. In October, Lee went alone to Dallas, got a job, and at the beginning of November moved his wife and daughter to Dallas. They remained in the Dallas area until April 1963, when Lee moved to New Orleans, leaving his wife and daughter in Irving, a suburb of Dallas, at the home of Ruth Paine, whom they had first met in February. His little family rejoined Lee in mid-May and they resided together in New Orleans until September 22 when Marina (who was eight months pregnant) and June returned to live at Ruth Paine's. They remained at Ruth Paine's even after Lee moved back to Dallas on October 3; and though Lee visited from time to time, it was at Ruth Paine's that Marina was living on October 20, when she gave birth to their second daughter, Rachel; and it was at Ruth Paine's that she was residing with their children on November 22, 1963.

From the time of their arrival from Russia, Lee and Marina had become acquainted with the growing number of people of the Russian-speaking community in the Dallas-Fort Worth area, who were attracted to each other by a common background, language and culture. With just one exception, Lee himself appears to have had only short-lived contacts with these people.

The exception was George de Mohrenschildt, who with his wife apparently began a friendship with the Oswalds sometime in the fall of 1962. The Warren Commission described the relationship between the couples as "close" and that Oswald had "appreciable respect" for George de Mohrenschildt. The House Committee provided an extensive biography relating the fascinating and exciting exploits of George de Mohrenschildt, from which the following is drawn.

De Mohrenschildt had an impressive pedigree. Amongst his ancestors was Baron Hilienfelt, a Baltic Swede who fought in the American Army of Independence; and an uncle, Ferdinand de Mohrenschildt, had been First Secretary of the last Russian Embassy in Washington under the Czarist Government. His father, Sergius Alexander von Mohrenschildt, a "Marshall of nobility" in Minsk Province, had served as director of Nobel interests in Czarist Russia. Following the Revolution, Sergius was jailed several times by the Communist regime and then was banished for life to Siberia, from where he escaped with his family to Poland. George's brother, Dimitri, had served in the Czarist Russian Imperial Navy. After the Revolution he joined anti-Communist groups for which he was jailed by the Communists and sentenced to death. Released in a prisoner exchange, Dimitri had emigrated to the United States in 1920 where he remained a "ferocious anti-Communist."

George had been about ten years of age when he fled with his parents from Russia to Poland. After attending a Polish cavalry military academy, he studied in Antwerp and attended the University of Liege from which he received a doctor's degree in international commerce in 1928. In 1938, he emigrated to the United States, where he went to work as a salesman for the Shumaker Co. in New York. The chief of export for the Shumaker Co., Pierre Fraiss, soon became one of de Mohrenschildt's best friends. Fraiss was connected with French intelligence, and before long de

Mohrenschildt was working for Fraiss collecting facts on people involved in pro-German activities. This intelligence work for Fraiss took him around the United States. It also involved contacting oil companies in the United States about selling oil to the French in competition against German oil supplies during the war. In 1944 de Mohrenschildt entered the University of Texas, from where he received a master's degree in petroleum geology and petroleum engineering in 1945. From that time on he became active as a petroleum engineer throughout the world.

It appears, though, that petroleum engineering may not have been all he was doing throughout the world. For example, following his trip in 1957 to Yugoslavia for the International Cooperation Administration, de Mohrenschildt was debriefed on that country on several occasions by the CIA in the person of their agent, J. Walton Moore. There were a number of further contacts between Moore and de Mohrenschildt for debriefing purposes during the ensuing years, at which some of the subjects discussed included China and Latin America. Interestingly enough De Mohrenschildt told the Warren Commission that he "asked Moore and Ft. Worth attorney Max Clark about Oswald to reassure himself that it was 'safe' for the De Mohrenschildt to assist Oswald." According to his testimony, De Mohrenschildt was told by one of the persons he talked to about Oswald, although he said he could not remember who it was, that "the guy seems to be OK." Since there is no indication who Clark was or that he had any contact at all with Oswald, the question arises as to what basis CIA agent Moore might have had for giving the "OK" to this returned defector. By 'happenstance,' at the time of the Bay of Pigs invasion de Mohrenschildt was in Guatemala City, the control center of the CIA's multi-million dollar invasion preparation operation.

One of de Mohrenschildt's world-wide contacts was with Clemard Joseph Charles, President of the Banque Commerciale d'Haiti. In early May 1963, Charles began a visit to the United States. Colonel Sam Kail, an Army Intelligence officer who was working in

Miami, contacted Dorothe Matlack of the office of the Army Chief of Staff for Intelligence. The work of Mrs. Matlack, who served as Assistant Director of the Office of Intelligence of the Army, included "human source collection of intelligence" and involved serving in a liaison capacity with the Central Intelligence Agency. Colonel Kail suggested that Mrs. Matlack talk to Charles when he visited Washington, DC, because of Charles' relationship to President Duvalier of Haiti and Haiti's strategic position relative to Cuba. On May 7, 1963, Mrs. Matlack met in the Capitol with Charles and de Mohrenschildt, apparently after having first made hotel reservations for them. Because of the potential political information Charles could give about the current situation in Haiti, she decided that the CIA should become the primary contact with Charles, and so she also arranged for Charles to meet with Tony Czaikowski of the CIA, whom she introduced as a professor from Georgetown University.

The House Select Committee related that, "A *Washington Post* Article by Norman Gale, dated September 29, 1964, reported that Haitian President Francois Duvalier had received two T-28 fighter plans from Dallas, Texas. The article stated the planes were flown to Haiti illegally. According to this article, Duvalier made down payment on the plans with a letter of credit drawn on the Banque Commerciale of Port-au-Prince, Haiti. The article identified Clemard Joseph Charles as president and principal stockholder of the bank and a close ally of Duvalier. The article stated that Charles visited the United States earlier in 1964 to buy boats and other weapons, and that he visited Dallas during that trip." ....

"In an air-gram dated May 2, 1967 from the Department of State to the American Embassy at Port au-Prince, Haiti, it was reported that a man named Edward Browder had leased a plane for one year starting on November 24, 1964 in the name of a phony company and had flown the plane to Port-au-Prince and left it there. The airgram reported also that Browder later cashed a check for $24,000 signed by Clemard Joseph Charles. Another airgram from the State Department to the Embassy dated May 25, 1967 verified that the check to Browder was drawn from the personal account of Clemard Joseph Charles at Manufacturers Hanover Trust Bank. "Edward Browder was interviewed by the House Committee at the Federal Penitentiary at MacNeill Island, Washington, where he was serving a 25-year sentence for securities violations. During his interview, Browder discussed a series of gun-running and smuggling operations he was involved in during the 1960s that were intended to result in the eventual overthrow or assassination of Fidel Castro. Browder stated that this work included assistance by the CIA in the form of money and operations. Browder said that during that period he did purchase at least two B-25 planes to be used in "smuggling operations" which would be used to assist the gun-running and raids against Cuba."

The House Committee interviewed Joseph Dryer, a Palm Beach, Florida, stockbroker who, they had learned, had known George de Mohrenschildt in Haiti. According to Dryer, during the 1950s and 60s, he, Clemard Joseph Charles, and George de Mohrenschildt were associated with a woman named Jacqueline Lancelot, who owned a well-known restaurant in Petionville, Haiti. Dryer said the restaurant was frequented by many American intelligence personnel from the American Embassy, and other foreigners. Lancelot, he said, had contact with the American intelligence operatives and passed them information about the Duvalier government. Dryer said that his relationship with Lancelot included passing messages for her to people in the United States whom Dryer assumed were connected in some way to the CIA. Dryer also told the Committee the following bit of hearsay information. He said that Lancelot had told him shortly after the Kennedy assassination that a "substantial" sum of money, $200,000 or $250,000, had been deposited in de Mohrenschildt's account in a Port-au-Prince bank (not Charles' bank). According to Dryer, Lancelot said her source of information was the person who handed out the funds at the bank; that the money was subsequently paid out, although she did not know to whom; and de Mohrenschildt left Haiti soon after.

De Mohrenschildt's friendship with Oswald surely made for a rather strange pairing. The House Committee provided a vivid description of the contrasts: "De Mohrenschildt was described as sophisticated and well educated, moving easily in the social and professional circles of oilmen and the so-called 'White Russian' community in Dallas, many of whom were avowed right-wingers. Oswalds 'lowly' background did not include much education or influence, and he was in fact shunned by the same Dallas Russian community that embraced de Mohrenschildt." When Oswald first moved to Dallas on October 9, 1962, before he even established a residence, he opened a post office box (#2915) at the Dallas General Post Office. His application for the box listed his address as that of George de Mohrenschildt's daughter, Alexandra de Mohrenschildt Taylor.

Finally, there is this intriguing "teaser" of the George de Mohrenschildt story. It appears that de Mohrenschildt had some type of association with a man named William Avery Hyde. This is an intriguing teaser because Hyde just happened to be the father of Ruth Paine, the woman with whom Marina and the children were permanently residing after September 1963. And on October 14, 1963 (18 days after the front page of the *Dallas Morning News* announced that JKF would be visiting Dallas in November), this same Ruth Paine placed a most fateful telephone call to Roy S. Truly, the superintendent of the Texas School Book Depository in downtown Dallas. As a direct result of that phone call, Lee Harvey Oswald began his employment at the Depository where, some five weeks later, John Fitzgerald Kennedy was assassinated.

CHAPTER 16

COVERT OPERATIONS

* * *

"In assessing the performance of the intelligence agencies in investigating President John F. Kennedy's assassination, one of the focuses of the Select Committee's investigation was whether the Warren Commission was supplied all the information necessary to conduct the 'thorough and independent investigation of the circumstances surrounding the assassination' which President Johnson had ordered. At the outset of its investigation, the Select Committee had evidence that the Warren Commission was not given information about CIA attempts to assassinate foreign leaders."

Senate Select Committee

As can be discerned from even our very brief glimpse of George de Mohrenschildt and his associates, American intelligence in the 50s and 60s might be described as being both 'passive' (receiving information) and 'active' (gun-running, etc.). But we have, to this point, seen just a tip of the iceberg of the 'active' side of the picture.

The Senate Select Committee stated, "In assessing the performance of the intelligence agencies in investigating President John F. Kennedy's assassination, one of the focuses of the Select Committee's investigation was whether the Warren Commission was supplied all the information necessary to conduct the "thorough and independent investigation of the circumstances surrounding the assassination" which President Johnson had ordered. At the outset of its investigation, the Select Committee had evidence that the Warren Commission was not given information about CIA attempts to assassinate foreign leaders." Before we move to the subject of active covert operations as they might apply to our discussions of the Kennedy case, it might prove informative to look at the subject of active covert operations of agents of the United States around the world in the years preceding the Kennedy murder.

Active, indeed extremely violent covert operations were part of the fabric of United States intelligence agencies, as is dramatically demonstrated by the following composite constructed from the Report of the Senate Select Committee to Study Government Operations with Respect to Intelligence Activities.

"Covert action is activity which is meant to further the sponsoring nation's foreign policy objectives, and to be concealed in order to permit that nation to plausibly deny responsibility."

"Following the end of World War II, many nations in Eastern Europe and elsewhere fell under Communist influence or control. The defeat of the Axis powers was accompanied by rapid disintegration of the Western colonial empires. World War II had no sooner ended than a new struggle began. The Communist threat, emanating from what came to be called the 'Sino-Soviet bloc,' led to a policy of containment intended to prevent further encroachment into the 'Free World.'

"United States strategy for conducting the Cold War called for the establishment of interlocking treaty arrangements and military bases throughout the world. Concern over the expansion of an aggressive Communist monolith led the United States to fight two major wars in Asia. In addition, it was considered necessary to wage a relentless cold war against Communist expansion wherever it appeared in the 'back alleys of the world.' This called for a full range of cover activities in response to the operations of Communist clandestine services."

"Events in the Dominican Republic appeared to offer an additional opportunity for the Russians and their allies. The Congo, freed from Belgian rule, occupied the strategic center of the African continent, and the prospect of Communist penetration there was viewed as a threat to American interests in emerging African nations. There was great concern that a Communist takeover in

Indochina would have a 'domino effect' throughout Asia. Even the election in 1970 of a Marxist president in Chile was seen by some as a threat similar to that of Castro's takeover in Cuba."

"From 1955 to 1970, the basic authority for cover operations was a directive of the National Security Council, NSC5412/2. This directive instructed the CIA to counter, reduce and discredit 'International Communism' throughout the world in a manner consistent with United States foreign and military policies. It also directed the CIA to undertake covert operations to achieve this end and defined covert operations as any covert activities related to propaganda, economic warfare, political action (including sabotage, demolition and assistance to resistance movements) and all activities compatible with the directive." "Beginning in 1955, the responsibility for authorizing CIA covert action operations lay with the Special Group, a subcommittee of a National Security Council composed of the President's Assistant for National Security Affairs, the Director of Central Intelligence, the Deputy Secretary of Defense and the Under Secretary of State for Political Affairs."

A glance at this Committee's discussion regarding covert actions conducted in the Congo and the Dominican Republic should prove instructive for our consideration of the material in our following chapters.

"In the summer of 1960, there was great concern at the highest levels in the United States government about the role of Patrice Lumumba in the Congo. Lumumba, who served briefly as Premier of the newly independent nation, was viewed with alarm by United States policy makers because of what they perceived as his magnetic public appeal and his leanings toward the Soviet Union.

"Under the leadership of Lumumba and the new President, Joseph Kasavubu, the Congo declared its independence from Belgium on June 30, 1960. In the turbulent month that followed, Lumumba threatened to invite Soviet troops to hasten the withdrawal of Belgian armed forces. The United Nations Security

Counsel requested Belgium's withdrawal and dispatched a neutral force to the Congo to preserve order. In late July, Lumumba visited Washington and received pledges of economic aid from Secretary of State Christian Herter. By the beginning of September, Soviet airplanes, trucks and technicians were arriving in the province where Lumumba's support was strongest."

"The evidence indicates that it is likely that President Eisenhower's expression of strong concern about Lumumba at a meeting of the National Security Council on August 18, 1960, was taken by Allen Dulles [Director of the CIA] as authority to assassinate Lumumba.

"The week after the August 18 NSC meeting, a presidential advisor reminded the Special Group of the 'necessity for very straightforward action' against Lumumba and prompted a decision not to rule out consideration of 'any particular kind of activity which might contribute to getting rid of Lumumba'. The following day, Dulles cabled a CIA Station Officer in Leopoldville, Republic of the Congo, that 'in high quarters' the 'removal' of Lumumba was 'an urgent and prime objective'. Shortly thereafter the CIA's clandestine service formulated a plot to assassinate Lumumba."

"In the summer of 1960, DDP (*Deputy Director for Plans*) Richard Bissell asked the Chief of the Africa Division, Bronson Tweedy, to explore the feasibility of assassinating Patrice Lumumba. Bissell also asked a CIA scientist, Joseph Scheider, to make preparations to assassinate or incapacitate an unspecified 'African leader.' Scheider procured toxic biological materials in response to Bissell's request, and was then ordered by Tweedy to take these materials to the Station Officer in Leopoldville."

"In mid-September, after losing a struggle for the leadership of the government to Kasavubu and Joseph Mobutu, Chief of Staff of the Congolese armed forces, Lumumba sought protection from the United Nations forces in Leopoldville."

"The evidence indicates that the ouster of Lumumba did not alleviate the concern about him in the United States government. Rather, CIA and high Administration officials continued to view him as a threat. During this period, CIA officers in the Congo advised and aided Congolese contacts known to have an intent to assassinate Lumumba. The officers also urged the 'permanent disposal' of Lumumba by some of these Congolese contacts. Moreover, the CIA opposed reopening Parliament after the coup because of the likelihood that Parliament would return Lumumba to power."

"In late September, Scheider delivered the lethal substances to the Station Officer in Leopoldville [Hedgman] and instructed him to assassinate Patrice Lumumba. The Station Officer testified that after requesting and receiving confirmation from CIA Headquarters that he was to carry out Scheider's instructions, he proceeded to take 'exploratory steps' in furtherance of the assassination plot."

"Scheider explained that the toxic material was to be injected into some substance that Lumumba would ingest: 'it had to do with anything he could get to his mouth, whether it was food or a toothbrush, so that some of the material could get in his mouth.'

"Hedgman said that the means of assassination was not restricted to use of toxic material provided by Scheider. He testified that he may have 'suggested' shooting Lumumba to Scheider as an alternative to poisoning. Scheider said it was his 'impression' that Tweedy and his Deputy empowered him to tell the Station Officer that he could pursue other means of assassination. Station Officer Hedgman testified that, although the selection of a mode of assassination was left to his judgment, there was a firm requirement that 'if I implemented these instructions it had to be a way which could not be traced back either to an American or the United States government.'

"Scheider's mission to the Congo was preceded and followed by cables from Headquarters urging the 'elimination' of Lumumba transmitted through an extraordinarily restricted 'Eyes Only' channel – including two messages bearing the personal signature of Allen Dulles." The "extraordinarily restricted" channel, known as The PROP channel, "indicated extraordinary sensitivity and restricted circulation at CIA Headquarters to Dulles, Bissell, Tweedy and Tweedy's Deputy. The PROP designator restricted circulation in the Congo to the Station Officer. Tweedy testified that the PROP channel was established and used exclusively for the assassination operation."

"Throughout the fall of 1960, while Lumumba remained in UN protective custody, the CIA continued to view him as a serious political threat. One concern was that if Parliament were re-opened and the moderates failed to obtain a majority vote, the 'pressures for Lumumba's return will be almost irresistible.' Another concern at CIA Headquarters was that foreign powers would intervene in the Congo and bring Lumumba to power. Lumumba was also viewed by the CIA and the Administration as a stalking horse for 'what appeared to be a Soviet effort to take over the Congo.'"

On October 15, 1960, Bronson Tweedy dispatched a cable "via the PROP channel for Hedgman's 'Eyes Only,' which prevented the message from being dispatched to anyone else, including the Ambassador." Amongst other things in this cable which dealt with the subject of the assassination of Lumumba, Tweedy requested "the Station Officer's reaction to the prospect of sending a senior CIA case officer to the Congo on a 'direct assignment' to concentrate entirely this aspect."

In his response two days later, Station Officer Hedgman "concluded this cable with the following cryptic recommendation, reminiscent of his testimony that he may have 'suggested' shooting Lumumba to Scheider as an alternative to poisoning: 'If Case Officer sent, recommend HQS pouch soonest high powered foreign make rifle with telescopic scope and silencer. Hunting good here when lights right. However as hunting rifles now forbidden, would keep rifle in office pending opening of hunting season.' Tweedy testified that the Station Officer's recommendation clearly referred to sending to the Congo via diplomatic pouch a weapon suited for assassinating Lumumba." "The oblique suggestion of shooting Lumumba at the 'opening of hunting season' could be interpreted as a plan to assassinate Lumumba as soon as he was seen outside the residence where he remained in UN Protective custody. Tweedy interpreted the cable to mean that 'an operational plan involving a rifle' had not yet been formulated by the Station Officer and that the 'opening of hunting season' would depend upon approval of such a plan by CIA headquarters."

"Michael Mulroney, a senior CIA officer in the Directorate for Plans, testified that in October 1960 he had been asked by Richard Bissell to go to the Congo to carry out the assassination of Lumumba." "At the time, Mulroney was the Deputy Chief of an extraordinarily secret unit within the Directorate of Plans." "Mulroney said that he refused to participate in an assassination operation, but proceeded to the Congo to attempt to draw Lumumba away from the protective custody of the UN guard and place him in the hands of Congolese authorities.

"According to Mulroney there was a 'very, very high probability' that Lumumba would receive capital punishment at the hands of the Congolese authorities. But he 'had no compunction about bringing him out and then having him tried by a jury of his peers.' Despite Mulroney's expressed aversion to assassination and his agreement to undertake a more general mission to 'neutralize' Lumumba's influence, Bissell continued pressing him to consider an assassination operation."

"Shortly after Mulroney's arrival in the Congo, he was joined by QJ/WIN a CIA agent with a criminal background. Late in 1960, WI/ROGUE, one of Hedgman's operatives, approached QJ/WIN with a proposition to join an 'execution squad.'" "WI/ROGUE was an 'essentially stateless' soldier of fortune, 'a forger and former bank robber.' The CIA sent him to the Congo after providing him with plastic surgery and a toupee so that Europeans traveling in the Congo would not recognize him. The CIA characterized WI/ROGUE as a man who 'learns quickly and carries out any assignment without regard for danger.' CIA's Africa Division recommended WI/ROGUE as an agent in the following terms: 'He is indeed aware of the precepts of right and wrong, but if he is given an assignment which may be morally wrong in the eyes of the world, but necessary because his case officer ordered him to carry it out, then it is right, and he will dutifully undertake appropriate action for its execution without pangs of conscience. In a word, he can rationalize all actions.'"

A November 14, 1960 PROP cable from the Station Officer to Tweedy states that a CIA agent had learned that Lumumba's "political followers in Stanleyville desire that he break out of his confinement and proceed to that city by car to engage in political activity *** Decision on breakout will probably be made shortly. Station expects to be advised by [agent] of [what] decision was made *** Station has several possible assets to use in event of breakout and studying several plans of action."

Lumumba left UN custody on November 27, 1960. A CIA Cable, Leopoldville to Director, the next day advised, "[Station] working with [Congolese Government] to get roads blocked and troops alerted [block] possible escape route."

A CIA Cable on November 29, 1960 read, "View change in location target, QJ/WIN anxious go Stanleyville and expressed desire execute plan by himself without using any apparatus."

The reply the following day from the Chief of the Africa Division to the Station Officer said, "Concur QJ/WIN go Stanleyville *** We are prepared consider direct action by QJ/WIN but would like your reading on security factors. How close would this place [the United States] to the action?"

"Early in December, Mobutu's troops captured Lumumba while he was traveling toward his stronghold at Stanleyville and imprisoned him."

"There is no doubt that the CIA and the Congolese government shared a concern in January 1961 that Lumumba might return to power, particularly since the Congolese army and police were threatening to mutiny if they were not given substantial pay raises. Station Officer Hedgman reported that a mutiny 'almost certainly would *** bring about [Lumumba] return power' and said he had advised the Congolese government of his opinion that the army garrison at Leopoldville 'will mutiny within two or three days unless drastic action taken satisfy complaints.'" "The next day, Hedgman cabled Headquarters: 'Station and Embassy believe present government may fall within few days. Result would almost certainly be chaos and return [Lumumba] to power.' Hedgman advised that reopening the Congolese Parliament under United Nations supervision was unacceptable because 'The combination of [Lumumba's] powers as demagogue, his able use of goon squads and propaganda and spirit of defeat within [government] coalition which would increase rapidly under such conditions would almost certainly insure [Lumumba] victory in Parliament *** Refusal take drastic steps at this time will lead to defeat of [United States] policy in Congo.'"

"On January 17, authorities in Leopoldville placed Lumumba and two of his leading supporters, Maurice Mpolo and Joseph Okito, aboard an airplane bound for Bakwanga. Apparently the aircraft was redirected in midflight to Elisabethville in Katanga Province 'when it was learned that United Nations troops were at Bakwanga airport.' On February 13, the government of Katanga reported that Lumumba and his two companions escaped the previous day and died at the hands of hostile villagers."

"The United Nations Commission on Investigation was 'not convinced by the version of the facts given by the provincial government of Katgana.' The Commission concluded instead that Lumumba was killed on January 17, almost immediately after his arrival to Katanga, probably with the knowledge of the central government and at the behest of the Katanga authorities: 'The

Commission wishes to put on record its view that President Kasavubu and his aides... should not escape responsibility for the death of Mr. Lumumba, Mr. Okito and Mr. Mpolo. For Mr. Kasavubu and his aides had handed over Mr. Lumumba and his colleagues to the Katanga authorities knowing full well, in doing so, that they were throwing them into the hands for their bitterest political enemies.'"

The Station Officer "clearly had prior knowledge of the plan to transfer Lumumba to a state where it was probable that he would be killed. Other supporters of Lumumba who had been sent to Bakwanga earlier by Leopoldville authorities 'were killed there in horrible circumstances and the place was known as the "slaughterhouse."' It was therefore improbable that Mr. Lumumba and his companions would have met a different fate at Bakwanga if they had been taken there.'"

"Hedgman acknowledged that the CIA was in close contact with some Congolese officials who 'quite clearly knew' that Lumumba was to be shipped to Katanga 'because they were involved.' But Hedgman said that these Congolese contacts 'were not acting under CIA instructions if and when they did this.'"

"Rafael Trujillo came to power in the Dominican Republic in 1930. For most of his tenure, the United States Government supported him and he was regarded throughout much of the Caribbean and Latin America as a protégé of the United States. Trujillo's rule, always harsh and dictatorial, became more arbitrary during the 1950s. As a result, the United States' image was increasingly tarnished in the eyes of many Latin Americans.

"Increasing American awareness of Trujillo's brutality and fear that it would lead to a Castro-type revolution caused United States officials to consider various plans to hasten his abdication or downfall. As early as February 1960, the Eisenhower Administration gave high level consideration to a program of covert aid to Dominican dissidents."

"During the spring of 1960, the US Ambassador to the Dominican Republic, Joseph Farland, made initial contact with... a group of dissidents regarded as moderate, pro-United States and desirous of establishing a democratic form of government." "During the course of a cocktail party in the Dominion Republic, a leading dissident made a specific request to Ambassador Farland for a limited number of rifles with telescopic sights. The Ambassador promised to pass on the request. He apparently did so after returning to Washington."

"Prior to his final departure from the Dominican Republic in May 1960, the Ambassador introduced his Deputy-Chief-of-Mission, Henry Dearborn, to the dissident leaders, indicating that Dearborn could be trusted. Then on June 16, 1960, CIA Headquarters cabled a request that Dearborn become the 'communications link' between the dissidents and CIA. The cable stated that Dearborn's role had the 'unofficial approval of [Assistant Secretary of State for Inter-American Affairs, Roy R.] Rubottom.' Dearborn agreed. He requested, however, that the CIA confirm the arrangement with the dissidents as being that the United States would 'clandestinely' assist the opposition to 'develop effective force to accomplish Trujillo overthrow,' but would not 'undertake any overt action itself against Trujillo government while it is in full control of Dominican Republic.' CIA Headquarters confirmed Dearborn's understanding of the arrangement."

"Events occurring during the summer of 1960 further intensified hemispheric opposition to the Trujillo regime. In June, agents of Trujillo tried to assassinate Venezuelan President Betancourt. As a result, the OAS (*Organization of American States*) censured the Trujillo government. At the same time, in August 1960 the United States interrupted diplomatic relations with the Dominican Republic and imposed economic sanctions. With the interruption of diplomatic relations, the United States closed its Embassy. Most American personnel, including the CIA Chief of Station, left the Dominican Republic. With the departure of the CIA

Chief of Station, Dearborn became *de facto* CIA Chief of Station and was recognized as such by both CIA and the State Department. Although in January 1961 a new CIA Chief of Station came to the Dominican Republic, Dearborn continued to serve as a link to the dissidents.

"Dearborne came to believe that no effort to overthrow the Trujillo government could be successful unless it involved Trujillo's assassination. He communicated this opinion to both the State Department and the CIA."

"On January 19, 1961, the last day of the Eisenhower Administration, Consul General Dearborn was advised that approval had been given to supplying arms and other materials to the Dominican dissidents."

"In a March 15, 1961 cable, a Station officer reported that Dearborn had asked for three .38 caliber pistols for issue to several dissidents." A June 7, 1961 CIA memorandum, "unsigned and with no attribution as to source, states that two of the three pistols were passed by a Station officer to a United States citizen who was in direct contact with the action element of the dissident group."

"In a March 26, 1961 cable to CIA Headquarters, the Station asked for permission to pass to the dissidents three 30 caliber M1 carbines. The guns had been left behind in the Consulate by Navy personnel after the United States interrupted formal diplomatic relations in August 1960 .....On March 31, 1961, CIA Headquarters cabled approval of the request to pass the carbines. The carbines were passed to the action group contact on April 7, 1961. Eventually, they found their way into the hands of one of the assassins, Antonio de la Maza."

"On April 7,1961, a Pouch Restriction Waiver Request and Certification was submitted seeking permission to pouch 'four M3 machine guns and 240 rounds of ammunition on a priority basis for issuance to a small action group to be used for self protection.' .... The Waiver Request was approved by Richard Bissell, as DDP, on

August 10 1961... The machine guns were pouched to the Dominican Republic and were received by the Station on April 19, 1961."

"By April 17, 1961, the Bay of Pigs invasion had failed. As a result, there developed a general realization that precipitous action should be avoided in the Dominican Republic until Washington was able to give further consideration to the consequences of a Trujillo overthrow and the power vacuum which would be created. A cable from Headquarters to the Station, on April 17, 1961, advised that it was most important that the machine guns not be passed without additional Headquarters approval." "Dearborn recalls receiving instructions that an effort be made to turn off the assassination attempt and testified that efforts to carry out the instructions were unsuccessful. In effect, the dissidents informed him that this was their affair and it could not be turned off to suit the convenience of the United States government.

"On April 30, 1961, Dearborn advised Headquarters that the dissidents had reported to him the assassination attempt was going to take place during the first week of May. The action group was reported to have in its possession three carbines, four to six 12-gauge shotguns and other small guns. Although they reportedly still wanted the machine guns, Dearborn advised Headquarters that the group was going to go ahead with what they had, whether the United States wanted them to or not."

A State Department memoranda dated May 15 "stressed that it was highly desirable for the United States to be identified with and to support the elements seeking to overthrow Trujillo. The attachment recommended that Consul General Dearborn inform the dissidents that if they succeed 'at their own initiative and on their own responsibility in forming an acceptable provisional government they can be assured that any reasonable request for assistance from the US will be promptly and favorably answered.'"

"Late in the evening of May 30, 1961, Trujillo was ambushed and assassinated near San Cristobal, Dominican Republic. The assassination closely paralleled the plan disclosed by the action group to American representatives in the Dominican Republic and passed on to officials in Washington at both the CIA and the State Department. The assassination was conducted by members of the action group, to whom the American carbines had been passed, and such sketchy information as is available indicates that one or more of the carbines was in the possession of the assassination group when Trujillo was killed. The evidence indicates, however, that the actual assassination was accomplished by handguns and shotguns."

CHAPTER 17

STRANGE BEDFELLOWS

* * *

"In August 1960, the CIA took steps to enlist members of the criminal underworld with gambling syndicate contacts to aid in assassinating Castro."

Senate Select Committee

The following material on Cuba is a composite constructed primarily from the Report of the Senate Select Committee to Study Government Operations with Respect to Intelligence Activities with some material from the House Report when that provides a more readable rendition.

"The fear of Communist expansion was particularly acute in the United States when Fidel Castro emerged as Cuba's leader in the late 1950s. His takeover was seen as the first significant penetration by the Communists into the Western Hemisphere. United States leaders, including most Members of Congress, called for vigorous action to stem the Communist infection in this hemisphere. These policies rested on widespread popular support and encouragement. Throughout this period, the United States felt impelled to respond to threats which were, or seemed to be, skirmishes in a global Cold War against Communism. Castro's Cuba raised the specter of a Soviet outpost at America's doorstep."

"Efforts against Castro did not begin with assassination attempts. From March through August 1960, during the last year of the Eisenhower Administration, the CIA considered plans to undermine Castro's charismatic appeal by sabotaging his speeches. According to the 1967 Report of the CIA's Inspector General, an official in the Technical Services Division (TSD) recalled discussing a scheme to spray Castro's broadcasting studio with a chemical which produced effects similar to LSD, but the scheme was rejected because the chemical was unreliable. During this period, TSD impregnated a box of cigars with a chemical which produced temporary disorientation, hoping to induce Castro to smoke one of the cigars before delivering a speech. The Inspector General also reported a plan to destroy Castro's image as 'The Beard' by dusting his shoes with thallium salts, a strong depilatory that would cause his beard to fall out. The depilatory was to be administered during a trip outside Cuba, when it was anticipated Castro would leave his shoes outside the door of his hotel room to be shined. TSD procured the chemical and tested it on animals, but apparently abandoned the scheme because Castro cancelled his trip." "A notation in the records of the Operations Division, CIA's Office of Medical Services, indicates that on August 16, 1960 an official was given a box of Castro's favorite cigars with instructions to treat them with lethal poison. The cigars were contaminated with a botulinum toxin so potent that a person would die after putting one in his mouth. The official reported that the cigars were ready on October 7, 1960; TSD notes indicate that they were delivered to an unidentified person on February 13, 1961. The record does not disclose whether an attempt was made to pass the cigars to Castro."

In August 1960, the CIA took steps to enlist members of the criminal underworld with gambling syndicate contacts to aid in assassinating Castro."

"The earliest concrete evidence of the operation is a conversation between DDP Bissell and Colonel Sheffield Edwards, Director of the Office of Security. Edwards recalled that Bissell asked him to locate someone to assassinate Castro. Bissell confirmed that he requested Edwards to find someone to assassinate Castro and believed that Edwards raised the idea of contacting members of a gambling syndicate operation in Cuba. Edwards assigned the mission to the Chief of the Operational Support Division of the Office of Security.

"Edwards and the Support Chief decided to rely on Robert A. Maheu to recruit someone 'tough enough' to handle the job. Maheu was an ex-FBI agent who had entered into a career as a private investigator in 1954. A former FBI associate of Maheu's was employed in the CIA's Office of Security and had arranged for the CIA to use Maheu in several sensitive cover operations in which 'he didn't want to have an Agency person or a government person get caught.' Maheu was initially paid a monthly retainer by the CIA of $500, but it was terminated after his detective agency became more lucrative. The Operational Support Chief had served as Maheu's case officer since the Agency first began using Maheu's services, and by 1960 they had become close personal friends."

"Sometime in late August or early September 1960, the Support Chief approached Maheu about the proposed operation. As Maheu recalls the conversation, the Support Chief asked him to contact John Rosselli, an underworld figure with possible gambling contacts in Las Vegas, to determine if he would participate in a plan to 'dispose' of Castro. The Support Chief testified, on the other hand, that it was Maheu who raised the idea of using Rosselli. Maheu had known Rosselli since the late 1950's." "At first Maheu was reluctant to become involved in the operation because it might interfere with his relationship with his new client, Howard Hughes. He finally agreed to participate because he felt that he owed the Agency a commitment." "The Support Chief testified that Maheu was told to offer money, probably $150,000, for Castro's assassination."

"According to Rosselli, he and Maheu met at the Brown Derby Restaurant in Beverly Hills in early September 1960. Rosselli testified that Maheu told him that 'high government officials' needed his cooperation in getting rid of Castro, and that he asked him to help recruit Cubans to do the job." "Maheu and Rosselli both testified that Rosselli insisted on meeting with a representative of the Government. A meeting was arranged for Maheu and Rosselli with the Support Chief at the Plaza Hotel in New York. The Inspector General's Report placed the meeting on September 14, 1960."

"It was arranged that Rosselli would go to Florida and recruit Cubans for the operation." "During the week of September 24, 1960 the Support Chief, Maheu, and Rosselli met in Miami to work out the details of the operation."

"After Rosselli and Maheu had been in Miami for a short time, and certainly prior to October 18, Rosselli introduced Maheu to individuals on whom Rosselli intended to rely: 'Sam Gold,' who would serve as a 'back-up, man' or 'key' man, and 'Joe,' whom 'Gold' said would serve as a courier to Cuba and make arrangements there." "The Support Chief testified that he learned the true identities of his associates one morning when Maheu called and asked him to examine the 'Parade' supplement to the *Miami Times*. An article on the Attorney General's ten most-wanted criminals list revealed that 'Sam Gold' was Momo Salvatore Giancana, a Chicago-based gangster, and 'Joe' was Santos Trafficante, the Cosa Nostra chieftain in Cuba."

Momo Salvatore Giancana was not exactly a candidate for monkhood. In addition to his more obvious disqualifications, Sam would have had serious problems with the vow of silence. The House Report informs us that an October 18, 1960 FBI memorandum read: "During a recent conversation with several friends, Giancana stated that Fidel Castro was to be done away with shortly, said it would occur in November. Moreover, Giancana said he had already met with the would-be assassin on three occasions, the last meeting taking place on a boat docked at the Fontainbleu Hotel, Miami Beach. Giancana stated everything had been perfected for killing Castro and that the assassin had arranged with a girl, not further described, to drop a 'pill' in some drink or food of Castro."

Nor was silence the only monk's vow with which Giancana would have had difficulty. He had a great fondness for the women. As we learn from the Senate Report, one of his girl friends in Las Vegas became the center of a bizarre event – bizarre if only because it was such an eerie precursor of the Watergate foul-up.

"In late October 1960, Maheu arranged for a Florida investigator, Edward DuBois, to place an electronic 'bug' in a room in Las Vegas and installed a tap on the phone. DuBois' employee, Arthur J. Balletti, flew to Las Vegas and installed a tap on the phone. The Support Chief characterized the ensuing events as a 'Keystone Comedy act.' On October 31, 1960, Balletti, believing that the apartment would be vacant for the afternoon, left the wiretap equipment unattended. A maid discovered the equipment and notified the local sheriff, who arrested Balletti and brought him to the jail. Balletti called Maheu in Miami, tying 'Maheu into this thing up to his ear.' Balletti's bail was paid by Rosselli."

"The Support Chief testified that during the early stages of negotiations with the gambling syndicate, Maheu informed him that a girl-friend of Giancana was having an affair with the target of the tap. Giancana wanted Maheu to bug that person's room; otherwise Giancana threatened to fly to Las Vegas himself. Maheu was concerned that Giancana's departure would disrupt the negotiations, and secured the Support Chief's permission for a bug to insure Giancana's presence and cooperation."

"Rosselli testified that Maheu had given him two explanations for the tap on different occasions: first, that Giancana was concerned that his girl-friend was having an affair; and second, that he had arranged the tap to determine whether Giancana had told his girl friend about the assassination plot, and whether she was spreading the story."

During the investigation of this affair, Colonel Edwards mislead the FBI, informing the Bureau that "The CIA would object to Maheu's prosecution because it might reveal sensitive information relating to the abortive Bay of Pigs invasion."

Clearly the placing of that tap had nothing whatsoever to do with the Bay of Pigs. Nonetheless, following the CIA assertion that it did, "Herbert J. Miller, Assistant Attorney General, Criminal Division, advised the Attorney General that the 'national interest' would preclude any prosecutions based upon the tap."

Another of Giancana's girl-friends, Judith Campbell Exner, reportedly was introduced to John F. Kennedy by Frank Sinatra, and a long-term relationship between her and JFK bloomed until it was brought to a sudden and unceremonious end when J. Edgar Hoover intervened.

The Committee circumspectly reported this affair as follows: "Evidence before the Committee indicates that a close friend of President Kennedy had frequent contacts with the President from the end of 1960 through mid-1962; FBI reports and testimony indicate that the President's friend was also a close friend of John Rosselli and Sam Giancana and saw them often during this same period." "White House telephone logs show 70 instances of phone contact between the White House and the President's friend, whose testimony confirms frequent phone contact with the President himself." "On February 27, 1962, Hoover sent identical copies of a memorandum to the Attorney General and Kenneth O'Donnell, Special Assistant to the President. The memorandum stated that information developed in connection with a concentrated FBI investigation of John Rosselli revealed that Rosselli had been in contact with the President's friend. The memorandum also reported that the individual was maintaining an association with Sam Giancana, described as 'a prominent Chicago underworld figure.' Hoover's memorandum also stated that a review of the telephone toll calls from the President's friend's residence revealed calls to the White House." "The association of the President's friend with the 'hoodlums' and that person's connection with the President was again brought to Hoover's attention in a memorandum preparing him for a meeting with the President planned for March 22, 1962... On March 22, Hoover had a private luncheon with President Kennedy. There is no record of what transpired at that luncheon. According to the White House logs, the last telephone contact between the White House and the President's friend occurred a few hours after the luncheon."

The 1978 House Committee Report gives the clearest rendition of the endeavors of The Senate Select Committee to attempt to verify the claim made by the Support Chief that he first learned the identities of Sam Gold and Joe because of an article in the "Parade" supplement of the *Miami Times*:

"The SSC [*Senate Select Committee*] conducted a search of supplements to all Miami newspapers for the requisite time period and could not locate any such article. The Committee consequently searched 'Parade' magazine for the fall of 1960, all of 1961, and all of 1962, the years that spanned the entire operation. The Committee found that on January 21,1962, 'Parade' published an article entitled 'The Untold Story: Our Government's Crackdown on Organized Crime,' written by Jack Anderson, which contained a listing of the top 10 hoodlums in the country as well as several photographs of mobsters, including Santos Trafficante. The article focused on the efforts of Attorney General Robert F. Kennedy's campaign against organized crime and mentioned both Giancana and Trafficante. Although this 'Parade' article appears to correspond with the Support Chief's and Maheu's descriptions, it is over one year past the beginning months of the operation. Indeed, it occurred 9 months after the completion of Phase I of the plots. Neither the SSC nor the [House] Committee has discovered any other articles pertaining to organized crime in Parade magazine or the supplements of any Miami newspaper for the alleged time period. It appears the Support Chief and Maheu are not telling the truth in an attempt to look for an ex-post facto reason for continuing the operation after the introduction of two of the top organized crime figures in the United States. Implicit in their contention is that while the CIA wished to solicit criminal sources to assassinate Castro, it would not knowingly have recruited any figures from the top echelon of organized crime." "Further, this CIA plot to assassinate Castro was necessarily a highly volatile and secret operation. Once Rosselli introduced additional contacts into the scene, it is not logical that the CIA would have neglected to verify the identities of such principals. On the contrary, it is more believable that the CIA ascertained the true identities of 'Sam Gold' and 'Joe' at an early stage and progressed consciously forward in the operation, confident that these two persons, in the words attributed to Colonel

Sheffield Edwards, were individuals 'tough enough' to handle the job."

The House Committee also provides the following information:

"After meeting several times in Miami and deciding upon poison pills as the method of assassination, the IG report [Inspector General] states that Trafficante made the arrangements for the assassination of Castro with one of his contacts inside Cuba on one of the trips he allegedly made to Havana, Cuba. This contact was Cuban official who held a position close to Castro. The IG report then stated that Rosselli passed the pills to Trafficante. Rosselli subsequently told the Support Chief that the pills were delivered to the Cuban official in Cuba. The Cuban official apparently retained the pills for a few weeks and then returned them since he was no longer in a position to fulfill any plan. The Cuban official was no longer in a position to kill Castro because he had lost his Cuban post. With the Cuban official unable to perform, the syndicate looked elsewhere. Rosselli next told the Support Chief, sometime during early 1961, that Trafficante knew a man prominent in the Cuban exile movement who could accomplish the job. After receiving approval, Trafficante approached this person about assassinating Castro and reported that he was receptive. The IG report stated that the Support Chief again distributed pills that eventually reached the Cuban exile leader."

The Senate Report provides the following information on a plan to poison Castro: "The Cuban claimed to have a contact inside a restaurant frequented by Castro .... The attempt met with failure. According to the Inspector General's Report, Edwards believed the scheme failed because Castro stopped visiting the restaurant where the 'asset' was employed."

The Senate Report went on to discuss the chronology of the anti-Castro plots:

"The Inspector General's Report divides the gambling syndicate operation into Phase I, terminating with the Bay of Pigs, and Phase II, continuing with the transfer of the operation to William Harvey in late 1961. The distinction between a clearly demarcated Phase I and Phase II may be an artificial one, as there is considerable evidence that the operation was continuous, perhaps lying dormant for the period immediately following the Bay of Pigs.

"In early 1961, Harvey was assigned the responsibility for establishing a general capability within the CIA for disabling foreign leaders, including assassination as a 'last resort.' The capability was called Executive Action and was later included under the cryptonym ZR/RIFLE." "Harvey's notes reflect that Bissell asked him to take over the gambling syndicate operation from Edwards and that they discussed the 'application of ZR/RIFLE program to Cuba' on November 16, 1961."

The following events are best summarized in the House Report which tells us:

"The Support Chief then introduced Harvey to Rosselli. During this phase, the CIA decided against using Giancana or Trafficante; instead, a person referred to as 'Maceo' entered the plot as the person who would help provide Castro contacts. In addition, the plots still utilized the services of the Cuban exile leader." "In June 1962 Rosselli reported to Harvey that the Cuban exile leader dispatched a three-man team to Cuba with the general assignment of recruiting others to kill Castro and, if the opportunity arose, to kill him themselves, maybe through the use of pills. In September 1962, Rosselli reported to Harvey in Miami that the 'medicine' was reported in place, that the three-man team was safe, and that the Cuban exile leader was prepared to dispatch another three-man team to infiltrate Castro's bodyguard. In December 1962, Rosselli and Harvey agreed that not much seemed to be occurring and by February 1963, Harvey terminated the plots."

Returning again to the Senate Report we learn that "Two plans to assassinate Castro were explored by Task Force W, the CIA section then concerned with covert Cuban operations, in early 1963. Desmond FitzGerald (now deceased), Chief of the Task Force, asked his assistant to determine whether an exotic seashell, rigged to explode, could be deposited in an area where Castro commonly went skin diving. The idea was explored by the Technical Services Division and discarded as impractical.

"A second plan involved having James Donovan (who was negotiating with Castro for the release of prisoners taken during the Bay of Pigs operation) present Castro with a contaminated diving suit …The Technical Services Division bought a diving suit, dusted the inside with a fungus that would produce a chronic skin disease (Madura foot), and contaminated the breathing apparatus with a tubercule bacillus. The Inspector General's Report states that the plan was abandoned because Donovan gave Castro a different diving suit on his own initiative. Helms testified that the diving suit never left the laboratory."

"In the fall of 1963, another operation against Castro began. Since early 1961, the CIA had had an important asset inside Cuba in the person of a highly-placed Cuban official who was referred to by the cryptonym AM/LASH …As a high-ranking leader who enjoyed the confidence of Fidel Castro, AM/LASH could keep the CIA informed of the internal workings of the regime. It was also believed that he might play a part in fomenting a coup within Cuba. From the first contact with AM/LASH until the latter part of 1963, it was uncertain whether he would defect or remain in Cuba. His initial request to the CIA and FBI for aid in defecting were rebuffed."

"Desmond FitzGerald, Chief of the Special Affairs Staff ….. met AM/LASH in late fall 1963 and promised him that the United States would support a coup against Castro. When later interviewed for the Inspector General's Report, FitzGerald recalled that AM/LASH repeatedly requested an assassination weapon, particularly a 'high-powered rifle with telescopic sights that could be used to kill

Castro from a distance.' FitzGerald stated that he told AM/LASH that the United States would have 'no part of an attempt on Castro's life.' However, a contemporaneous memorandum by the case officer involved states 'C/SAS [FitzGerald] approved telling AM/LASH he would be given a cache inside Cuba. Cache could, if he requested it, include high-powered rifles with scopes.' AM/LASH was told on November 22 1963 that the cache would be dropped in Cuba."

"Another device offered to AM/LASH was a ballpoint pen rigged with a hypodermic needle. The needle was designed to be so fine that the victim would not notice its insertion. ... Helms confirmed that the pen was manufactured 'to take care of a request from him that he have some device for getting rid of Castro, for killing him, murdering him, whatever the case may be.' On November 22, 1963, FitzGerald and the case officer met with AM/LASH and offered him the poison pen, recommending that he use Blackleaf-40, a deadly poison which is commercially available. The Inspector General's Report noted that 'it is likely that at the very moment President Kennedy was shot, a CIA officer was meeting with a Cuban agent... and giving him an assassination device for use against Castro.'"

CHAPTER 18

CASTRO RETALIATION?

* * *

"Castro warned against the United States 'aiding terrorist plans to eliminate Cuban leaders.' He stated, according to Harker, that US leaders would be in danger if they promoted any attempt to eliminate the leaders of Cuba."

House Select Committee

In a section entitled CIA PLOTS AGAINST CASTRO, the House Committee relates as follows: "In early January 1967, Edward Morgan approached Columnist Drew Pearson, related the background of the plots, posed the possibility that the plots could have provoked a Castro retaliation, and asked Pearson to inform Chief Justice Earl Warren of the operation. Warren subsequently informed Secret Service Director James J. Rawley who in turn notified the FBI. Morgan informed the committee that Roselli initially approached him complaining of excessive FBI surveillance ever since he had been involved in this patriotic venture. Roselli also informed Morgan that Castro had retaliated for these plots by assassinating President Kennedy. After receiving this information the FBI decided not to investigate the allegation further. Following the publication of the Jack Anderson and Drew Pearson articles of March 3 and 7, 1967, however, where the theory of retaliation first gained public notoriety, President Johnson ordered the FBI to investigate the matter. The FBI consequently interviewed Edward Morgan on March 20, 1967.

The Senate Committee had stated: "On March 21, 1967, the Washington Field Office sent FBI Headquarters ten copies of a blind memorandum reporting on the interview. This memorandum can be summarized as follows:

"1. The lawyer had information pertaining to the assassination, but that it was necessary for him in his capacity as an attorney to invoke the attorney-client privilege since the information in his possession was derived as a result of that relationship.

"2. His clients, who were on the fringe of the underworld, were neither directly nor indirectly involved in the death of President Kennedy, but they faced possible prosecution in a crime not related to the assassination and through participation in such crime they learned of information pertaining to the President's assassination.

"3. His clients were called upon by a governmental agency to assist in a project which was said to have the highest governmental approval. The project had as its purpose the assassination of Fidel Castro. Elaborate plans were made including the infiltration of the Cuban government and the placing of informants within key posts in Cuba.

"4. The project almost reached fruition when Castro became aware of it; by pressuring captured subjects he was able to learn the full details of the plot against him and decided 'if that was the way President Kennedy wanted it, he too could engage in the same tactics.'

"5. Castro thereafter employed teams of individuals who were dispatched to the United States for the purpose of assassinating President Kennedy. The lawyer stated that his clients obtained this information 'from "feedback" furnished by sources close to Castro,' who had been initially placed there to carry out the original project.

"6. His clients were aware of the identity of some of the individuals who came to the United States for this purpose and he understood that two such individuals were now in the State of New Jersey.

"7. One client, upon hearing the statement that Lee Harvey Oswald was the sole assassin of President Kennedy 'laughs with tears in his eyes and shakes his head in apparent disagreement.'

"8. The lawyer stated if he were free of the attorney-client privilege, the information that he would be able to supply would not directly identify the alleged conspirators to kill President Kennedy. However, because of the project to kill Fidel Castro, those participating in the project, whom he represents, developed through feedback information that would identify Fidel Castro's counter-assassins in this country who could very well be considered suspects in such a conspiracy."

"The transmittal slip accompanying this memorandum noted, 'No further investigation is being conducted by the Washington Field Office unless it is advised to the contrary by the Bureau. Had the interviewing agents known of the CIA-underworld plots against Castro, they would have been aware that the lawyer had clients who had been active in the assassination plots." "Neither the Field agents who interviewed the lawyer nor the Headquarters supervisor agents assigned to the assassination case could provide any explanation for the Bureau's failure to conduct any follow-up investigation. When they were informed of the details of CIA assassination efforts against Castro, each of these agents stated that the allegations and specific leads provided should have been investigated to their logical conclusions."

The concept of a Castro retaliation theory has been discounted on a number of rationalizations which can be summarized thusly:

(1) That Castro has denied it.

(2) That it would not make sense for Castro to do it.

(3) That Morgan's client was manipulating the facts.

(4) That Castro didn't know about the US plots against him.

The first two items invite the following questions:

(1) Why would anyone believe Castro's denial?

(2) What is the basis to assume that Castro would have been so logical?

The third item refers to the fact that one of Morgan's clients was John Rosselli, who was at the time trying to avoid multiple problems with law enforcement. There is no doubt that given such a source, one must take any information with a large grain of salt. However, the fact that the source is a mobster such as Rosselli does not necessarily mean the information is untrue. Indeed, if the government really believed that such a source necessarily made information untrue, they would have to drop a very large percentage of their criminal prosecutions since they are based on "turning" someone. The fact is that much of law enforcement is premised on the reality that only when a Rosselli is being threatened by some penalty to be imposed upon himself, will he divulge information as to others. Moreover, the first part of the information that Morgan was supplying is now known to be true.

Consideration of the balance of Morgan's information leads us to item four, namely, the proposition that Castro could not have known about US plots against him and so would have had no reason to retaliate.

It will be recalled that an intricate part of the CIA-Mafia plot against Castro involved Salvatore Trafficante's role as a courier. The House Committee reported: "To support the description of Trafficante as a courier, the IG Report states that, 'At that time the gambling casinos were still operating in Cuba, and Trafficante was making regular trips between Miami and Havana on syndicate business.'" "If Trafficante was actually traveling between Miami an Havana, the implications are interesting. He was either willing to risk being detained again or had acquired assurance from the Cuban Government regarding his safety. In any event, the presence of Trafficante during the fall of 1960 in Cuba raises the possibility of a more cooperative relationship between himself and the Cuban Government than believed previously. Such a relationship during the period when Trafficante was scheming to assassinate Castro invites the theory that Trafficante was possibly informing the Cuban Government of activities in the Miami area in general and of the plots in particular. In return for such information, Trafficante could have been promised lost gambling operations as well as support and a Cuban sanctuary for the smuggling of contraband into the United States."

Trafficante was not the only potential source for Castro to learn of the US plots against his life. Joseph Langosch, the Chief of Counter-Intelligence for the CIA's Special Affairs Staff in 1963 (the component responsible for CIA operations against the Government of Cuba and the Cuban Intelligence Services) told the House Select Committee that "The AM/LASH operation prior to the assassination of President Kennedy was characterized by the special affairs staff, Desmond FitzGerald and other senior CIA officers as an assassination operation initiated and sponsored by the CIA... As of 1962 it was highly possible that the Cuban Intelligence Services were aware of AM/LASH and his association with the CIA."

Any questions that Castro knew of the US plots against his life would seem to be resolved by this quote from the material from the House Select Committee in a section entitled, "Debut of the Retaliation Theory." This section begins with the following information: "The genesis of this theory can be attributed to an interview that Premier Castro held on September 7, 1963 with Associated Press Reporter Daniel Harker. In that interview, Castro warned against the United States "aiding terrorist plans to eliminate Cuban leaders". He stated, according to Harker, that US leaders would be in danger if they promoted any attempt to eliminate the leaders of Cuba."

None of this proves that President Kennedy was assassinated by Castro in retaliation for US Assassination plots against him.

However, possible Castro retaliation plots are not the only Cuban aspect to our story. In fact, in one fashion or another, Cuba would seem to lie at the very center of this web.

CHAPTER 19
ANTI-CASTRO CUBANS

* * *

"Assassination was part of the ambience of that time".

CIA Chief, JM/WAVE Station

The House Select Committee conducted an exhaustive study entitled ANTI-CASTRO ACTIVITIES AND ORGANIZATIONS from which the following is extracted.

"The Committee ascertained that as a consequence of the efforts, the failure and the eventual unwillingness of the Kennedy administration to liberate Cuba from Castro, these persons and organizations acquired the means, motive and opportunity to assassinate the President."

"If it can be said to have a beginning, the anti-Castro Cuban exile movement was seeded in the early-morning hours of New Year's Day 1959 when a DC-4 lifted from the fog-shrouded Camp Columbia airfield in Havana. Aboard the plane was Fulgencio Batista, the military dictator of Cuba for the previous 6 years. Batista was fleeing the country, his regime long beset by forces from within and without, now crumbling under pressure from rebel forces sweeping down from the mountains. When dawn came, the bells tolled in Havana and, 600 miles away, Fidel Castro Ruz began his triumphal march to the capital. For seven days Castro and his 26th of July Movement rebels moved down Cuba's Central Highway while thousands cheered and threw flowers in his path. Castro finally arrived in Havana on January 8 and characteristically gave a speech. Clad in his green fatigue uniform while three white doves, which someone had dramatically released, circled above him, Castro boldly proclaimed: 'There is no longer an enemy!'

"That was not true, of course, and he knew it. A hard core of Batistianos had fled the country early, many long before their leader, and were already concocting counter-revolutionary plots from their refuges in the United States, the Dominican Republic and elsewhere.

"And it was not very long after Castro took power that a sense of betrayal began to grow among those who had once been his strongest supporters. As each day went by it became more apparent that Castro's revolution was, as one chronicler noted, 'leading inexorably toward an institutionalized dictatorship in which individuals were contemptuously shorn of their rights and dissenters were met with charges of treasonable conduct, counter-revolutionary activity or worse.' Then, too, there was a large number of public executions. Within 2 weeks of his reign, Castro shot 150 ex-Batista officials. Within three months, there were at least 506 executions.

"The disillusionment for many Cubans deepened when it became obvious that the form of Castro's rule was turning toward Communism and that Castro's attitude toward the United States was engendering a hostile relationship. The publishing of Castro's Agrarian Reform Law in May 1959, was a significant sign. It was far more radical than had been expected and was obviously designed to strip both Cuban and American-owned sugar firms of their immensely valuable cane lands. A few weeks later the chief of Castro's air force, Major Pedro Diaz-Lanz, resigned, charging 'there was Communist influence in the armed forces and Government.' Then, when Castro's own hand-picked president, Manuel Urrutia, announced at a press conference that he rejected the support of the Communists and said, 'I believe that any real Cuban revolutionary should reject it openly,' Castro immediately forced him to resign and accused him of actions 'bordering on treason.'

"And so, after the broken pledges of free elections and a free press, the mass trials and executions, the assumption of unlimited power and the bellicose threats against the United States, it slowly became apparent to many Cubans that Fidel Castro was not the political savior they had expected.

"Then, on October 19, 1959, there occurred an incident which precipitated the information of the first organized anti-Castro opposition within Cuba. Major Huber Matos, one of Castro's highest ranking officers and considered by most Cubans to be one of the key heroes of the revolution, resigned from the Army in protest against the increasing favoritism shown to known Communists. The next day Matos was arrested, charged with treason, subsequently tried and sentenced to 20 years in prison. Shortly afterward, Castro himself called a secret meeting of the National Agrarian Reform Institute managers at which he outlined a plan to communize Cuba within three years. There the suspicions of Dr. Manuel Artime, the manager in Oriente Province, were confirmed. 'I realized,' Artime later said, 'that I was a democratic infiltrator in a Communist government.'

"Artime returned to Oriente and began organizing students and peasants to fight against Castro and Communism. By early November each province in Cuba had an element of Artime's new underground movement. It was called the Movimiento de Recuperacion Revolucionaria (MRR). It was the first anti-Castro action group originating from within Castro's own ranks.

"By the summer of 1960, it had become obvious both within and without Cuba that the foundation for an eventual confrontation between Castro and anti-Castro forces had been laid. The Eisenhower administration had canceled the Cuban sugar quota. Soviet first deputy chairman Anastas Mikoyan had visited Havana and Raul Castro had gone to Moscow. Ernesto 'Che' Guevara had proclaimed publicly that the revolution was on the road set by Marx, and Allen Dulles of the Central Intelligence Agency had said in a speech that Communism had perverted Castro's revolution. By then, Castro had seized more than $700 million in US property within Cuba.

"On March 17, 1960, President Eisenhower authorized the CIA to organize, train and equip Cuban refugees as a guerilla force to overthrow Castro. Soon it became common knowledge within Cuba that a liberation army was being formed and that a political structure in exile had been created. As the flight from Cuba increased in size and fervor, the exile community in the United States grew in spirit and confidence."

"By April 1961, the more than 100,000 Cubans who had fled Castro's revolution lived in anticipation of its overthrow. They had been buoyed in that hope by public pronouncements of support from the US Government. In his State of the Union Address, President Kennedy had spoken of 'the Communist base established 90 miles from the United States,' and said that 'Communist domination in this hemisphere can never be negotiated.' In addition, the Cuban exiles had been organized, directed and almost totally funded by agencies of the US Government, principally the CIA.

"From an historical perspective, in light of its later radical change, the attitude of the Cuban exiles toward the US Government prior to the Bay of Pigs is especially significant. Author Haynes Johnson who in writing a history of the invasion collaborated with the top Cuban leaders, including brigade civilian chief Manuel Artime, described that attitude in detail: 'From the beginning, the Cuban counter-revolutionists viewed their new American friends with blind trust. Artime was no exception. He, and later virtually all of the Cubans involved, believed so much in the Americans – or wanted so desperately to believe – that they never questioned what was happening or expressed doubts about the plans. Looking back on it, they agree now that their naiveté was partly genuine and partly reluctance to turn down any offer of help in liberating their country. In fact, they had little choice; there was no other place to turn. Some, of course, were driven by other motives: political power and personal ambition were involved. Even more important was the traditional Cuban attitude toward America and Americans. To Cubans the United States was more than the colossus of the north, for the two countries were bound closely by attitudes, by history, by geography and by economics. The United States was great and powerful, the master not only of the hemisphere but perhaps of the world, and it was Cuba's friend. One really didn't question such a belief. It was a fact; everyone knew it. And the mysterious, anonymous, ubiquitous American agents who dealt with the Cubans managed to strengthen that belief.'

"This 'blind trust' by the Cuban exiles in the US Government prior to the Bay of Pigs was specifically noted by the military commander of the 2506 Brigade, Joe (Pepe) Perez San Roman: 'Most of the Cubans were there,' he said, 'because they knew the whole operation was going to be conducted by the Americans, not by me or anyone else. They just trusted the Americans. So they were going to fight because the United States was backing them.'

"The debacle at the Bay of Pigs was not only military tragedy for the anti-Castro Cuban exiles but also a painful shattering of their confidence in the US Government. The exile leaders claimed the failure of the invasion was a result of the lack of promised air support, and for that they directly blamed President Kennedy. Particularly galling to them was Kennedy's public declaration to Soviet Premier Khrushchev at the height of the invasion, when the Brigade was being slaughtered in the swamps of Bahia de Cochinos: 'I repeat now that the United States intends no armed intervention in Cuba.'

"Even those exile leaders who were willing to rationalize the extent of Kennedy's responsibility were dissuaded when Kennedy himself admitted the blame. Cuban Revolutionary Council leader Manuel Antonio de Varona, in his executive session testimony before the Committee, told of the President gathering the Council members together at the White House when it became clear that the invasion was a disaster. Varona recalled: 'We were not charging Mr. Kennedy with anything; we just wanted to clarify. We knew that he didn't have any direct knowledge of the problem, and we knew he was not in charge of the military effects directly. Nevertheless, President Kennedy, to finish the talks, told us he was the one – the only one responsible.'

"A few days after that meeting, the White House issued a public statement declaring that President Kennedy assumed 'sole responsibility' for the US role in the action against Cuba.

"The acceptance of responsibility did not cut the bitter disappointment the Cuban exiles felt toward the US Government and President Kennedy. Much later, captured and imprisoned by Castro, Brigade Commander San Roman revealed the depth of his reaction at the failure of the invasion: 'I hated the United States,' he said, 'and I felt that I had been betrayed. Every day it became worse and then I was getting madder and madder and I wanted to get a rifle and come and fight against the US.'

"Prominent Cuban attorney Mario Lazo wrote a book caustically titled *Dagger in the Heart*. Lazo wrote: 'The Bay of Pigs defeat was wholly self-inflicted in Washington. Kennedy told the truth when he publicly accepted responsibility ... The heroism of the beleaguered Cuban Brigade had been rewarded by betrayal, defeat, death for many of them, long and cruel imprisonment for the rest. The Cuban people and the Latin American nations, bound to Cuba by thousands of subtle ties of race and culture, were left with feelings of astonishment and disillusionment, and in many cases despair. They had always admired the United States as strong, rich, generous – but where was its sense of honor and the capacity of its leaders? The mistake of the Cuban fighters for liberation was that they thought too highly of the United States. They believed to the end that it would not let them down. But it did.'

"President Kennedy was well aware of the bitter legacy left him by the Bay of Pigs debacle. It is not now possible to document the changes in Kennedy's personal attitude brought about by the military defeat, but the firming of US policy toward Cuba and the massive infusion of US aid to clandestine anti-Castro operations in the wake of the Bay of Pigs was editorially characterized by Taylor Branch and George Crile in *Harper's Magazine* as 'the Kennedy Vendetta.'

"What can be documented is the pattern of US policy between the period of the Bay of Pigs failure in April 1961 and the Cuban missile crisis in October 1962. That pattern, replete with both overt and covert maneuvers, had a significant effect on the reshaping of Cuban exile attitudes and, when it was abruptly reversed, could have provided the motivation for involvement in the assassination of President Kennedy.

"In retrospect, the period between the Bay of Pigs and the Cuban missile crisis can be considered the high-water mark of anti-Castro activity, almost every manifestation of the US policy providing a reassurance of support of the Cuban cause. As a matter of fact, only a few days after the Bay of Pigs invasion, President Kennedy delivered a particularly hard-line address before the American Society of Newspaper Editors on the implications of Communism in Cuba. 'Cuba must not be abandoned to the Communists,' he declared. In appealing for support from Latin America, he indicated that the United States would expect more from the nations of the hemisphere with regard to Cuba and asserted that the United States would not allow the doctrine of non-intervention to hinder its policy. Said Kennedy, 'Our restraint is not inexhaustible,' and spoke of Cuba in the context of the 'new and deeper struggle.'

'When Castro, in a May Day speech, declared Cuba to be a socialist nation, the State Department retorted that Cuba was a full-fledged member of the Communist bloc.

"Another US response was the establishment of the Alliance for Progress, after years of relatively little attention to Latin America's economic and social needs. President Kennedy gave the Alliance concept a memorable launching in a speech in March 1961 when he called for vigorous promotion of social and economic development in Latin America through democratic means and, at the same time, pledged substantial financial and political support.

"While the campaign to broaden its Cuban policy base was being pursued, the United States was proceeding on another course. In one of the first unilateral efforts to isolate Cuba from its allies, the United States in September 1961 announced it would stop assistance to any country that assisted Cuba. In December, Kennedy extended the denial of Cuba's sugar quota through the first half of 1962.

"Meanwhile, the secret policy aimed at removing Castro through assassination continued as FBI chief J. Edgar Hoover informed Attorney General Robert Kennedy in May that the CIA had used the Mafia in 'clandestine efforts' against Castro. In that month, poison pills to be used in a plot to kill Castro were passed to a Cuban exile in Miami by a Mafia figure. In November 1961, Operation Mongoose, designed to enlist 2,000 Cuban exiles and dissidents inside Cuba to overthrow Castro was initiated.

"Although the bitter after-taste of the Bay of Pigs invasion lingered in the Cuban exile community, those who remained active in the fight against Castro came to realize that these subsequent actions of the Kennedy administration were manifestations of its determination to reverse the defeat. What Kennedy had euphemistically termed 'a new and deeper struggle' became, in actuality, a secret war ...."

"The nerve center of the United States' 'new and deeper struggle' against Castro was established in the heartland of exile activity, Miami. There, on a secluded, heavily wooded 1,571-acre tract that was part of the University of Miami's south campus, the CIA set up a front operation, an electronics firm called Zenith Technological Services. Its code name was JM/WAVE and it soon became the largest CIA installation anywhere in the world outside of its headquarters in Langley, Virginia. The JM/WAVE station had, at the height of its activities in 1962, a staff of more than 300 Americans, mostly case officers. Each case officer employed from 4 to 10 Cuban 'principal agents' who, in turn, would each be responsible for between 10 and 30 regular agents. In addition, the CIA set up 54 front corporations – boat shops, real estate firms, detective agencies, travel companies, gun shops – to provide ostensible employment for the case officers and agents operating outside of JM/WAVE headquarters. It also maintained hundreds of pieces of real estate, from small apartments to palatial homes, as 'safe houses' in which to hold secret meetings. As a result of its JM/WAVE operation, the CIA became one of Florida's largest employers. It was the JM/WAVE station that monitored, more or less controlled, and in most cases funded the anti-Castro groups. It was responsible for the great upsurge in anti-Castro activity and the lifted spirits of the Cuban exiles as American arms and weapons flowed freely through the training camps and guerilla bases spotted around south Florida. Anti -Castro raiding parties that left from small secret islands in the Florida Keys were given the 'green light' by agents of the JM/WAVE station. The result of it all was that there grew in the Cuban exile community a renewed confidence in the US Government's sincerity and loyalty to its cause.

"Then came the Cuban missile crisis. The more fervent Cuban exiles were initially elated by the possibility that the crises might provoke a final showdown with Castro. For several months there had been increasing pressure on President Kennedy to take strong measures against the build-up of the Soviet presence in Cuba, which was becoming daily more blatant. In a report issued at the end of March 1962, the State Department said that Cuba had received from the Soviet Union $100 million in military aid for the training of Cuban pilots in Czechoslovakia and that the Soviet Union also had provided from 50 to 75 Mig fighters as well as tons of modern weapons for Cuba's ground forces. Fortifying the Cuban exiles' hope for action was the fact that the increasing amounts of Soviet weapons moving into Cuba became the dominant issue in the news in the succeeding months, leading to congressional calls for action and a series of hard-line responses from President Kennedy. In September, Kennedy declared that the United States would use 'whatever means may be necessary' to prevent Cuba from exporting 'its aggressive purposes by force or threat of force' against 'any part of the Western Hemisphere.'

"The fervent hope of the Cuban exiles – that the Cuban missile crisis would ultimately result in the United States smashing the Castro regime – was shattered by the manner in which President Kennedy resolved the crisis. Cuba itself was relegated to a minor role as tough negotiations took place between the United States and Soviet Union, specifically through communication between President Kennedy and Premier Khrushchev. The crisis ended when President Kennedy announced that all IL-28 bombers were being withdrawn by the Soviets and progress was being made on the withdrawal of offensive missiles and other weapons from Cuba. In return, Kennedy gave the Soviets and the Cubans a 'no invasion' pledge.

"If Kennedy's actions at the Bay of Pigs first raised doubts in the minds of the Cuban exiles about the President's sincerity and determination to bring about the fall of Castro, his handling of the missile crisis confirmed those doubts. Kennedy's agreement with Khrushchev was termed 'a violation' of the pledge he had made 3 days after the Bay of Pigs invasion that the United States would never abandon Cuba to Communism. Wrote one prominent exile: 'For the friendly Cuban people, allies of the United States, and for hundreds of thousands of exiles eager to stake their lives to liberate their native land, it was a soul-shattering blow.'

"The bitterness of the Anti-Castro exiles was exacerbated by the actions the US Government took to implement the President's 'no invasion' pledge. Suddenly there was a crackdown on the very training camps and guerilla bases which had been originally established and funded by the United States, and the exile raids which once had the Government's 'green light' were now promptly disavowed and condemned. On March 31, 1963, a group of anti-Castro raiders were arrested by British police at a training site in the Bahamas. The US State Department admitted it had given the British the information about the existence of the camp. That same night another exile raiding boat was seized in Miami Harbor. On April 3, the Soviet Union charged the United States 'encourages and bears full responsibility' for two recent attacks on Soviet ships in Cuban ports by anti-Castro exile commandos. The United States responded that it was 'taking every step necessary to insure that such attacks are not launched, manned or equipped from US territory.' On April 5, the Coast Guard announced it was throwing more planes, ships and men into its efforts to police the straits of Florida against anti-Castro raiders. As a result of the crackdown, Cuban exile sources declared that their movement to rid their homeland of Communism had been dealt 'a crippling blow' and that they had lost a vital supply link with anti-Castro fighters inside Cuba. There were numerous other indications of the US crackdown on anti-Castro activity following the missile crisis. The Customs Service raided what had long been a secret training camp in the Florida Keys and arrested the anti-Castro force training there. The FBI seized a major cache of explosives at an anti-Castro camp in Louisiana. Just weeks later, the US Coast Guard in cooperation with the British Navy captured another group of Cuban exiles in the Bahamas. In September, the Federal Aviation Administration issued 'strong warning' to six American civilian pilots who had been flying raids over Cuba. Shortly afterward, the Secret Service arrested a prominent exile leader for conspiring to counterfeit Cuban currency destined for rebel forces inside Cuba. In October, the Coast Guard seized 4 exile ships and arrested 22 exile raiders who claimed they were moving their operations out of the United States.

"The feeling of betrayal by the Cuban exiles was given reinforcement by prominent sympathizers outside their community, as well as by Kennedy's political opponents. Captain Eddie Rickenbacker, chairman of the Committee for the Monroe Doctrine, asserted: 'The Kennedy administration has committed the final betrayal of Cuban hopes for freedom by its order to block the activities of exiled Cuban freedom fighters to liberate their nation from Communism.' Senator Barry Goldwater accused Kennedy of 'doing everything in his power' to keep the flag of Cuban exiles 'from ever flying over Cuba again.' Richard Nixon urged the end of what he called the 'quarantine' of Cuban exiles.

"Of course, the most strident reactions came from within the anti-Castro community itself. Following the US Government's notification that it would discontinue its subsidy to the Cuban Revolutionary Council, its president, Jose Miro Cardona, announced his resignation from the council in protest against US policy. The Cuban exile leader accused President Kennedy of 'breaking promises and agreements' to support another invasion of Cuba. Miro Cardona said the change in American policy reflected the fact that Kennedy had become 'the victim of a master play by the Russians.'"

"Against the pattern of US crackdown on Cuban exile activity during this period, however, emerges a counter-grain of incidents that may have some bearing on an examination of the Kennedy assassination. These incidents involve some extremely significant Cuban exile raids and anti-Castro operations which took place, despite the crackdown, between the time of the missile crisis and the assassination of the President."

"In retrospect, this much is clear. With or without US Government support and whether or not in blatant defiance of Kennedy administration policy, there were a number of anti-Castro action groups which were determined to continue – and, in fact, did continue-their operations. The resignation of Miro Cardona actually split the Cuban Revolutionary Council down the middle and precipitated a bitter dispute among the exile factions. The more moderate contended that without US support there was little hope of ousting Castro and that the exiles should concentrate their efforts in mounting political pressure to reverse Washington's shift in policy. Other exile groups announced their determination to continue the war against Castro and, if necessary, to violently resist the curtailment of their para-military activities in the Kennedy administration. In New Orleans, for instance, Carlos Bringuier, the local leader of the Cuban Student Directorate (DRE) who, coincidentally, would later have a contact with Lee Harvey Oswald, proclaimed, in the wake of the Miro Cardona resignation, that his group 'would continue efforts to liberate Cuba despite action by the United States to stop raids originating from US soil.'

"The seeds of defiance of the Kennedy administration may have been planted with the exiles even prior to the Bay of Pigs invasion. In his history of the invasion, Haynes Johnson revealed that shortly before the invasion, 'Frank Bender,' the CIA director of the invasion preparations, assembled the exile leaders together at the CIA's Guatemala training camp: 'It was now early in April and Artime was in the camp as the civilian representative of the Revolutionary Council. Frank called Pepe (San Roman) and (Erneido) Oliva again. This time he had startling information. There were forces in the administration trying to block the invasion, and Frank might be ordered to stop it. If he received such an order, he said, he would secretly inform Pepe and Oliva. Pepe remembers Frank's next words this way: 'If this happens you come here and make some kind of show, as if you were putting us, the advisers, in prison, and you go ahead with the program as we have talked about it, and we will give you the whole plan, even if we are your prisoners.' ... Frank then laughed and said: 'In the end we will win.'

"That, then, is the context in which the Committee approached the question of whether or not the assassination of President Kennedy was a conspiracy involving anti-Castro Cuban exiles.

"It also considered the testimony of the CIA's chief of its Miami JM/WAVE station in 1963, who noted, '"assassination" was part of the ambience of that time.'"

As the quote attributed to "Frank Bender" makes clear, there was rather less than total respect and admiration for President Kennedy by at least some CIA personnel. This was, it should be noted, not a one-way street. Although Kennedy accepted "sole responsibility' for the Bay of Pigs debacle, privately he blamed the

CIA. The word "privately" as used here should not be misunderstood to mean "secretly;" it really is used to distinguish Kennedy's true feelings from his "official" statements. He didn't make much of a secret about his disdain for the CIA, which was such that, as the House Report relates, he vowed to "splinter the agency into a thousand pieces."

The net result of all of this was that John Kennedy would up with at least two sets of enemies who shared mutual interests and the capacity for violence.

CHAPTER 20

KENNEDY HAD ENEMIES

* * *

"In Georgia, the marquee of a movie theatre showing PT109
read 'See how the Japs almost got Kennedy.'"

House Select Committee

Elements of the CIA, and anti-Castro Cubans, were not John Kennedy's only bitter enemies. In a section entitled AT HOME: A TROUBLED LAND, the House Committee related as follows:

"In an era when the United States was confronted with intractable, often dangerous, international and domestic issues, the Kennedy administration was inevitably surrounded by controversy as it made policies to deal with the problems. it faced. Although a popular President, John F. Kennedy was reviled by some, an enmity inextricably related to his policies."

"Kennedy appointed Blacks to high administration posts and to Federal judgeships. He gave Attorney General Robert F. Kennedy his sanctions for vigorous enforcement of civil rights laws to extend voting rights, end segregation and fight discrimination."

"Violence erupted soon after Kennedy took office. In May 1961, the Congress of Racial Equality staged a series of freedom rides in Alabama in an effort to integrate buses and terminals. One bus was burned by a mob in Anniston, Alabama. An angry segregationist crowd attacked demonstrators in Montgomery, Alabama, and several persons were injured. Attorney General Kennedy ordered several hundred US marshals to Montgomery to protect the demonstrators. National Guardsmen with fixed bayonets scattered a mob that tried to overwhelm the marshals, who were protecting a mass meeting at a Black church where civil rights leader Martin Luther King, Jr. was speaking."

"Trouble exploded again in 1962 when James Meredith, a 29-year old Black Air Force veteran, gained admission to the all-white University of Mississippi. Meredith had been refused admission despite Federal court orders requiring that he be enrolled. The Kennedy administration supported an effort to force compliance by the State, but Governor Ross Barnett was equally determined to defy the orders. In his fourth attempt to enroll at the university, Meredith arrived in Oxford on September 30, escorted by 300 US marshals. He was met by a mob of 2,500 students and segregationist extremists who howled, "Two-four-one-three, we hate Kennedy. The hecklers attacked the marshals with tear gas. A bloody night-long riot that left two dead and scores injured was quelled only after Federal troops had been dispatched by President Kennedy.'

"Blacks continued demonstrations for equal rights in the spring of 1963. In April and May, Dr. King led an attack on what he called 'the most segregated city in the United States,' Birmingham, Alabama. Demonstrators were met by police dogs, electric cattle prods and fire hoses."

"In June 1963, Alabama Governor George Wallace, in defiance of a Federal court order, stood on the steps of the University of Alabama to prevent the admission of two Black students. Wallace bowed, however, to National Guard troops that had been federalized by the President ... In the same month, Medgar Evers, the NAACP field secretary in Mississippi, was shot to death in front of his home in Jackson, Mississippi."

"On August 28, 1963, an inter-racial group of more than 200,000 persons joined 'The March for Jobs and Freedom' in Washington, DC, to urge the Congress to pass the comprehensive civil rights legislation the Kennedy administration envisioned. Violence shattered the hopeful mood in the wake of the Washington march when a bomb exploded on September 17 at the Sixteenth Street Baptist Church in Birmingham, Alabama during a Sunday School session. Four young Black girls were killed and 23 other persons were injured."

"In October, *Newsweek* magazine reported that the civil rights issue alone had cost Kennedy 3.5 million votes, adding that no Democrat in the White House had ever been so disliked in the South. In Georgia, the marquee of a movie theatre showing *PT109* read "See how the Japs almost got Kennedy.""

"As the policies of the Kennedy administration broke new ground, political extremists in the United States seemed increasingly willing to resort to violence to achieve their goals. In an address at the University of Washington in Seattle on November 16, 1961, President Kennedy discussed the age of extremism: two groups of frustrated citizens, one urging surrender and the other urging war. He said: 'It is a curious fact that each of these extreme opposites resembles the other. Each believes that we have only two choices: appeasement or war, suicide or surrender, humiliation or holocaust, to be either Red or dead.'

"The radical right condemned Kennedy for his 'big Government' policies, as well as his concern with social welfare and civil rights progress. The ultra-conservative John Birch Society, Christian Anti-Communist Crusade led by Fred C. Schwarz, and the Christian Crusade led by Rev. Billie James Hargis attracted an anti-Kennedy following. The right wing was incensed by Kennedy's transfer of General Edwin A. Walker from his command in West Germany to Hawaii for distributing right-wing literature to his troops. The paramilitary Minutemen condemned the administration as 'soft on Communism' and adopted guerilla warfare tactics to prepare for the fight against the Communist foe. At the other extreme, the left labeled Kennedy a reactionary disappointment, a tool of the 'power elite.'"

There was, however, another domestic issue which presented President Kennedy with, perhaps, his foremost enemy – an enemy all the more dangerous to him since it had contacts with, and could mobilize and utilize segments of, his other enemies.

CHAPTER 21

ENEMY #1, THE MOB

* * *

"The Committee found that these three cases ...had identifiable similarities. In two of the cases, the assailant was himself murdered soon after the crime. The persons recruited to carry out the acts could be characterized as dupes or tools. The intent was ...for disguising the true identity of the conspirators, and to place the blame on generally nondescript individuals."

House Select Committee

The following material is drawn from the House Committee's special volume on organized crime:

"Up to the 1960s the Italian groups of organized crime were in an enviable position. They had an organization that few believed existed and about which little was known. It's leaders – and hence the organization itself – were protected by low-level members who actually performed the criminal acts, many of which Federal and other agencies considered to be beyond their purview or legislative mandate. At best, organized crime was assigned a low priority at State and local levels of law enforcement, and even this was easily nullified by corruption and politics. At the Federal level, even where there was concern, effective action was hampered by inadequate enabling legislation."

"The only major national investigation to be conducted during the period from prohibition until the late 1950s was that of the Senate Select Committee to Investigate Organized Crime in Interstate Commerce, chaired by Senator Estes Kefauver. The Committee held hearings in major cities across the country. It built up a substantial body of knowledge that indicated that there was a national and highly successful syndicate known as the Mafia, involved in a wide range of criminal activities throughout the United States and abroad. Violence was key to its success, as was corruption, and it was completely ruthless. As a result of the Committee's findings, Congress passed some gambling legislation, similar investigations were precipitated at the State and local levels, and in 1954, the Federal Government took further action by setting up the Organized Crime and Racketeering Section in the Department of Justice. Its main function was to coordinate the effort against organized crime, but it found little cooperation from other agencies.

"It was in 1957 that organized crime once again came into national attention. On November 14 a significant meeting took place outside the village of Apalachin, New York. The aftermath was perhaps not what the participants had anticipated, for not only was the cloak of secrecy partially pulled aside, but the event ultimately led to the greatest campaign to date against organized crime. On that day, Sergeant Edgar Crosswell of the New York State Police noted that a large number of people were converging on the estate of Joseph Barbera, Sr., many from far away. Crosswell had long been interested in Barbera, at the time the distributor for a major soda bottling company. Barbera had come from northern Pennsylvania, where he had a long police record that included two arrests for homicide (he was not convicted of either). Because the meeting was on private property, no direct police action could be taken. Crosswell himself watched the entrance from nearby. A tradesman from the village, while making a delivery, noticed Crosswell and alerted those at the meeting. Many of Barbera's guests elected to depart. Some did so by car and were detained, once on public roads, for the purpose of identification. Others who fled onto adjoining posted acreage were picked up for possible trespass. Most of those who remained on Barbera's estate could not be identified.

In all, 63 people were detained and identified. Local hotel records, auto rental contracts and one report of a motor vehicle accident provided investigators with the names of still others. The evidence showed that they had come from New England, New York,

New Jersey, Pennsylvania, Florida, Missouri, Texas, Colorado, Ohio, Illinois, and northern and southern California. They included many of the leading organized crime figures, such as Santos Trafficante, Vito Genovese, Carmine Galante, John Ormento and Sam Giancana." "The evidence supported a conclusion that the gathering was to have been a national meeting of... criminals and their associates."

"Because a number of attendees at the Apalachin meeting were directly or indirectly involved in union affairs, some were called before the Senate Select Committee on Improper Activities in the Labor or Management Fields, chaired by Senator John L. McClellan. These hearings became known as the McClellan Committee hearings. Senator John F. Kennedy was a member of this Committee; his brother, Robert F. Kennedy, was its chief counsel "

"By 1960, the FBI had accumulated substantial knowledge about Italian organized criminal groups . . . Nevertheless, the FBI did not make organized crime a top priority until the Kennedy administration arrived in Washington . . . With the advent of [the Kennedy] administration, organized crime investigations were assigned a high priority . . . As a first step, Robert Kennedy dramatically expanded the number of attorneys in the Organized Crime and Racketeering Section of the Criminal Division of the Justice Department and made clear to the FBI that organized crime was to be a high priority. The category within which these investigations were carried at Justice was shown in FBI files to be AR, or anti-racketeering. He also put together a list of 40 organized crime figures who were to be targeted for investigation. This was soon followed by a second list of 40. The Attorney General quickly requested new legislation to improve the Department's ability to attack organized crime."

"The scope and success of this campaign by the Kennedy administration can be easily seen in the following statistics and charts on staffing, investigations, and prosecution:

Between 1960 (prior to the Kennedy administration) and 1963, there was:

(1) A 250 % increase in the number of attorneys – from 17 to 60.

(2) More than a 900 % increase in days in the field - from 660 to 6,172.

(3) A 1,250 % increase in days in grand jury – from 100 to 1,353. ,

(4) A 1,700 % increase in days in court – from 61 to 1,081.

From 1961 to 1963, there was:

(5) A 500 % increase in defendants indicted – from 121 to 615;

(6) A 400 % increase in defendants convicted – from 73 to 288."

"As the year 1963 progressed, there were many signs that the constant pressure was taking its toll." As the House Committee stated in its final report: "The zeal of the Kennedy brothers signified the roughest period for organized crime in Department of Justice history. Historian Arthur Schlesinger, Jr., wrote in *Robert Kennedy and His Times* that, as a result of the Attorney General's pressure, 'the national Government took on organized crime as it had never been done before.' Schlesinger observed: 'in New York, Robert Morgenthau, the Federal Attorney, successfully prosecuted one syndicate leader after another. The Patriarca gang in Rhode Island and the De Cavalcante gang in New Jersey were smashed. Convictions of racketeers by the Organized Crime Section [together with] the Tax Division steadily increased – 96 in 1961, 101 in 1962, 373 in 1963. So long as John Kennedy sat in the White House, giving his Attorney General absolute backing, the underworld knew that the heat was on.'

"The Attorney General focused on targets he had become acquainted with as counsel for the Rackets Committee. He was particularly concerned about the alliance of the top labor leaders and racketeers as personified by Teamster President James R. Hoffa. Schlesinger wrote that 'the pursuit of Hoffa was an aspect of the war against organized crime.' He added: 'the relations between the Teamsters and the syndicate continued to grow. The FBI electronic microphone, planted from 1961 to 1964, in the office of Anthony Giacalone, a Detroit hood, revealed Hoffa's deep if wary involvement with the local mob. For national purposes a meeting place was the Rancho La Costa Country Club near San Clemente, California, built with $27 million in loans from the Teamsters pension fund; its proprietor, Morris B. Dalitz, had emerged from the Detroit [sic. Cleveland] underworld to become a Las Vegas and Havana gambling figure. Here the Teamsters and the mob golfed and drank together.'

"Here they no doubt reflected that, as long as John Kennedy was President, Robert Kennedy would be unassailable.'"

Schlesinger may well be right that Jimmy Hoffa came to realize that the key was John, not Robert, since John could always replace Robert; but if John were gone, Robert was out of office. However, the House Select Committee found that "Hoffa and at least one of his Teamster lieutenants, Edward Partin, apparently did, in fact, discuss the planning of an assassination conspiracy against President Kennedy's brother, Attorney General Robert F. Kennedy, in July or August of 1962." "In an interview with the Committee, Partin reaffirmed the account of Hoffa's discussion of a possible assassination plan, and he stated that Hoffa had believed that having the Attorney General murdered would be the most effective way of ending the Federal Government's intense investigation of the Teamsters and organized crime. Partin further told the Committee that he suspected that Hoffa may have approached him about the assassination proposal because Hoffa believed him to be close to various figures in Carlos Marcello's syndicate organization. Partin, a Baton Rouge Teamsters official with a criminal record, was then a leading Teamsters Union official in Louisiana. Partin was also a key Federal witness against Hoffa in the 1964 trial that led to Hoffa's eventual imprisonment.

"While the committee did not uncover evidence that the proposed Hoffa assassination plan ever went beyond its discussion, the committee noted the similarities between the plan discussed by Hoffa in 1962 and the actual events of November 22, 1963.

"While the Committee was aware of the apparent absence of any finalized method or plan during the course of Hoffa's discussion about assassinating Attorney General Kennedy, he did discuss the possible use of a lone gunman equipped with a rifle with a telescopic sight, the advisability of having the assassination committed somewhere in the South, as well as the potential desirability of having Robert Kennedy shot while riding in a convertible." "Edward Partin told the Committee that Hoffa believed that by having Kennedy shot as he rode in a convertible, the origin of the fatal shot or shots would be obscured.

"The context of Hoffa's discuss with Partin about an assassination conspiracy further seemed to have been predicated upon the recruitment of an assassin without any identifiable connection to the Teamster organization or Hoffa himself."

The special organized crime volume of the House Committee Report informs us that by 1963, "Santos Trafficante's gambling operations in Florida were in trouble." "Sam Giancana in Chicago was also feeling the pressure. Giancana's concern could be readily understood. For some time he had been the subject of the intense coverage by the FBI. By the spring of 1963, it had become 'bumper-to-bumper,' almost 24 hours per day – while driving, on the golf course, in restaurants, wherever he was . . . As a consequence, Giancana was staying away from his home base in Chicago to a significant degree, and it was creating problems."

"Later in July 1963, on two weekends, Sam Giancana and Phyllis McGuire, the singer, were together at the Cal-Neva Lodge on Lake Tahoe, Nevada. One of these weekends Frank Sinatra, who owned 50 percent of the Lodge (as well as having an interest in the Sands in Las Vegas) was with them. On August 2, 1963 Giancana and McGuire were also guests at Frank Sinatra's Palm Springs, California, home, having flown there on Sinatra's plane. These and other similar facts appeared in the Chicago newspapers and other media and resulted in action by the Nevada Gaming Commission, which had listed Giancana as a person not to be allowed in any premises licensed for gambling. Sinatra refused to deny his close relationship with Giancana and decided to sell his interests rather than run the risk of a suspended license. Later that month, the FBI learned of rumblings in the higher echelons of organized crime in Chicago over Giancana's absenteeism and bad publicity."

Other La Cosa Nostra leaders were also experiencing difficulties, but few more than Carolos Marcello. The House Committee Report describes the position of Marcello within the national crime syndicate as follows: "The FBI determined in the 1960s that because of Marcello's position as head of the New Orleans Mafia family (the oldest in the United States, having first entered the country in the 1880s), the Louisiana organized crime leader had been endowed with special powers and privileges not accorded to any other La Cosa Nostra leaders. As the leader of the 'first family' of the Mafia in America, according to FBI information, Marcello had been the recipient of the extraordinary privilege of conducting syndicate operations without have to seek the approval of the national commission."

In a special section dealing exclusively with Carlos Marcello, the House Committee relates, 'The exact place of Marcello's birth on February 6, 1910 has long been in doubt, and at one point was a central question in a lengthy deportation proceeding. Nevertheless, it is generally believed that Marcello was born in Tunis, North Africa, with the name Calogero Minacore. Marcello's first contact with the law came on November 29, 1929, when he was arrested at the age of 19 by New Orleans police as an accessory before and after the robbery of a local bank. The charges were subsequently dismissed. Less than 6 months later, on May 13, 1930, he was convicted of assault and robbery and was sentenced to the State penitentiary for 9 to 14 years. He served less than 5 . . . In 1935, after receiving a pardon by the Governor of Louisiana, Marcello's early underworld career continued, with charges being filed against him for a second assault and robbery, violation of Federal Internal Revenue laws, assault with intent to kill a New Orleans police officer, and yet another assault and robbery. Marcello was not prosecuted on the various charges. In 1938, as part of what Federal agents described as 'the biggest marihuana ring in New Orleans history,' Marcello was arrested and charged with the sale of more than 23 pounds of illegal substance. Despite receiving another lengthy prison sentence and a $76,830 fine, Marcello served less than 10 month and arranged to settle his fine for $400. Other charges were brought against Marcello over the next several years, stemming from such alleged offenses as narcotics sale, a high speed automobile chase, and assaulting an investigative reporter; these were never prosecuted, and the records have since disappeared.

"During the 1940s, Marcello became associated with New York Mafia leader Frank Costello in the operation of a slot machine network. Costello was then regarded by some authorities as one of the most influential leaders of organized crime in the United States and was commonly referred to in the newspapers as the Mafia's 'boss of all bosses' or 'prime minister of the underworld.' Marcello's association with Costello in various Louisiana gambling activities had come about following a reported agreement between Costello and Senator Huey Long that allowed for the introduction of slot machines into New Orleans.

"Marcello was also involved in Louisiana gambling through his family-owned Jefferson Music Company, which came to dominate the slot machine, pinball and juke box trade in the New Orleans area. By the late 1940s, in an alliance with Joseph Poretta, Marcello had taken control of the largest racing wire service in New Orleans, the Southern News Service and Publishing Co., which served Louisiana's prosperous gambling network. Marcello and other associates also gained control of the two best-known gambling casinos in the New Orleans area, the Beverly Club and New

Southport Club; the Beverly Club brought Marcello into partnership with the syndicate financier, Meyer Lansky.

"By the late 1950s, the Nola Printing Co. of New Orleans, a gambling wire service controlled by the Marcello interests, was serving bookmakers and relay centers throughout the State of Louisiana, as well as areas as diverse as Chicago, Houston, Miami, Hot Springs, Indianapolis and Detroit and cities in Alabama and Mississippi.

"In a statement prepared for the House Judiciary Committee in 1970, [Aaron M. Kohn, the managing director of the Metropolitan Crime Commission of New Orleans and a former FBI agent] outlined the continuing expansion of Marcello's holdings during the 1940s and 1950s: 'Marcello and his growing association developed their capital or bankroll through extensive gambling, including casinos, slot machines, pinball, handbooks, layoff, football pools, dice card games, roulette and bingo; also narcotics, prostitution, extortion, clip -joint operations, B-drinking, marketing stolen good, robberies, burglaries and thefts. Their criminal enterprise required, and had, corrupt collusion of public officials at every critical level including police, sheriffs, justices of the peace, prosecutors, mayors, governors, judges, councilmen, licensing authorities, State legislators, and at least one Member of Congress.'

'When Marcello appeared as a witness before the Kefauver Committee on January 25, 1951, he invoked the fifth amendment and refused to respond to questioning on his organized crime activities. Subsequently convicted of contempt of Congress for refusing to respond to the directions of the chair, Marcello was later successful in having his conviction overturned. In its final report, the Kefauver Committee concluded that Marcello's domination of organized crime in Louisiana had come about in large part due to the 'personal enrichment of sheriffs, marshals, and other law enforcement officials' who received payoffs for 'their failure to enforce gambling laws and other statutes relating to vice.' The Kefauver report further noted that, 'In every line of inquiry, the Committee found... the trail of Carlos Marcello.'"

"The Kefauver report also raised the question of why Marcello who 'has never become a citizen,' had not been deported. In early 1953, partly as a result of the national attention he received from the Kefauver Committee investigation, Marcello finally became the subject of deportation proceedings."

"Carlos Marcello was called to testify before the McClellan Committee on March 24, 1959, during the Committee's extended investigation of labor racketeering and organized crime. Serving as chief counsel to the Committee was Robert F. Kennedy; his brother, Senator John F. Kennedy, was a member of the Committee. In response to Committee questioning, Marcello again invoked the fifth amendment in refusing to answer any questions relating to his background, activities, and associates. At the conclusion of Marcello's appearance before the Committee, Senator Sam Ervin of North Carolina requested of the Chair permission to ask the New Orleans underworld leader one final question: 'I would like to know how you managed to stay in the United States for 5 years, 9 months and 24 days after you were found ordered deported as an undesirable person.' Marcello's response to the question – 'I wouldn't know' – provoked Ervin to state that 'The American people's patience ought to run out on this' and that 'those who have no claim to any right to remain in America, who come here and prey like leeches upon law-abiding people out to be removed from this country.' Senator Karl Mundt joined in Ervin's denunciation, urging prompt action by the Attorney General, and Senator Carl Curtis further remarked to Marcello that, 'I think you ought to pack up your bags and voluntarily depart.'"

"Carlos Marcello and his syndicate became a primary target of investigation by the Department of Justice during the Kennedy administration. Attorney General Robert F. Kennedy viewed him as one of the most powerful and threatening Mafia leaders in the Nation and ordered that the Justice Department focus on him, along with other figures such as Teamster President Hoffa and Chicago Mafia leader Sam Giancana.

"In Marcello's case, the intent of the Kennedy administration was made known even before Inauguration Day January 20, 1961. On December 29, 1960, the *New Orleans States-Item* reported that Attorney General designate Kennedy was planning specific actions against Marcello. An FBI report from that period noted: 'On January 12, 1961, a [source] advised that Carlos Marcello is extremely apprehensive and upset and has [been] since the *New Orleans States-Item* newspaper on December 28, 1960 published a news story reporting that... Robert F. Kennedy stated he would expedite the deportation proceedings pending against Marcello after Kennedy takes office in January 1961.'

"The Bureau's La Cosa Nostra file for 1961 noted that Marcello flew to Washington, DC shortly after the inauguration of President Kennedy and was in touch with a number of political and business associates. While there he placed a telephone call to the office of at least one Congressman. Bureau records further indicate that Marcello initiated various efforts to forestall or prevent the anticipated prompt deportation action. An FBI report noted that Marcello may have tried a circuitous approach. Through a source, the Bureau learned of another Mafia leader's account of how Marcello had reportedly proceeded. Philadelphia underworld leader, Angelo Bruno discussed a specified attempt by Marcello to forestall an action by the immigration authorities. According to the Philadelphia underworld leader Marcello had enlisted his close Mafia associate, Santos Trafficante of Florida, in the reported plan. Trafficante in turn contacted Frank Sinatra to have the singer use his friendship with the Kennedy family on Marcello's behalf. This effort met with failure and may even have resulted in intensified Federal efforts against Marcello."

"On March 3, 1961, General Joseph Swing of the Immigration and Naturalization Service advised the FBI that: 'The Attorney General had been emphasizing the importance of taking prompt action to deport notorious hoodlums. In this connection, the Marcello case is of particular interest. A final order of deportation has been entered against Marcello but this fact is being held in strictest confidence.' On the afternoon of April 4, 1961, 8 years after he was ordered deported, Carolos Marcello was finally ejected from the United States. As he walked into the INS office in New Orleans for his regular appointment to report as an alien, he was arrested and handcuffed by INS officials. He was then rushed to the New Orleans airport and flown to Guatemala. Marcello's attorneys denounced the deportation later that day, terming it 'cruel and uncivilized,' and noted that their client had not been allowed to telephone his attorney or see his wife." "On April 10, 1961, 6 days after he was deported, the Internal Revenue service filed a $835,396 tax lien against Marcello and his wife. On April 23, news reports disclosed that Marcello was being held in custody by Guatemalan authorities in connection with what were reported to be false citizenship papers he had presented on arrival there April 6. On May 4, Guatemalan President Miguel Fuentes ordered that Marcello be expelled; he was driven to and released at El Salvador border late that night. On May 19, 1961, a Federal court in Washington ruled that Marcello's deportation was fully valid and denied a motion by his attorneys that it be declared illegal. With that ruling, Marcello's re-entry to the country was prohibited.

"Less than 2 weeks later, Marcello secretly gained entry into the United States. On June 2, 1961, confirming widespread rumors that their client had somehow slipped back in, Marcello's attorney's announced he had returned and was in hiding. Federal investigators have never been able to establish in detail his means of entry. On June 5, 1961, after Attorney General Kennedy dispatched 20 Federal agents to Shreveport, Louisiana, to conduct a search for Marcello, the Louisiana crime leader voluntarily surrendered in New Orleans and was ordered held in an alien detention center at McAllen, Texas. On June 8, a Federal grand jury indicted him for illegal re-entry; on July 11, the INS ruled he was an undesirable alien and once again ordered him deported. On June 16, 1961, the FBI received a report that a US Senator from Louisiana might have sought to intervene on Marcello's behalf. This Senator had reportedly received 'financial aid from Marcello' in the past and was sponsoring a Louisiana official for a key INS position from which assistance might be rendered."

"On October 30, 1961, Attorney General Kennedy announced the indictment of Marcello by a Federal grand jury in New Orleans on charges of conspiracy in falsifying a Guatemalan birth certificate and committing perjury." "On December 20, 1961, with Marcello free on a $10,000 bond, the five-member Board of Immigration Appeals upheld the deportation order against Marcello, denying another appeal by Marcello attorneys that it be declared invalid. In October 1962, a Bureau of Narcotics report described Marcello as 'one of the Nations leading racketeers' and noted that he was 'currently under intense investigation by the Internal Revenue Service Intelligence Division for tax fraud.' The report also noted that Marcello was then instituting a further legal step to forestall deportation. Marcello's attorneys had filed a legal writ in an effort to set aside his Federal conviction on narcotics charges from 24 years earlier. This conviction was one of the key factors in the ongoing deportation proceedings against him. On October 31, 1962, a Federal court ruled against Marcello's attempt to have the 1938 drug conviction nullified. The court said that his claim that he had no counsel present when he pled guilty to the narcotics charge on October 29, 1938, was false, as was his claim that he had not known of his rights and could not afford an attorney.

"On February 15, 1963, in apparent response to Attorney General Kennedy's request for continuing action against Marcello, FBI Director J. Edgar Hoover directed the New Orleans FBI office to intensify its coverage of Marcello and his organization. He ordered that a 'special effort' be made to upgrade the level of the investigation of Marcello, and suggested increased use of informants as well as the possible initiation of electronic surveillance . . . Two unsuccessful attempts were made to effect such surveillance, failures attributable in all likelihood to the security system employed by Marcello at the various locations from which he operated."

"On November 4, 1963, Marcello went on trial in New Orleans on Federal charges of conspiracy in connection with his alleged falsification of a Guatemalan birth certificate. Eighteen days later, on November 22, 1963, he was acquitted. The news of President Kennedy's murder in Dallas reached the courtroom shortly before the verdict was announced."

The above review makes clear that by 1963, top Mafia leaders and their labor cronies had been the subjects of an unprecedented, unremitting, relentless campaign against them; a campaign which could not be terminated by merely getting rid of Robert Kennedy, who could be replaced with a like-minded person by President Kennedy, whose program this was.

The House Report informs us that the Kefauver Committee had stated among its conclusions: "The domination of the Mafia is based fundamentally on 'muscle' and 'murder.' The Mafia is a secret conspiracy against law and order which will ruthlessly eliminate anyone who stands in the way of its success in any criminal enterprise in which it is interested. It will destroy anyone who betrays its secrets. It will use any means available – political influence, bribery, intimidation, et cetera, to defeat any attempt on the part of law enforcement to touch its top figures."

Information of perhaps more than passing interest to our story is provided by the House Select Committee in the discussion of the 1930 crime which resulted in Marcellos's first conviction – a grocery story robbery – which had been personally planned by the then 20-year old Carlos Marcello, using an interesting method of operation:

"Aaron M. Kohn, the managing director of the Metropolitan Crime Commission of New Orleans and a former FBI agent testified:

"Marcello had shielded his own complicity in the crime by inducing two juveniles to carry out the robbery... Marcello and a confederate had supplied the juveniles with a gun and instructions on their 'getaway.'

"The plan had gone awry when the two were later apprehended and pressured by authorities to identify the 'higher-ups.'"

"Kohn also noted that Marcello 'was referred to as a Fagin' in press accounts at the time, in an apparent reference to the Dickens character who recruited juveniles to carry out his crimes."

Organized crime had become somewhat more sophisticated by mid-century, as the House Committee noted in its final report:

"The committee studied the Kennedy assassination in terms of the traditional forms of violence used by organized crime and the historic pattern of underworld slayings. While the murder of the President's accused assassin did in fact fit the traditional pattern - a shadowy man with demonstrable organized crime connections shoots down a crucial witness - the method of the President's assassination did not resemble the standard syndicate killing. A person like Oswald - young, active in controversial political causes, apparently not subject to the internal discipline of a criminal organization - would appear to be the least likely candidate for the role of Mafia hit man, especially in such an important murder. Gunmen used in organized crime killings have traditionally been selected with utmost deliberation and care, the most important considerations being loyalty and a willingness to remain silent if apprehended. These are qualities best guaranteed by past participation in criminal activities. There are, however, other factors to be weighed in evaluating the method of possible operation in the assassination of President Kennedy.

"While the involvement of a gunman like Oswald does not readily suggest organized crime involvement, any underworld attempt to assassinate the President would in all likelihood have dictated the use of some kind of cover, a shielding or disguise.

"The committee made the reasonable assumption that an assassination of a President by organized crime could not be allowed to appear to be what it was.

"Traditional organized crime murders are generally committed through the use of killers who make no effort to hide the fact that organized crime was responsible for such murders or 'hits.' While syndicate-authorized hits are usually executed in such a way that identification of the killers is not at all likely, the slayings are nonetheless committed in what is commonly referred to as the 'gangland style.' Indeed, an intrinsic characteristic of the typical mob execution is that it serves as a self-apparent message, with the authorities and the public readily perceiving the nature of the crime as well as the general identity of the group or gang that carried it out.

"The execution of a political leader-most particularly a President would hardly be a typical mob execution and might well necessitate a different method of operation.

"The overriding consideration in such an extraordinary crime would be the avoidance of any appearance of organized crime complicity."

"In its investigation, the Committee noted three cases, for the purposes of illustration, in which the methodology employed by syndicate figures was designed to insulate and disguise the involvement of organized crime. These did not fit the typical pattern of mob killing, as the assassination of a President would not. While the atypical cases did not involve political leaders, two of the three were attacks on figures in the public eye.

"In the first case, the acid blinding of investigative reporter Victor Riesel in April 1956, organized crime figures in New York used a complex series of go-betweens to hire a petty thief and burglar to commit the act. Thus, the assailant did not know who had actually authorized the crime for which he had been recruited. The use of such an individual was regarded as unprecedented, as he had not been associated with the syndicate, was a known drug user, and outwardly appeared to be unreliable. Weeks later, Riesel's assailant was slain by individuals who had recruited him in the plot."

"The second case, the fatal shooting of a well-known businessman, Sol Landie, Kansas City, Missouri, on November 22 1970, involved the recruitment, through several intermediaries, of four young Black men by members of the local La Cosa Nostra family. Landie had served as a witness in a Federal investigation of gambling activities directed by Kansas City organized crime leader Nichols Civella. The men recruited for the murder did not know who had ultimately ordered the killing, were not part of the Kansas City syndicate, and had received instructions through intermediaries to make it appear that robbery was the motive for the murder. All of the assailants and two of the intermediaries were ultimately convicted.

"The third case, the shooting of New York underworld leader Joseph Colombo before a crowd of 65,000 people in June 1971, was carried out by a young Black man with a petty criminal record, a nondescript loner who appeared to be alien to the organized crime group that had recruited him through various go-betweens. The gunman was shot to death immediately after the shooting of Colombo, a murder still designated unsolved."

"The Committee found that these three cases, each of which is an exception to the general rule of organized crime executions, had identifiable similarities.

- Each case was solved, in that the identity of the perpetrator of the immediate act became known.

- In two of the cases, the assailant was himself murdered soon after the crime.

- In each case, the person who wanted the crime accomplished recruited the person or person who made the attack through more than one intermediary.

- In each case, the person suspected of inspiring the violence was a member of, or connected to, La Cosa Nostra.

- In each case, the person or persons hired were not professional killers, and they were not part of organized criminal groups.

- In each case, the persons recruited to carry out the acts could be characterized as dupes or tools who were being used in a conspiracy they were not fully aware of.

- In each case, the intent was to insulate the organized crime connection, with a particular requirement for disguising the true identity of the conspirators, and to place the blame on generally nondescript individuals."

Does the above suggest that people such as Marcello had learned by their earlier mistakes that it is not sufficient to be a "Fagin" since they are still at risk for being implicated unless their dupe is then wiped out, eliminating the trail back to them?

CHAPTER 22

JACK RUBY, MOBSTER

* * *

"The committee also examined allegations that, even before the 1947 move to Dallas, Ruby had been personally acquainted with two professional killers for the organized crime syndicate in Chicago, David Yaras and Lenny Patrick

"Yaras and Patrick were, in fact, notorious gunmen, having been identified by law enforcement authorities as executioners for the Chicago mob and closely associated with Sam Giancana, the organized crime leader in Chicago"

House Select Committee

The House Committee Report relates that, "The committee, as did the Warren Commission, recognized that a primary reason to suspect organized crime of possible involvement in the assassination was Ruby's killing of Oswald. For this reason, the committee undertook an extensive investigation of Ruby and his relatives, friends and associates to determine if there was evidence that Ruby was involved in crime, organized or otherwise, such as gambling and vice, and if such involvement might have been related to the murder of Oswald. The evidence available to the committee indicated that Ruby was not a 'member' of organized crime in Dallas or elsewhere, although it showed that he had a significant number of associations and direct and indirect contacts with underworld figures, a number of whom were connected to the most powerful La Cosa Nostra leaders. Additionally, Ruby had numerous associations with the Dallas criminal element."

"In the years since the assassination, there had been allegations that Ruby was involved in organized crime's 1947 attempt to move into Dallas, perhaps as a front-man for the Chicago racketeer. While Ruby apparently did not participate in the organized crime move to Dallas in 1947, he did establish himself as a Dallas nightclub operator around that time. His first club was the Silver Spur, which featured country and western entertainment. Then he operated the Sovereign, a private club that failed and was converted into the Carousel Club, a burlesque house with striptease acts. Ruby, an extroverted individual, acquired numerous friends and contacts in and around Dallas, some of whom had syndicate ties."

"The committee also examined allegations that, even before the 1947 move to Dallas, Ruby had been personally acquainted with two professional killers for the organized crime syndicate in Chicago, David Yaras and Lenny Patrick. The committee established that Ruby, Yaras and Patrick were in fact acquainted during Ruby's years in Chicago, particularly in the 1930s and 1940s. Both Yaras and Patrick admitted, when questioned by the FBI in 1964, that they did know Ruby, but both said that they had not had any contact with him for 10 to 15 years."

"On the other hand, the committee established that Yaras and Patrick were, in fact, notorious gunmen, having been identified by law enforcement authorities as executioners for the Chicago mob and closely associated with Sam Giancana, the organized crime leader in Chicago who was murdered in 1975. Yaras and Patrick are believed to have been responsible for numerous syndicate executions. including the murder of James Ragan, a gambling wire service owner. The evidence implicating Yaras and Patrick in syndicate activities is unusually reliable. Yaras, for example, was overheard in a 1962 electronic surveillance discussing various underworld murder contracts he had carried out and one he had only recently been assigned. While the committee found no evidence that Ruby was associated with Yaras or Patrick during the 1950s or 1960s, it concluded that Ruby had probably talked by telephone to Patrick during the summer of 1963."

"Included among Ruby's closest friends was Lewis McWillie."
"An appendix to the Warren Report included the following:` Ruby apparently met McWillie in about 1950 when McWillie operated`a Dallas nightclub. McWillie, whom Ruby said he idolized, supervised

234

gambling activities at Havana's Tropicana Hotel in 1959 and later was employed in a managerial capacity in a Las Vegas gambling establishment." "McWillie moved from Dallas to Cuba in 1958 and worked in gambling casinos in Havana until 1960. In 1978, McWillie was employed in Las Vegas, and law enforcement files indicate he had business and personal ties to major organized crime figures, including Meyer Lansky and Santos Trafficante." "McWillie admitted being acquainted with several organized crime and gambling figures, including R. D. Matthews, a Dallas and Las Vegas gambler; Joseph Civello, a Dallas organized crime leader (now deceased); and Sam Yaras, the brother of organized crime figure, Dave Yaras." "Ruby traveled to Cuba on at least one occasion to visit McWillie. McWillie testified to the committee that Ruby visited him only once in Cuba, and that it was a social visit. The Warren Commission concluded this was the only trip Ruby took to Cuba, despite documentation in the Commission's own files indicating Ruby made a second trip."

"Both Ruby and McWillie claimed that Ruby's visit to Cuba was at McWillie's invitation and lasted about a week in the late summer or early fall of 1959. The committee, however, obtained tourist cards from the Cuban Government that show Ruby entered Cuba on August 8, 1959, left on September 11, reentered on September 12 and left again on September 13, 1959. These documents supplement records the committee obtained from the Immigration and Naturalization Service (INS) indicating that Ruby left Cuba on September 11, 1959, traveling to Miami, returned to Cuba on September 12, and traveled on to New Orleans on September 13, 1959. The Cuban Government could not state with certainty that the commercial airline flights indicated by the INS records were the only ones Ruby took during the period."

"Other records obtained by the committee indicate that Ruby was in Dallas at times during the August 8 to September 11, 1959, period. He apparently visited his safe deposit box on August 21, met with FBI Agent Charles W. Flynn on August 31, and returned to the safe deposit box on September 4. Consequently, if the tourist card documentation, INS, FBI, and bank records are all correct, Ruby had to have made at least three trips to Cuba. While the records appeared to be accurate, they were incomplete. The committee was unable to determine, for example, whether on the third trip, if it occurred, Ruby traveled by commercial airline or some other means. Consequently, the committee could not rule out the possibility that Ruby made more trips during this period or at other times. Based on the unusual nature of the 1-day trip to Miami from Havana on September 11-12 and the possibility of at least one additional trip to Cuba, the committee concluded that vacationing was probably not the purpose for traveling to Havana, despite Ruby's insistence to the Warren Commission that his one trip to Cuba in 1959 was a social visit.

"The committee reached the judgment that Ruby most likely was serving as a courier for gambling interests when he traveled to Miami from Havana for 1 day, then returned to Cuba for a day, before flying to New Orleans. This judgment is supported by the following:

- McWillie had made previous trips to Miami on behalf of the owners of the Tropicana, the casino for which he worked, to deposit funds;

- McWillie placed a call to Meyer Panitz, a gambling associate in Miami, to inform him that Ruby was coming from Cuba, resulting in two meetings between Panitz and Ruby; There was a continuing need for Havana casino operators to send their assets out of Cuba to protect them from seizure by the Castro government; and,

- The 1-day trip from Havana to Miami was not explained by   Ruby, and his testimony to the Warren Commission about his   travels to Cuba was contradictory.

"The committee also deemed it likely that Ruby at least met various organized crime figures in Cuba, possibly including some who had been detained by the Cuban government."

BOOK FOUR

* * *

THE WEB TIGHTENS

CHAPTER 23
CURIOUS ACTIVITIES

* * *

*The evidence demonstrates that there were at least three other
people involved with Oswald in the Walker shooting So, the
same man who -with a number of conspirators - couldn't hit a
stationary target silhouetted in a window across the yard from
him with his rifle propped up on a fence, then went out with
no conspirators and managed from a high angle to hit a target
at least twice as it was moving away from him.*

For someone who, out of disillusionment with Soviet life, had
picked up his family and left Russia, Lee Harvey Oswald thereafter
continued to manifest some remarkable interests.

The Warren Commission reported: "He wrote to the Soviet
Embassy in Washington for information on how to subscribe to
Russian periodicals and for 'any periodicals or bulletins which you
may put out for the benefit of your citizens living for a time in the
U.S.A.'. He subsequently subscribed to several Russian journals. In
December 1962 the Soviet Embassy received a card in Russian signed
'Marina and Lee Oswald,' which conveyed New Year's greetings
and wishes for 'health success and all of the best to the employees at
the Embassy.'"

"Soon after his return to this country Oswald had started to
correspond with the Communist Party U.S.A. and the Socialist
Workers Party He subscribed to the Worker in August 1962. He
wrote for additional literature from these organizations and
attempted to join the Socialist Workers Party which however had no
branch in Texas."

"Oswald also wrote the Socialist Workers Party offering his
assistance in preparing posters From this organization too he
received the response that he might be called upon if needed He was

asked for further information about his photographic skills which he does not appear to have ever provided. Oswald did obtain literature from the Socialist Workers Party however and in December 1962 he entered a subscription to the affiliated publication the Militant."

"He sought advice from the central committee of the Communist Party U.S.A. in a letter dated August 28 1963 about whether he could 'continue to fight handicapped as it were by my past record * * * [and] compete with anti-progressive forces above ground or whether in your opinion I should always remain in the back ground i.e. underground.' Stating that he had used his 'position' with what he claimed to be the local branch of the Fair Play for Cuba Committee to 'foster communist ideals,' Oswald wrote that he felt that he might have compromised the FPCC and expressed concern lest 'Our opponents could use my background of residence in the U.S.S.R against any cause which I join by association they could say the organization of which I am a member is Russian controlled etc.' In reply Arnold Johnson advised Oswald that while as an American citizen he had a right to participate in such organizations as he wished 'there are a number of organizations including possibly Fair Play which are of a very broad character and often it is advisable for some people to remain in the background not underground.'"

The Warren Commission cited the above material to support the picture of Oswald as an avowed and active communist even upon his return to the United States. Perhaps so.

But, might the above sound like "all talk and no action?" Might it allow consideration of the possibility that Oswald was "papering the file?" "Building credentials?" In other words, as discussed regarding Nosenko, was Oswald building a "Legend," supplying people with a fabricated identity?

The following appears in a section the Warren Commission entitled: PRIOR ATTEMPT TO KILL, The Attempt on the Life of Maj. Gen Edwin A. Walker:

"At approximately 9 p.m. on April 10 1963 in Dallas Tex. Maj. Gen. Edwin A. Walker, an active and controversial figure on the American political scene since his resignation from the U.S Army in 1961 narrowly escaped death when a rifle bullet fired from outside his home passed near his head as he was seated at his desk. There were no eyewitnesses although a 14-year-old boy in a neighboring house claimed that immediately after the shooting he saw two men in separate cars drive out of a church parking lot adjacent to Walker's home. A friend of Walker's testified that two nights before the shooting he saw 'two men around the house peeking in windows.' General Walker gave this information to the police before the shooting but it did not help solve the crime Although the bullet was recovered from Walker's house, in the absence of a weapon it was of little investigatory value. General Walker hired two investigators to determine whether a former employee might have been involved in the shooting. Their results were negative. Until December 3 1963 the Walker shooting remained unsolved."

"In her testimony before the Commission in February 1964, Marina Oswald stated that when Oswald returned home on the night of the Walker shooting, he told her that he had been planning the attempt for 2 months. He showed her a notebook 3 days later containing photographs of General Walker's home and a map of the area where the house was located. Although Oswald destroyed the notebook, three photographs found among Oswald's possessions after the assassination were identified by Marina Oswald as photographs of General Walker's house. Two of these photographs were taken from the rear of Walker's house. The Commission confirmed, by comparison with other photographs, that these were, indeed, photographs of the rear of Walker's house. An examination of the window at the rear of the house, the wall through which the bullet passed, and the fence behind the house indicated that the bullet was fired from a position near the point where one of the photographs was taken. The third photograph identified by Marina Oswald depicts the entrance to General Walker's driveway from a back alley. Also seen in the picture is the fence on which Walker's assailant apparently rested the rifle."

The Warren Commission set forth the following details regarding a letter determined to have been written by Lee Harvey Oswald, including the Commission's conclusion that, "It is clear that the note was written while the Oswalds were living in Dallas before they moved to New Orleans in the spring of 1963." The Warren Commission ascertained that the letter was written in Russian by Oswald on the evening of the shooting of General Walker, and set forth the content of the letter as follows:

"In translation, the note read as follows:

1. This is the key to the mailbox which is located in the main post office in the city on Ervay Street. This is the same street where the drugstore, in which you always waited is located. You will find the mailbox in the post office which is located 4 blocks from the drugstore on that street. I paid for the box last month so don't worry about it.

2. Send the information as to what has happened to me to the Embassy and include newspaper clippings (should there be anything about me in the newspapers). I believe that the Embassy will come quickly to your assistance on learning everything.

3. I paid the house rent on the 2d so don't worry about it.

4. Recently I also paid for water and gas.

5. The money from work will possibly be coming. The money will be sent to our post office box. Go to the bank and cash the check.

6. You can either throw out or give my clothing, etc. away. Do not keep these. However, I prefer that you hold on to my personal papers (military, civil, etc.).

7. Certain of my documents are in the small blue valise.

8. The address book can be found on my table in the study should need same.

9. We have friends here. The Red Cross also will help you [Red Cross in English].

10. I left you as much money as I could, $60 on the second of the month. You and the baby [apparently] can live for another 2 months using $10 per week.

11. If I am alive and taken prisoner, the city jail is located at the end of the bridge through which we always passed on going to the city (right in the beginning of the city after crossing the bridge)."

The Warren Commission concluded that:

"On April 10 1963 Oswald shot at Maj. Gen Edwin A. Walker (Resigned U.S Army) demonstrating once again his propensity to act dramatically and in this instance violently in furtherance of his beliefs. The shooting occurred 2 weeks before Oswald moved to New Orleans and a few days after he had been discharged by the photographic firm."

"As indicated in chapter IV Oswald had been planning his attack on General Walker for at least 1 and perhaps as much as 2 months. He outlined his plans in a notebook and studied them at considerable length before his attack."

The House Committee provides the following further detail: "Police located a 14-year-old boy in Walker's neighborhood who said that after hearing the shot, he climbed a fence and looked into an alley to the rear of Walker's home. The boy said he then saw some men speeding down the alley in a light green or light blue Ford, either a 1959 or 1960 model. He said he also saw another car, a 1958 Chevrolet, black with white down the side, in a church parking lot adjacent to Walker's house. The car door was open, and a man was bending over the back seat, as though he was placing something on the floor of the car.

"On the night of the incident, police interviewed Robert Surrey, an aide to Walker. Surrey said that on Saturday, April 6, at about 9 p.m., he had seen two men sitting in a dark purple or brown 1963 Ford at the rear of Walker's house. Surrey also said the two men

243

got out of the car and walked around the house. Surrey said he was suspicious and followed the car, noting that it carried no license plate."

Thus, the official reports look at the Walker event as a very simple, straightforward proposition: Oswald shot at Walker, thereby demonstrating his propensity for violence, such as assassinating President Kennedy.

Upon analysis, however, the relationship between the Walker incident and the murder of JFK is not quite so simple nor quite so straightforward.

For example, we have seen repeated examples of Oswald creating evidences of his bona fides as a left-wing activist. Can you think of better credentials for a left-wing activist than having attempted to kill that right wing hero, General Walker?

- And, to prove it was me, look at the map I drew and these photos I took while planning it. And look at this letter I wrote to my wife, when I knew that I might be jailed or killed as I undertook this valiant effort on behalf of our side.

If we are to assume that the Walker incident was a true assassination attempt by Oswald, we must be willing to believe the following:

On 11/22/63, Oswald:

- at least twice hit a moving target

- a few hundred yards away

- moving away from him

- at a steep downward angle

- from a 6th floor window

On 4/11/63, Oswald:

- could not hit a stationary target

- on a level shooting field

- sitting at a desk

- only a short backyard away

- with his rifle propped up on a fence.

How is one supposed to reconcile the conclusion that Oswald was acting alone in killing Kennedy with the fact that every bit of the credible evidence makes it absolutely clear that Lee Harvey Oswald was not acting alone in this Walker incident? The evidence demonstrates that there were at least three others involved with Oswald in this Walker conspiracy: there were "some" in the car in the alley and at least two in the car in the church parking lot where a man was putting something on the back floor (it is uncontroverted that Oswald did not drive).

So, the same man who -with a number of co-conspirators-couldn't hit a stationary target silhouetted in a window across the yard from him with his rifle propped up on a fence, then went out with no conspirators & managed from a dramatically high angle to hit a target at least twice (one a head shot) as it was moving away from him?

Let us compare the Walker and Kennedy events:

Does the official reconstruction of the events surrounding the Walker case tell us anything about the character, the personality of the presumed gunman in the Walker shooting?

Does the official reconstruction of the events surrounding the Kennedy case tell us anything about the character, the personality of the presumed gunman in the Kennedy shooting?

Make believe for a moment that you had never heard the official conclusions that Oswald did both. Given the character traits displayed in the first event as compared to the character traits displayed in the second event, would you think it was the same man involved in each?

Assuming for these purposes that the Walker event was not a sham, let us examine for a moment the character and personality of Oswald as described in the Walker case and contrast it with the character and personality of Oswald as described in the Kennedy case.

In the Walker case, Oswald is reported by the Warren Commission to have done the following acts:

1- he plans the shooting over a two month period;

2- he creates a notebook for the event;

3- he draws a map of the site;

4- he takes photos of the site;

5- he writes a very detailed letter to his wife including how she and the baby are provided for;

6- he has a number of co-conspirators in the activity.

In the Kennedy case, Oswald is reported to have done the following:

1- although he now has a second child, he does nothing to provide for his wife or children;

2- he acted on his own;

3- he acted without plans, maps, photos;

4- the earliest he can be demonstrated to have planned the act would the day before, Thursday morning November 21, when he asked his co-employee, Frazier for a ride to Irving that night. (How could he be sure Frazier could give him a lift that night? How could he be sure Frazier wasn't taking the day off on Friday?)

Does scenario #1 sound like the same "M.O" as scenario #2? If scenario #1 and scenario #2 involved the same man, is there reason to question whether scenario #1 might have been part of creating a "Legend?"

The Warren Commission provides the following information: "During the period Oswald was in New Orleans, from the end of April to late September 1963, he was engaged in activity purportedly on behalf of the now defunct Fair Play for Cuba Committee (FPCC), an organization centered in New York which was highly critical of US policy toward the Cuban Government under Fidel Castro. In May 1963, after having obtained literature from the FPCC, Oswald applied for and was granted membership in the organization.

"When applying for membership, Oswald wrote to National headquarters that he had 'been thinking about renting a small office at my own expense for the purpose of forming a FPCC branch here in New Orleans. Could you give me a charter?'"

We should note that this offer to rent an office at his own expense was being made by a man who at the most – accepting the generous financial reconstruction of the Warren Committee – ended up the month of May with a grand total of $129.58 to his name.

The FPCC responded to the effect that even if Oswald were able to organize the few members FPCC had in the New Orleans area, he would still need an equal number of new members just to be able to conduct a legal executive board for the chapter. They also strongly recommended against opening an office for a number of reasons, not the least of which was that having an identifiable location made it too easy for the 'lunatic fringe' on the other side to make trouble. Their suggestion was to use a Post Office box instead of an address.

On June 3, 1962, Oswald opened box No. 30061 at the Lafayette Square Substation in New Orleans. However, it seems clear that this was not in response to the suggestion of FPCC. For one thing, he had already been using a PO box, having maintained one at the General Post Office while in Dallas. Moreover, on this box he now opened in New Orleans, he did not list FPCC as one of the additional names entitled to receive mail at that box; he listed only Marina Oswald and A. J. Hidell (one of Oswald's aliases).

Oswald thereafter informed national headquarters that against their advice he had decided "to take an office from the very beginning," and that he was going to have membership cards printed, which he did. He wrote three further letters to the New York office, in one of which he discussed his activity in passing our circulars on the street.

On at least three occasions, Oswald did, in fact, distribute commercially printed literature consisting of handbills demanding "Hands of Cuba" in large letters and application forms for his FPCC chapter. Once while doing so, he was arrested and fined for being involved in a disturbance with a man named Carlos Bringuier and other anti-Castro Cuban refugees (These events are more fully explored in chapters 24 & 25). His activities received some attention in the New Orleans and he twice appeared on a local radio program representing himself as a spokesman for the Fair Play for Cuba Committee.

Despite these activities, the FPCC chapter which Oswald purportedly formed in New Orleans was entirely fictitious. So, again the question, fact or Legend?

Nor is there any evidence that Oswald ever opened an office as he claimed to have done. Although literature he was passing out contained the rubber stamp imprint "FPCC, 544 Camp St., New Orleans, La.," investigation has established that neither the Fair Play for Cuba Committee nor Lee Harvey Oswald ever maintained an office at that address.

This address puzzle is particularly mystifying, since Oswald was passing out literature presumably designed to win over converts to his pro-Castro group. Should he win people over, presumably he would like them to contact him. Why, then, would he list on the literature an address with which he had no connection – an address where he could not be contacted – when he had a post office box he could have listed where they could have contacted him (just as headquarters had suggested). The way he did it, how would someone reading the literature bearing the 544 Camp Street address have contacted Oswald in order to join him? Fact or Legend?

The Warren Commission presented a picture of Oswald as absolutely, positively pro-Castro – no ifs, no ands, no buts. Reading the work of the Commission, one would be justified in believing that there was absolutely no doubt on this issue. Perhaps so.

However, doesn't the available evidence cry out for full exploration of at least the following two alternative possibilities on this issue:?

1 -was Oswald <u>pretending</u> to be pro-Castro?

2 -was Oswald a tool for anti-Castro activists regardless of what his personal beliefs were?

The Senate Report on JFK Act, July 22, 1992, reported at p.90 in the Final Report of the Asassination Records Review Board (1998):

"The Committee has found … the FBI investigation, as well as the CIA inquiry [into the Kennedy assassination], was deficient on the specific question of the significance of Oswald's contacts with pro-Castro and anti-Castro groups for many months before the assassination.

The Senate Select Committee, stated the following in their section entitled, "THE INGREDIENTS OF AN ANTI-CASTRO CUBAN CONSPIRACY:"

"Was the John F. Kennedy assassination a conspiracy involving anti-Castro Cuban exiles? The committee found that it was not easy to answer that question years after the event, for two reasons. First, the Warren Commission decided not to investigate further the issue despite the urging of staff counsel involved with that evidence and the apparent fact that the anti-Castro Cuban exiles had the means, motivation, and opportunity to be involved in the assassination. In addition the area of possible Cuban exile involvement was one in which the Warren Commission was not provided with an adequate investigative background. Despite knowledge of Oswald's apparent interest in pro-Castro and anti-Castro activities and top level awareness of certain CIA assassination plots, the FBI ... made no special investigative effort into questions of possible Cuban Government or Cuban exile involvement in the assassination independent of the Oswald investigation. There is no indication that the FBI or the CIA directed the interviewing of Cuban sources or of sources within the Cuban exile community.

"Nevertheless, even from the paucity of evidence that was available to them in 1964, two staff attorneys for the Warren Commission speculated that Lee Harvey Oswald, despite his public posture as a Castro sympathizer, was actually an agent of anti-Castro exiles.

"Pressing for further investigation of that possibility, Assistant Counsel William Coleman and W .David Slawson wrote a memorandum to the Commission stating: "The evidence here could lead to an anti-Castro involvement in the assassination on some sort of basis as this: Oswald could have become known to the Cubans as being strongly pro-Castro. He made no secret of his sympathies, and so the anti-Castro Cubans must have realized that law enforcement. authorities were also aware of Oswald's feelings and that, therefore, if he got into trouble, the public would also learn of them ...Second, someone in the anti-Castro organization might have been keen enough to sense that Oswald had a penchant for violence ... On these facts, it is possible that some sort of deception was used to encourage Oswald to kill the President when he came to Dallas . . . The motive of this would, of course, be the expectation that after the President was killed Oswald would be caught or at least his identity ascertained, the law enforcement authorities and the public would then blame the assassination on the Castro government and a call for its forceful overthrow would be irresistible...."

"It is important in considering the possibility of anti-Castro Cuban involvement in the Kennedy assassination to recall the political and emotional conditions that affected the Cuban exile communities in Miami, New Orleans, and Dallas while Kennedy was President."

Had the Warren Commission more fully investigated the situation, and fully pursued & explored the evidence without preconceived conclusions, they would have had before them the material discussed in the following chapters.

CHAPTER 24
THE FBI & OSWALD

* * *

"There are basically three kinds of 'notional' or fictitious organizations. All three were used in COINTELPRO attempts to factionalize."

Senate Select Committee

"The third type of "notional" was the wholly fictitious organization, with no actual members, which was used as a pseudonym for mailing letters or pamphlets."

Senate Select Committee

"The Fair Play for Cuba Committee is the principal outlet for pro-Castro propaganda and agitation on the part of US nationals sympathetic to the Castro regime."

J. Edgar Hoover

Oswald made a great show of writing to the Soviet Embassy to advise them that the FBI was trying to inhibit his activities on behalf of the Fair Play for Cuba Committee.

Reference was made in chapter 23 to events involving Carlos Bringuier. The Warren Commission had reasoned that Oswald had met Bringuier "by presenting himself as hostile to Premier Castro in an apparent attempt to gain information about anti-Castro organizations operating in New Orleans." Perhaps so.

However, infiltration is not a one-way street. Consider, for example, the FBI's counter-intelligence program against the Communist Party (COINTELPRO).

The Senate Select Committee in a section entitled COINTELPRO: THE FBI'S COVERT ACTION PROGRAMS AGAINST AMERICAN CITIZENS informs us that COINTELPRO was begun in 1956, then expanded by a March 1960 directive to make a greater effort to prevent Communist infiltration (COMINT). This program against the Communist Party, USA (CPUSA COINTELPRO) was supplemented by SWP COINTELPRO, initiated on October 12, 1961 and directed against the Socialist Workers Party, which was targeted because of its '"open" espousal of its lines "through running candidates for public office" and its direction and/or support of "such causes as Castro's Cuba and integration problems arising in the South." White Hate groups including the Ku Klux Klan also merited their own COINTELPROs.

Among the favorite COINTELPRO methods was the use of fictitious organizations. The Senate Select Committee described this routine as follows.

"There are basically three kinds of 'notional' or fictitious organizations. All three were used in COINTELPRO attempts to factionalize.

"The first kind of 'notional' was the organization whose members were all Bureau informants. Because of the Committee's agreement with the Bureau not to reveal the identity of informants, the only example which can be discussed publicly is a proposal which, although approved, was never implemented. That proposal involved setting up a chapter of the WEB DuBois Club in a Southern city which would be composed entirely of Bureau informants and fictitious persons. The initial purpose of the chapter was to cause the CPUSA expense by sending organizers into the area, cause the Party to fund Bureau coverage of out-of-town CP meetings by paying the informants' expenses, and receiving literature and instructions. Later, the chapter was to begin to engage in deviation from the Party line so that it would be expelled from the main organization 'and then they could claim to be the victim of a Stalinist-type purge.' It was anticipated that the entire operation would take no more than 18 months.

"The second type of 'notional' was the fictitious organization with some unsuspecting (non-informant) members. For example,

Bureau informants set up a Klan organization intended to attract membership away from the United Klans of America. The Bureau paid the informant's personal expenses in setting up the new organization, which had, at its height, 250 members.

"The third type of 'notional' was the wholly fictitious organization, with no actual members, which was used as a pseudonym for mailing letters or pamphlets. For instance, the Bureau sent out newsletters from something called 'The Committee for Expansion of Socialist Thought in America' which attacked the CPUSA from the 'Marxist right' for at least two years."

To the discussion of this last type of "notional," we can add that obviously the setting up of such a fictitious organization can manufacture some very nice credentials for someone looking to pass himself off as something he is not.

Passing out pro-Castro literature on the street, getting into an altercation with anti-Castro Cubans, getting arrested for same, and supporting Castro in a debate on radio will all do wonders for showcasing someone as pro-Castro.

An FBI intelligence program aimed at Castro sympathizers had originally begun in 1960. After the Bay of Pigs invasion in 1961, the FBI intensified its coverage of pro-Castro Cuban activities. Particular attention came to be paid to the Fair Play for Cuba Committee.

As the Senate Select Committee related, "FBI field offices were advised [on April 27, 1961] that 'increasing anti-United States attitudes and demonstrations stemming from the Cuban situation and "cold war" tensions are a cause for concern' and that pro-Castro groups might 'react militantly to an emergency situation.' In particular, the activities of the Fair Play for Cuba Committee revealed 'the capacity of a nationality group organization to mobilize its efforts in such a situation so as to arrange demonstrations and influence public opinion.' Hence, all field offices were to 'be most alert to the possibility of demonstrations by nationality groups which could lead to incidents involving violence.'"

On July 25, 1961, "Director Hoover submitted a report to President Kennedy's Special Assistant for National Security, McGeorge Bundy, on the status of the internal security programs of the Interdepartmental Intelligence Conference." The report (in part) stated, "The Fair Play for Cuba Committee is the principal outlet for pro-Castro propaganda and agitation on the part of US nationals sympathetic to the Castro regime. There are indications that this organization is receiving funds from the Cuban Government. In addition, investigation has shown that this group has been heavily infiltrated by the Communist Party, USA (CPUSA), and the Socialist Workers Party (SWP) . . . In fact, some chapters of the group have been directly organized by and under the complete control of the CPUSA or the SWP."

The FBI has consistently denied that Oswald was an undercover agent, which may well be the case. However, there are certain things which would seem to have to be disregarded before wholeheartedly accepting such assurances.

Oswald's actions in 1959 (defection to the Soviet Union in 1959; informing the American Embassy in Moscow that he was going to renounce his American citizenship and apply for Soviet citizenship; and his statement that he intended to reveal radar secrets to the Soviet Union) required, per FBI procedures, that a "security case" be opened with Oswald as the subject. That was indeed done, and the security case was, as it should have been, still open when Oswald re-defected in 1962.

The Bureau indicates that it wasn't until almost three weeks after his return from Russia that they first interviewed Oswald. This was done by Special Agents John W. Fain and B. Tom Carter at the Fort Worth FBI office on June 26, 1962, at which time they say that Oswald denied he had told State Department officials at the American Embassy in Moscow that he was going to renounce his

American citizenship, apply for Soviet citizenship, and reveal radar secrets to the Soviets.

Moreover, Fain told the House Select Committee, when he asked Oswald to take a polygraph test, Oswald refused to even be polygraphed on whether he had dealings with Soviet intelligence. Fain did not report Oswald's refusal to be polygraphed when he testified before the Warren Commission on May 6, 1964, "despite," as the Senate Committee observed, "detailed questioning by Commission members Ford and Dulles as to the discrepancies in Oswald's statements and Fain's reaction to them."

A second interview on August 16, 1962 (this time by Fain and Special Agent Arnold J. Brown, in the back seat of Fain's automobile) yielded similar denials.

These agents all described Oswald as giving incomplete answers and demonstrating a bad attitude towards the Bureau: he was said to be cold, arrogant, uncooperative and evasive. Despite Oswald's reported attitude and demonstrable lies, the Bureau closed the Oswald security case on August 26, 1962.

The Senate Committee commented that, "Although wide-ranging interviews were a basic investigative technique commonly used by the Bureau to develop background information on subjects of security investigations, no neighborhood or employment sources were checked in Oswald's case, nor was his wife interviewed.

Allegedly, "The FBI did not interview Marina Oswald prior to the assassination" despite the existence of a "Bureau program which monitored the activities of Soviet immigrants and repatriates to detect possible foreign intelligence ties."

"Oswald's subscribing in September 1962 to the *Worker*, which the Bureau characterized as 'an east coast Communist Newspaper', came to the attention of the New York Field Office on September 28, 1962 (presumably through surveillance at that newspaper). This act, the Bureau concedes, contradicted statements attributed to Oswald in his FBI interviews that he was 'disenchanted with the Soviet

Union.' Yet despite this, Oswald's security case was not re-opened. After the assassination, FBI Assistant Director Gale agreed that had standard Bureau procedures been followed, 'In light of Oswald's defection, the case should have been re-opened at the first indication of Communist sympathy or activity (i.e., September 1962).'

Then, on March 26, 1963, the Oswald security case was re-opened, purportedly as a result of his subscription to the *Worker* the previous September. It is interesting to note, however, that shortly after Oswald received this official certification that he was a security problem, he wrote a letter to the Fair Play for Cuba Committee claiming that he had passed out FPCC literature in Dallas with a placard around his neck reading "Hands Off Cuba – Viva Fidel".

"Despite the fact that the Oswald security case was now ostensibly re-opened as of the end of March 1963, Marina Oswald was still not interviewed by the Bureau, the alleged reason for this being that there was information that Oswald had been drinking to excess and beating his wife, and that the relevant FBI manual provision required a 'cooling off' period. After the assassination, FBI Director Hoover agreed that this could only be characterized as 'an asinine excuse', and Assistant Director Gale conceded that, in fact, the best time to get information from her would be after she was beaten up by her husband.'"

Approximately a week to ten days before the Kennedy assassination, Oswald is said to have delivered a note addressed to FBI agent James P. Hosty at the FBI office in Dallas. Despite the other evidence indicating that the FBI had intentionally stayed away from Marina, Hosty said that Lee's note was threatening or complaining in nature, ordering Hosty to stop bothering Oswald's wife.

It should be remembered that during this period of time Oswald had been making a great show of writing to the Soviet Embassy to advise them that the FBI was trying to inhibit his activities on behalf of the Fair Play for Cuba Committee. The question does come to mind as to whether Oswald sent anyone other than the FBI a copy of this threatening letter complaining about FBI harassment of his wife. It surely would seem to have added to his credentials as a pro-Castro advocate.

However, we will never know what was really in Oswald's note, because *following* the assassination – under the order, he said, of J. Gordon Shanklin, head of the Dallas FBI office – Agent Hosty destroyed Oswald's note.

The House Committee informs us that, seemingly curious for someone who wanted nothing to do with the FBI, "After his arrest following the Kennedy assassination, it was found that Oswald's address book contained the name, address, telephone number and automobile license plate number of Special Agent James P. Hosty. "

CHAPTER 25

FACT OR FICTION?

* * *

While he was in the New Orleans jail on August 10, 1963, in relation to the altercation with the anti-Castro Cubans, Lee Harvey Oswald – by his own request – was paid an official visit by FBI agent Quigley.

House Select Committee

The FBI persistently and consistently described Oswald as uncooperative and, indeed, highly antagonistic toward the Bureau. He wanted nothing to do with them. Perhaps so.

Consider, however, the testimony of a man named Adrian Alba, who told the House Select Committee that as an employee and part owner of the Crescent City Garage in New Orleans, he had, in the summer of 1963, become acquainted with Lee Harvey Oswald, who at that time worked next door at the Reily Coffee Co. Oswald had spent many of his working hours at the garage, where he read gun magazines and discussed guns with Alba.

Alba related that one day an FBI agent entered his garage and requested to use one of the Secret Service cars garaged there. The FBI agent showed Alba his credentials, and Alba allowed him to take a Secret Service car, a dark green Studebaker. Later that day or the next day, Alba says he saw the FBI agent in the car handing a white envelope to Oswald in front of the Reily Coffee Co. There was no exchange of words, Alba says, and Oswald, in a bent position, turned away from the car window and held the envelope close to his chest as he walked to the Reily Coffee Co. Alba says he believes he observed a similar transaction a day or so later as he was returning from lunch, but on this occasion he was farther away and failed to see what was handed to Oswald.

A factor which must be considered in evaluating the credibility of Alba is the fact that he did not relate his account of the transactions between Oswald and the FBI agent when he testified before the Warren Commission in 1964. He explained to the Committee in 1978 that he first remembered these incidents in 1970, when his memory was triggered by a television commercial showing a merchant running to and from a taxi to assist a customer. Alba's failure to relate this information to the Warren Commission unarguably may be a reason in and of itself to disbelieve him. On the other hand, it doesn't necessarily mean his story is untrue, any more than the fact that agent Fain failed to tell the Warren Commission that Oswald refused a polygraph means that is not true.

However, in evaluating the FBI's story as to Oswald's dealings with them, there is an undisputed fact which must be evaluated, because it is seemingly so inconsistent with the Bureau's position that Oswald was un-cooperative, antagonistic, and wanted nothing to do with them. Given that posture, how does one rationalize the fact – which the Bureau concedes to be true – that while he was in the New Orleans jail on August 10, 1963, in relation to the altercation with the anti-Castro Cubans, Lee Harvey Oswald – by his own request – was paid an official visit by FBI agent Quigley? It would appear that the FBI-Oswald relationship might be bit more intricate than the Bureau has claimed.

Another relationship that might upon close examination prove to be rather more byzantine is that of Oswald with Carlos Bringuier. It has been mentioned above in chapter 23 that Oswald was arrested and fined for being involved in a disturbance with anti-Castro Cuban refugees. The disturbance with anti-Castro Cubans referred to was described by the Warren Commission as follows.

"On August 5, he visited a store managed by Carlos Bringuier, a Cuban refugee and avid opponent of Castro and the New Orleans delegate of the Cuban student directorate. Oswald indicated an interest in joining the struggle against Castro. He told Bringuier that he had been a Marine and was trained in guerilla warfare, and that he was willing not only to train Cubans to fight Castro but also to join the fight himself. The next day Oswald returned to the store and left his 'Guidebook for Marines' for Bringuier.

"On August 9, Bringuier saw Oswald passing out Fair Play for Cuba leaflets. Bringuier and his companions became angry and a dispute resulted. Oswald and the three Cuban exiles were arrested for disturbing the peace. Oswald spent the night in jail and was interviewed by a lieutenant of the New Orleans Police Department . . On August 16, Oswald, assisted by at least one other person who was a hired helper, again passed out Fair Play for Cuba literature, this time in front of the International Trade Mart. That night, television newscasts ran pictures of Oswald's activities . . . William Stuckey, a radio broadcaster with a program called *Latin Listening Post,* had long been looking for a member of the Fair Play for Cuba Committee to appear on his program. He learned of Oswald from Bringuier . . . Stuckey arranged for a debate between Oswald and Bringuier on a 25-minute daily public affairs program called *Conversation Carte Blanche* which took place on August 21."

A number of questions arise from this scenario. Let's start at the end. A radio broadcaster has long been looking for a member of the Fair Play for Cuba Committee to appear on his program. Presumably one good reason why he has not found any is there are none in New Orleans. Now, suddenly, Oswald gets to be the public voice for Fair Play for Cuba. How? Well, he gets recommended for the job by Carlos Bringuier, who happens to be the man Oswald went out of his way to deceive; who happens to be the man who got into a fight with Oswald as a result of Oswald's double-dealing. Does this tale ring true?

Does it ring true when we add in the fact that while in jail following the fight with Bringuier, Oswald asks for and receives a visit by an agent from the FBI, an organization that Oswald is overtly treating as an enemy. No one has ever explained this visit by agent Quigley, but it is clear that Oswald sent for him.

Remember, this entire scenario never comes into being if Oswald had not first gone to see Bringuier. That is, of course, if we believe that this entire Oswald/Bringuier story actually took place - that it as not contrived. If the official position is that it really happened, shouldn't someone have asked a simple question such as: Why would Oswald go to see Bringuier in the first place?

Might one possible reason be that Oswald was going out of his way to entice Bringuier into attacking him? Logically, shouldn't the next question be: Why would Oswald want Bringuier to attack him? Would being attacked by this "avid opponent of Castro and the New Orleans delegate of the Cuban student directorate" serve to give Oswald standing as an avid pro-Castro figure? For what purpose? To get the attention of who? Was this to add to Oswald's Legend?

If Oswald is really a pro-Castro zealot, why would he be going in to schmooze with this anti-Castro zealot? Why would Oswald be trying to convince Bringuier that he was anti-Castro? Why would Oswald be indicating to Bringuier that "he had an interest in joining the struggle against Castro?" Why would he have told Bringuier "that he had been a Marine and was trained in guerilla warfare and that he was willing not only to train Cubans to fight Castro but also to join the fight himself?" And, remember, this was not a single visit. Why did Oswald the next day return to the store and leave his 'Guidebook for Marines' for Bringuier?

Given all that the official reports have concluded as to Oswald's beliefs, shouldn't someone have thought through the logical questions such as: Do we believe Oswald was trying to set the stage for Bringuier to attack him out of anger for being deceived? - or do we believe that Oswald was trying to con Bringuier into believing Oswald was indeed anti-Castro for other reasons?

This second possibility carries with it the need to accept that Oswald could believe that Bringuier would not shortly thereafter find out that Oswald was not anti-Castro. That Bringuier would not find out that he was passing out leaflets & application forms for his non-existent FPFC chapter - listing as its address the non-existent office at 544 Camp St.

However, it might be of some passing interest for us to note that there was a need on the part of the FBI to find people who could inveigle their way into the anti-Castro groups.

The Senate Select Committee informs us that on May 23, 1961, shortly after the Bay of Pigs, FBI field offices were instructed that "The failure of the recent invasion attempt by Cuban rebel forces has accentuated the problem of investigating anti-Castro and pro-Castro groups and individuals in the United States. In addition to discharging our security and criminal responsibilities we are faced with the necessity of acquiring and providing other agencies informative and valid intelligence data relative to the objectives and activities of both factions as well as data regarding key personalities . . . In order to discharge these investigative and intelligence responsibilities with maximum effectiveness it is essential that particular attention be afforded the development on a broadly expanded basis of sources and informants in a position to provide knowledgeable data regarding pro-Castro and anti-Castro activities."

The Senate Committee said: "After the missile crisis, CIA operations against Cuba apparently decreased, while operations by Cuban exile groups on their own continued. On March 18, 1963, there was a reported attack on a Soviet vessel off the northern coast of Cuba by members of two exile groups, Alpha 66, and the Second National Front of Escambray. There was another reported attack on a Soviet vessel off the northern coast of Cuba on the evening of March 26-27, 1963, by members of another anti-Castro group, Commandos L-66.

"This apparently caused considerable concern within the U.S. Government that such activity by Cuban exile groups could produce confrontation with the Soviets. One witness stated, 'the whole apparatus of government, Coast Guard, Customs, Immigration and

Naturalization, FBI, CIA, were working together to try to keep these operations from going to Cuba.'

"These moves to restrict exile activities had an impact on New Orleans at the time Lee Harvey Oswald was living there. As reported on page one of the *New Orleans Times-Picayune* on August 1, 1963, the FBI seized more than a ton of dynamite, 20 bomb casings, napalm material and other devices at a home in the New Orleans area on July 31. Newspaper interest in the seizure continued with prominent articles in the *Times-Picayune* on August 2 and August 4.

"The Warren Commission learned that, on August 5, Oswald contacted a Cuban exile in New Orleans, Carlos Bringuier, offering to help in training anti-Castro forces. Then on August 7, Oswald returned and left his Marine Corps training manual for Bringuier. Two days later, Bringuier saw Oswald handing out pro-Castro literature, which resulted in fighting and their arrest. Oswald subsequently appeared on a radio debate with Bringuier, again taking a pro-Castro position." *(Attention of the reader is directed to the fact that while the Senate Committee did not state a cause and effect relationship, the material in this paragraph was placed by them in a section discussing "Moves to Restrict Exile Activities.")*

The Senate Committee continued the above material as follows: "Additional FBI reports provided to the Warren Commission detailed other facts connected to this anti-Castro activity in New Orleans at the time of Oswald's contact with Bringuier. On July 24, according to FBI reports, ten Cuban exiles arrived in New Orleans from Miami. These ten joined an existing group of exiles at a 'training camp' north of New Orleans, which was directed by the same individuals who were involved in procuring the dynamite the FBI seized. By late July, some 28 Cuban exiles were at the training camp, allegedly awaiting transportation to Guatemala where they would work for a lumber company.

"Some of those who owned the land on which the Cuban exiles were staying became concerned about the FBI interest in the

266

anti-Castro activities and ordered them to leave. Carlos Bringuier was called upon to assist in getting this group back to Miami."

"Although this was the extent of the Warren Commission investigation of this incident, at least one FBI report, on the seizure of materials, which was not provided the Warren Commission, raises additional questions about the purpose of Oswald's contact with Bringuier. Indeed, Bringuier himself believed Oswald was attempting to infiltrate the anti-Castro movement in order to report its activities to pro-Castro forces."

This last item cites as its authority the Warren Report testimony of Carlos Bringuier. The Warren Commission had set forth this last item in a context that might lead one to believe that Bringuier from the start believed Oswald was attempting to infiltrate his organization on behalf of pro-Castro forces. A careful reading of the actual testimony of Carlos Bringuier might lead one to conclude that the Warren Commission was being rather selective as to just what part of Bringuier's testimony they would utilize to support the conclusion they wished to promulgate.

The following are excerpts from the testimony of Carlos Bringuier. The questioning is by Wesley J. Liebeler, Assistant Counsel to the Warren Commission:

"Mr. LIEBELER. Did there come a time when you met Lee Harvey Oswald?

Mr. BRINGUIER. Yes.

Mr. LIEBELER. Tell us when that was, and the circumstances of the event.

Mr. BRINGUIER. Well, the first day that I saw Lee Harvey Oswald was on August 5, 1963, but before we go deeper in this matter about Oswald, I think that I would like to explain to you two things that I think will facilitate the Commission to understand my feeling at that moment.

Mr. LIEBELER. That is perfectly all right. Go ahead.

Mr. BRINGUIER. And you see, in August 24, 1962, my organization, the Cuban Student Directorate, carry on a shelling of Havana, and a few days later when person from the FBI contacted me here in New Orleans-his name was Warren C. de Brueys. Mr. de Brueys was talking to me in the Thompson Cafeteria. At that moment I was the only one from the Cuban Student Directorate here in the city, and he was asking to me about my activities here in the city, and when I told him that I was the only one, he didn't believe that, and he advised me-and I quote, 'We could infiltrate your organization and find out what you are doing here.' My answer to him was, 'Well, you will have to infiltrate myself, because I am the only one.' And I want to put this out, because after the assassination of Mr. Kennedy, when I was interviewed, I told something that some part of the press or some persons now are trying to use to tell that maybe Oswald was a man from the FBI or the CIA. I will go into that later on. After that, after. my conversation with de Brueys, I always was waiting that maybe someone will come to infiltrate my organization from the FBI, because I already was told by one of the FBI agent that they will try to infiltrate my organization. Next thing is this: On August 2, 1963, I receive in my store — I have over there the office of the delegation too, the visit of two Cubans, who told me that they had already desert from one Anti-Castro training camp that was across Lake Pontchartrain here in New Orleans. Until that moment I did not know nothing about that Anti-Castro training camp here in the city, and they told me that that Anti-Castro training camp was a branch of the Christian Democratic Movement-that is another Anti-Castro organization-and they told me that they had the fear inside the training camp that there was a Castro agent inside that training camp. A few days before, too, the police found here in New Orleans about 1 mile from that training camp a big lot of ammunition and weapons and all those things, and when Oswald came to me on August 5 I had inside myself the feeling, well, maybe this is from the FBI, or maybe this is a Communist, because the FBI already had told me that maybe they will infiltrate my organization, but that feeling-I only had that feeling on August 5, because 4 days later I was convinced that Oswald was not an FBI agent and that he was a Pro-Castro agent. When I told that to the press after the assassination, I saw in some magazines that I was not sure if he was an FBI or not, and that is not the truth, because on August 9, 3 months before the assassination, I was sure that he was a Pro- Castro and not an FBI. I want to have that clear."

The reader will please note that the encounter was on August 5, but it was not until 4 days later that Bringuier "was convinced that Oswald was not an FBI agent and that he was a pro-Castro agent." 4 days after August 5 was August 9. What happened on August 9? Well, picking up in a subsequent answer of Bringuier, we can get some context that the Warren Commission appears to have ignored or intentionally omitted:

BRINGUIER: … on August 9 I was coming back to the store at 2 o'clock in the afternoon, and one friend of mine with the name of Celso Hernandez came to me and told me that in Canal Street there was a young man carrying a sign telling "Viva Fidel" in Spanish, and some other thing about Cuba, but my friend don't speak nothing in English, and the only thing that he understood was the "Viva Fidel" in Spanish. He told me that he was blaming the person in Spanish, but that the person maybe didn't understood what he was telling to him and he came to me to let me know what was going on over there. At that moment was in the store another Cuban with the name of Miguel Cruz, and we went all three with a big sign that I have in the store in color. The sign is the Statue of Liberty with a knife in the back, and the hand, knifing her in the back, has the initials of the Soviet Union, and it said, "Danger. Only 99 Miles from the United States Cuba Lies in Chains." We pick up the sign and we went to Canal Street to find the guy. We were walking all Canal Street to Rampart Street, but we could not find him. We were asking to different people in the street, but nobody saw him, nobody told us, Yes, I saw him, or, He went to this side. I decided to get a Canal streetcar to search for him, and we went in the Canal streetcar until about the 2700 block of Canal Street, and we came back in the Canal streetcar, but we could not find him at that moment. I went back to the store. but just 3 or 4 minutes later one of my two friends, Miguel Cruz, came back running and told me that the guy was another time in Canal Street and that Celso was watching him over there. I went over there with the sign another time, and I was surprised when I recognized that the guy with the sign hanging on the chest. said, "Viva Fidel" and "Hands off Cuba," was Lee Harvey Oswald....

BRINGUIER: ....When I saw that was Oswald and he recognized me, he was also surprised, but just for a few seconds. Immediately he smiled to me and he offered the hand to shake hands with me. I became more angry and I start to tell him that he don't have any face to do that, with what face he was doing that, because he had just came to me 4 days ago offering me his service and that he was a Castro agent, and I start to blame him in the street. That was a Friday around 3 o'clock at this moment, and many people start to gather around us to see what was going on over there. I start to explain to the people what Oswald did to me, because I wanted to move the American people against him, not to take the fight for myself as a Cuban but to move the American people to fight him, and I told them that that was a Castro agent, that he was a pro-Communist, and that he was trying to do to them exactly what he did to us in Cuba, kill them and send their children to the execution wall. Those were my phrases at the moment.

The people in the street became angry and they started to shout to him. "Traitor ! Communist! Go to Cuba! Kill him !" and some other phrases that I do not know if I could tell in the record.

Mr. LIEBELER. You mean they cursed at him, they swore at him?

Mr. BRINGUIER. That is right, some bad phrases, bad words.

Mr. LIEBELER. Yes.

Mr. BRINGUIER. And at that moment, one of the Americans push him by one arm. One policeman came. When policeman came to me and asked me to keep walking and to let Oswald distribute his literature that he was handing out he was handing out yellow leaflets of the Fair Play for Cuba Committee, New Orleans Chapter-and I told to the policeman that I was Cuban, I explained to him what Oswald did to me, and I told him that I don't know if was against the law, but that I will not leave that place until Oswald left and that I will make some trouble.

The policeman left, I believe going to some place to call the headquarters, and at one moment my friend Celso took the literature from Oswald, the yellow sheets, and broke it and threw it on the air. There were a lot of yellow sheets flying. And I was more angry, and I went near Oswald to hit him. I took my glasses off and I went near to him to hit him, but when he sensed my intention, he put his arm down as an X, like this here (demonstrating).

Mr. LIEBELER. He crossed his arms in front of him?

Mr. BRINGUIER. That is right, put his face and told me, "O.K. Carlos, if you want to hit me, hit me." At that moment, that made me to reaction that he was trying to appear as a martyr if I will hit him, and I decide not to hit him, and just a few seconds later arrive two police cars, and one of the policeman over there was Lieutenant Gaillot, G-a-i-l-l-o-t. They put Oswald and my two friends in one of the police cars, and I went with Lieutenant Gaillot in the other police car to the First District of Police here in New Orleans. When we were in the First District of Police, we were in the same room. One small room over there, and some of the policemen start to question Oswald if he was a Communist, what he was doing that, and all those things, and Oswald at that moment-that was in front of myself -was really cold blood. He was answering the questions that he would like to answer, and he was not nervous, he was not out of control, he was confident in himself at that moment over there. One of the questions that they asked to him was about his organization, the Fair Play for Cuba, and I saw him showing some papers that - I believe they were the credentials of the Fair Play for Cuba Committee, that the Fair Play for Cuba Committee is a national organization, and when he told that, he was so kind of proud that it was not a small group but a national group all over the United States, and they asked of him the name of the members. No. Excuse me.

Before they asked him if he has any office. He told them no, that there were they were holding the meetings in different house, different homes? different members of the organization one night in one house, another night in another house, but in front of me he didn't told nothing about any office. When they asked him about the name of the members, he answered that he could not tell the name of the members in front of myself, because he will not like to let me know who were the ones who were helping him here in the city, and at that moment the police came out of the room and that was the last time that I saw him that day."

Thus, rather than the impression stated by the Warren Commission, it would seem more accurate to state that Bringuier's testimony was to the effect that on August 5. he was suspect that Oswald might be an infiltrator, either from the FBI or a communist group. But that four days later, Bringuier become convinced that Oswald was a communist because Oswald had credentials and flyers proclaiming him to be a member of a non-existent New Orleans Fair Play for Cuba organization. This, of course, would beg the question as to why Oswald was pretending to be a member of a pretend communist group. Which brings us full circle back to the lengthy exploration discussed above of "notional" organizations, and building "credentials" and the like.

The Senate Committee in their section on Cuba and the Intelligence Agencies, states: "A report of the Miami Office of the FBI [dated October 3, 1963] revealed some of the information the FBI had on this incident:

"On June 14, 1963, information was received that a group of Cuban exiles had a plan to bomb the Shell refinery in Cuba. On June 15, United States Customs Agents seized a twin Beechcraft airplane on the outskirts of Miami, Florida, along with a quantity of explosives. [. . . , . . . , . . ., 'A' and . . . , along with American [. .] were involved and detained, but not arrested, by the United States Customs Agents. It was ascertained that [. . .] supplied the money and explosives for this operation. [He] is well known as a former gambling concession operator in Havana. On July 19, 1963, [. . .] advised that there was another plan to bomb Cuba, using bomb casings and dynamite located on the outskirts of New Orleans, Louisiana. On July 31, 1963, the Federal Bureau of Investigation (FBI) at New Orleans, Louisiana, obtained a search warrant and seized 2,400 pounds of dynamite and 20 bomb casings near Lacombe, Louisiana. This material was located on the property of [. . .], brother of [. . .], [of] Miami Beach and former operator of a casino in the Nacional Hotel, Havana, Cuba. Investigation determined that this dynamite was purchased at Collinsville, Illinois, by ['B'] for 'A,' who was involved in the June 14, 1963 seizures at Miami. 'A' transported the dynamite to New Orleans in a rented trailer. Also involved in this bomb plot were[. . .]. [. . .] advised on June 14, 1963, 'B' of Collinsville, Illinois, recently arrived in Miami, Florida, in a Ford station wagon with a load of arms for sale. American adventurers and mercenaries, [. . .] and [. . .], took 'B' around to meet the different Cuban exile leaders in Miami. On another occasion, an intelligence agency conducted a sensitive operation which developed information on the location of arms caches and training camps in another country. That information was given to the other country, which then raided the camps and seized the materials. Raids and seizures such as these apparently were commonplace throughout the summer and fall of 1963. Those individuals apparently sponsoring this activity were angered by these raids and seizures."

Just as there is more than one type of notional organization, so there is more than one type of covert action. One type of covert action is called a "False Flag" operation, which is designed to deceive the public in such a way that the activities appear to have been carried out by some other entity which will then be blamed for the activity. It derives from the concept of a military unit flying the flag of a country other than their own as a deception.

There were at least two false flag operations in this era that are of interest to our discussion. They were Operation Northwoods and Operation Mongoose. These two false flag operations were seriously proposed by the military leaders of the United States, the goal of each being to create pretexts that would justify the U.S. invading Cuba in the early 1960's. These are discussed here not because they were implemented, for they were not implemented– indeed they were rejected outright by President Kennedy, who earned the significant ire of many of the zealots who had dreamed up these proposals. The purpose of discussing these proposals here is to give the reader a glimpse as to the deep anti-Castro obsession of many people at that time, as well as an insight into the extent they would go to accomplish their goals including dangerous, not to say violent actions in their schemes.

The previously secret documents detailing these false flag operations were made public in November 1997, by the John F. Kennedy Assassination Records Review Board. The proposals called for committing various acts of terrorism in a manner designed to be blamed on Castro. The goal was specifically to deceive the American public who would be expected to seek retaliation against Castro, thereby creating public support for a war against Cuba. The goals also included justifying an invasion of Cuba in the eyes of the rest of the world: "The desired resultant from the execution of this plan would be to place the United States in the apparent position of suffering defensible grievances from a rash and irresponsible government of Cuba and to develop an international image of a Cuban threat to peace in the Western Hemisphere."

Operation Northwoods was a proposal of the Joint Chiefs of Staff, signed on their behalf by the Chairman of the Joint Chiefs of Staff, Lyman Lemnitzer, and submitted as to the Secretary of Defense, Robert McNamara. Just a few of the proposals comprising Operation Northwood were:

1. Develop a Communist Cuban terror campaign in the Miami area, in other Florida cities and even in Washington, DC.

2. U.S. personnel to disguise themselves as agents of the Cuban government and to engage in terrorist attacks on the U.S. base at Guantanamo Bay.

3. Sink a boatload of Cubans en route to Florida (real or simulated).

4. Friendly forces disguised as Cuban agents would hijack an American passenger plane containing American passengers. The plane would drop down off the radar screen and be replaced by a pilotless aircraft, which would crash, purportedly killing all the passengers. The real passenger plane would be secretly flown back to the United States.

5. A "Remember the Maine" incident - blowing up a US ship in Guantanamo Bay and blaming Cuba.

6. Foster attempts on lives of Cuban refugees in the United States even to the extent of wounding, in instances to be widely publicized.

7. Create an incident which will make it appear that Cuban MIGs have destroyed a USAF aircraft over international waters in an unprovoked attack.

8. Hijackings and bombings followed by the introduction of phony evidence that would implicate the Cuban government.

9. Real or simulated actions against various U.S. military and civilian targets.

10. Exploding a few plastic bombs in carefully chosen spots, the arrest of Cuban agents and the release of prepared documents.

Operation Mongoose was comprised of twelve proposals in a February 1962 memorandum entitled "Possible Actions to Provoke, Harass or Disrupt Cuba." This memorandum, written by Brig. Gen. William H. Craig, was submitted to the Chief of Operations of the

Cuba Project, Brig. Gen. Edward Lansdale. Amongst the proposals of Operation Mongoose were:

1. A plan to create an incident which has the appearance of an attack on U.S. facilities (GMO) in Cuba, thus providing an excuse for use of U.S. military might to overthrow the current government of Cuba.

2. A plot to blame Castro if the 1962 Mercury manned space flight carrying John Glenn crashed, the objective being to provide irrevocable proof that, should the Mercury manned orbit flight fail, the fault lies with Cuba. This was to be accomplished by manufacturing various pieces of evidence which would prove electronic interference on the part of the Cubans.

* * *

Even after General Lemnitzer was fired by President Kennedy as the Chairman of the Joint Chiefs of Staff following his submission of Operation Northwoods, the Joint Chiefs of Staff still planned false -flag pretext operations at least into 1963

.

CHAPTER 26
THE RETURN OF SVENGALI

* * *

"The Clinton witnesses were credible and significant. They established an association of an undetermined nature between Ferrie, Shaw and Oswald less than 3 months before the assassination."

House Select Committee

Also extremely active in Sergio Arcacha Smith's anti-Castro group was a man we have met previously –the man who had been Lee Harvey Oswald's commander in the Civil Air Patrol – David Ferrie.

As discussed previously, despite what Oswald had told the Fair Play for Cuba Committee headquarters about renting an office, and despite his stamp on literature he was distributing stating that FPCC was located at 544 Camp Street, investigation following the assassination revealed that neither the FPCC nor Lee Harvey Oswald had ever rented an office at that address.

Troubled by questions such as why Oswald would list an address with which he had absolutely no relationship, the House Select Committee conducted its own investigation and produced a section focusing on the possibility of a connection between Oswald and 544 Camp Street.

It turns out that the building located at 544 Camp Street, the Newman Building, occupied a corner lot where Camp Street meets Lafayette Street. The Camp Street address was the main entrance for two tenants who have no relation to our story.

The Lafayette address, however, was the main entrance of Guy Banister Associates, a private investigative firm. Guy Banister, after a 20-year career, had retired from the FBI in 1954 to become assistant superintendent for the New Orleans Police Department. After a falling out with the mayor of New Orleans, Banister had left public service and formed his own private detective agency.

According to FBI files, Banister had become excessively involved in anti-Communist activities after his separation from the Bureau, and testified before various investigating bodies about the dangers of Communism. Early in 1961, Banister helped draw up a charter for the Friends of Democratic Cuba, an organization set up as the fund-raising arm of Sergio Arcacha Smith's branch of the Cuban Revolutionary Council [CRC].

The FBI files also indicate that Banister was running background investigations on those Cuban students at Louisiana State University who sought to join Smith's anti-Castro group, ferreting out any pro-Castro sympathizers among them.

Also extremely active in Sergio Arcacha Smith's anti-Castro group was a man we have met previously – the man who had been Lee Harvey Oswald's commander in the Civil Air Patrol – David Ferrie.

The House Committee tells us that Ferrie shared Banister's anti -Communism and anti-Castro fervor. In fact, Ferrie had actually had to be asked "to discontinue his remarks at a speaking engagement in July 1961 before the New Orleans chapter of the Military Order of World Wars. His topic was the Presidential administration and the Bay of Pigs fiasco. The organization put a stop to Ferrie's remarks when he became too critical of President Kennedy."

Ferrie had not bothered to renew his CAP commander charter when it ran out in 1954, although he continued to wear the insignia of the CAP on his fatigues. He did renew his commander charter in 1959, when he augmented his cadet's standard CAP rifle training by instituting an association with the New Orleans Cadet Rifle Club.

Ferrie also started a group called the "Falcon Squadron", composed of Ferrie's closet CAP associates. A group within this group, the "Omnipotents", was allegedly starting to train cadets in what to do in the event of a major attack on the United States.

Ferrie's job and ownership of an airplane enabled him to travel around the country with relative ease. He told officials he frequently traveled to Texas and other parts of the South, including Miami. He also visited New York on occasion. The amount of time Ferrie spent in these cities could not be determined. In August 1959, while in Miami, Ferrie was put under a 24-hour surveillance by customs agents who believed he was involved in gun smuggling. Following a brief investigation, it was determined that Ferrie was not involved in any illegal activity, but merely planning an outing for his "scouts". The investigation was dropped.

Ferrie also became involved in other activities. In 1959, he had found an outlet for his political fanaticism in the anti-Castro movement. By early 1961, Ferrie and a young man whom Ferrie had first met in the CAP, Layton Martens, were working with Sergio Arcacha Smith, head of the Cuban Revolutionary Front delegation in New Orleans.

Ferrie soon became Smith's eager partner in counter-revolutionary activities. He reportedly built two miniature submarines, which he planned to use for an attack on Havana Harbor, obtained several rifles and mortars for the proposed invasion, and was reportedly teaching Cubans how to fly. Further, several of Ferrie's cadets claimed to have taken trips to Cuba in Ferrie's airplane.

Ferrie was also involved with Arcacha Smith, adventurer Gordon Novel and Layton Martens in a raid on a munitions dump in Houma, Louisiana. Others who were said to have participated in the raid, in which various weapons, grenades and ammunition were stolen, were Andrew Blackmon, a Ferrie associate and former CAP cadet, and Guy Banister, whose involvement may have been limited to storing the stolen material.

In September 1961, the US Border Patrol received information that Ferrie was attempting to purchase a C-47 airplane for $30,000 and reportedly had a cache of arms.in the New Orleans area. The report was never verified.

Arcacha Smith wrote to Eastern Airlines' then-president Eddie Rickenbacker on Ferrie's behalf requesting a 60- or 90-day leave with pay for full-time work for the CRC. The request was denied. Nevertheless, Ferrie's vacation in April 1961 coincided with the Bay of Pigs invasion. Ferrie's role, if any, is not known.

Guy Banister did investigative work both directly for Ferrie and for Ferrie's lawyer, G. Wray Gill, in connection with the charges brought against Ferrie by Eastern Airlines, his employer, and by the New Orleans police alleging crimes against nature, and extortion. In return, Ferrie provided Banister research services, such as analysis of autopsy reports.

Ferrie and Banister also worked together over some period of time with attorney Gill for the defense of another of Gill's clients who was involved in a deportation case – Carlos Marcello.

"Ferrie's involvement with Marcello may have begun as early as the spring of 1961. An unconfirmed Border Patrol report of February 1962 alleges that Ferrie was the pilot who flew Marcello back into the United States from Guatemala after he had been deported in April 1961 as part of the US Attorney General Robert Kennedy's crackdown on organized crime. This may have helped Ferrie establish an enduring relationship with the Marcello organized crime family.

The return of Marcello to the United States coincided chronologically with Ferrie's activities with the Cuban Revolutionary Council. According to Carlos Quiroga, a Cuban who had been involved with the CRC, Ferrie often provided Arcacha Smith with funds, stating 'Ferrie lent him [Arcacha Smith] money when he needed it for his family . . . He [Ferrie] had $100 bills around all the time', even after he lost his job with the airlines."

As a result of his work with Guy Banister, David Ferrie spent a good deal of time at Banister's office at the Newman Building, and he and Banister were frequent customers at Mancuso's coffee shop on the first floor. Less than a block away were the Reily Coffee Co., where Oswald worked, and the Crescent City Garage, whose owner, Adrian Alba, testified that he had often seen Oswald in Mancuso's.

Following his much-publicized altercation and subsequent debate with the anti-Castro leader, Carlos Bringuier, near the end of August 1963, Oswald largely passed out of sight in New Orleans until mid-September.

During this period, Oswald reportedly appeared in Clinton, Louisiana, where a voting rights demonstration organized by the Congress of Racial Equality was in progress. Clinton, the county seat of East Feliciana Parish, was about 130 miles from New Orleans.

There were six witnesses in Clinton who saw Oswald there, "among them a State representative, a deputy sheriff and a registrar of voters" . . . In addition to the physical descriptions they gave that matched that of Oswald, other observations of the witnesses tended to substantiate their belief that he was, in fact, the man they saw. For example, he referred to himself as "Oswald", and he produced his Marine Corps discharge papers as identification.

The reason Oswald had to produce identification was because he was applying to be registered as a voter in East Feliciana Parish. But, as far as we know, he produced legitimate identification, so that none of the papers he produced contained an address that would quality him to be registered as a resident of East Felicia Parish. Apparently, the pretext he offered was that he had been seeking employment at East Louisiana State Hospital, in nearby Jackson, Louisiana, and had been told that his job would depend on his becoming a registered voter, and so he had come to Clinton for that purpose. He was, it would appear, unsuccessful in attempting to be registered as a voter in East Feliciana Parish.

Some of the witnesses said that Oswald was accompanied by two older men whom they identified as [David] Ferrie and [a man named Clay] Shaw.'

The House Select Committee found that "the Clinton witnesses were credible and significant . . . If the witnesses were not only truthful but accurate as well in their accounts, they established an association of an undetermined nature between Ferrie, Shaw and Oswald less than 3 months before the assassination."

There the matter has stood since then: "an association of an undetermined nature" involving Oswald, David Ferrie and a third man. In other words, a mystery. But perhaps there are a few potential clues that have been overlooked.

The central question would seem to be: Was it only a mere coincidence that a "big-city boy" like Oswald happened to be applying to be registered as a voter out in East Feliciana Parish, just at the very time that an organized Black voting registration drive was taking place in that parish?

Perhaps so. But let's look at a little background.

The Senate Committee, in a special volume on the Federal Bureau of Investigation, relates that in the late 50s and early 60s, in addition to its own mandate, the FBI had "the role of an investigative agency, acting for the Justice Department, required by law to serve the Civil Rights Division, which was in turn charged with the responsibility of enforcing Federal laws with respect to civil rights . . . [T]he Civil Rights Division was to enforce the Civil Rights Acts of 1957 and 1960 – a twin responsibility to go after (A) public officials who practiced racial discrimination in registration or voting, and (B) anyone, public official or private citizen, who interfered with registration or voting by threats, intimidation or coercion by any means.

"In 1960 the Department of Justice believed that there was massive wide-spread racial discrimination in voting in five Deep South States (Alabama, Georgia, Louisiana, Mississippi and South Carolina) and in some counties in Florida, North Carolina and Tennessee.

"Shortly after the Civil Rights Act of 1960 went into effect, record demands were made for 15 counties in [five] states – McCormick, Hampton and Claredon Counties, South Carolina; Webster, Fayette and Early Counties, Georgia; Wilcox, Sumpter and Montgomery Counties, Alabama; East Feliciana, Quachita and East Carroll Parishes, Louisiana; and Boliva, Leflore, and Forrest Counties, Mississippi.'"

By 1964, "The result of four years of work was a tremendous accumulation of proof of racial discrimination of voting throughout the States of Alabama, Mississippi and Louisiana."

An example of one aspect of the Bureau's activity in this field is the June 27, 1963 memorandum on the subject 'Racial Matters' which FBI Headquarters sent to the Special Agents in charge of all field offices; in part, the memorandum reads: "In order that the Bureau's information will be complete and absolutely current, it is essential that all offices promptly [send] information concerning racial demonstrations . . . arrests arising out of racial problems, results of court action, and any other pertinent information. Steps shall be taken to furnish pertinent information so that it will be received prior to midnight on the day of occurrence . . . When activities continue throughout the night, the Bureau is to be telephonically advised of the current status of the activities before 7 a.m., Eastern Daylight Savings Time.

"Each office must also assume responsibility for following up scheduled racial activity and promptly advising the Bureau of subsequent developments. Whenever the Bureau has been advised that a meeting, demonstration or other pertinent activity will take place, coverage must be continued and the Bureau promptly informed as to whether the anticipated activity actually occurred, and pertinent details of what transpired. If a planned racial activity is cancelled or postponed, the Bureau should also be promptly advised."

Given the above background, together with the other information we know now about Lee Harvey Oswald, it would seem appropriate to at least entertain the following questions:

- Might Oswald's business in Clinton have been part of the coverage of this Black voting registration drive organized by the Congress of Racial Equality, such as is mandated in the 'Racial Matters' memo sent from FBI headquarters to all field offices only two months earlier?

- Might the purpose of having Oswald apply to be registered as a voter in East Feliciana Parish, be to test whether an outside white would be treated better than local Blacks?

The so-called "Clinton Sightings" of Oswald have significance beyond the possibility that they tie the FBI to Oswald, for they rather firmly tie the supposed pro-Castro Communist, Oswald, together with the staunch anti-Communist, anti-Castro partisan, David Ferrie.

Nor is this the only evidence tying Oswald and Ferrie together in this fateful period of time. There is a fascinating link which has been largely overlooked despite the fact that there are credible witnesses to its existence.

A Ferrie associate named Layton Martens told the police that after the assassination, W. Wray Gill (Carlos Marcello's lawyer, for whom Ferrie had been doing some work) had "come by to relay a message to Ferrie that his library card was found among Oswald's effects." The House Select Committee dismissed this with the comment that 'Marten's story was unsubstantiated'.

However, they subsequently relate that. "Oswald's former landlady in New Orleans, Mrs. Jesse Garner told the Committee she recalled that Ferrie visited her home on the night of the assassination and asked about Oswald's library card" And, "A neighbor of Oswald's, Mrs. Dorris Eames, told New Orleans district attorney investigators in 1968 that Ferrie had come by her house after the assassination, inquiring if Mr. Eames had any information regarding Oswald's library card. Eames told Ferrie he had seen Oswald in the public library but apparently had no information about the library card Oswald used."

Why would Ferrie be asking questions about the library card of the deceased Lee Harvey Oswald? Was Ferrie some kind of ghoulish collector of library cards of infamous people? Perhaps. On the other hand, is there any possibility that Ferrie had ever handled that library card? Does Ferrie's interest in this card point to the possibility of an active association between Oswald and Ferrie in this period of time?

CHAPTER 27

CLOSET ANTI-COMMUNIST?

* * *

"The result of Veciana and Bishop re-establishing contact eventually led to Veciana's founding of Alpha 66..."

Alpha 66 became one of the most active of the anti-Castro exile groups..."

"When Veciana arrived for the meeting, Bishop was there talking with [a young man]...."

"Veciana testified that he recognized the young man with Bishop as Lee Harvey Oswald after seeing photographs of him following the Kennedy assassination."

House Select Committee

The Clinton sightings are not Oswald's only possible contact with virulent anti-Castro Cuban zealots.

Antonio Veciana Blanch was the founder of Alpha 66 which, "throughout 1962 and most of 1963, was one of the most militant of the exile groups. Its repeated hit-and-run attacks had drawn public criticism from President Kennedy in the spring of 1963, to which Veciana replied, "We are going to attack again and again"'.

Veciana told the House Select Committee that originally he had been recruited to work against the Castro Government in the middle of 1960, by a man who called himself Maurice Bishop, who purported to be with a construction firm headquartered in Belgium. Veciana related that prior to the time the American Embassy in Cuba was closed in January 1961, Bishop had suggested that he go there and contact certain officials for help in his anti-Castro activity. Veciana recalled that one of the names Bishop had given him was Sam Kail.

The House Committee ascertained that Colonel Sam Kail "served as the US Army attaché at the US Embassy in Havana from June 3,1958 until the day the Embassy closed, January 4, 1961. His primary mission as military attaché was that of intelligence. Later, in February 1962, he was transferred to Miami where he was in charge of the unit that debriefed newly-arrived Cuban refugees. Although he reported directly to the Chief of Army Intelligence in Washington, Kail said he assumed his unit was actually functioning for the CIA." (The Committee doesn't mention that Kail, as we know, was also involved with Clemard Charles, the friend of George de Mohrenschildt.)

Veciana says that in mid-1961 he fled Cuba because Bishop told him Castro's agents were becoming suspicious of his activities.

"Shortly after he settled in Miami, Veciana testified, Bishop contacted him again" "Early in their relationship in Miami, Bishop asked Veciana to monitor the activities of an anti-Castro operation called 'Cellula Fantasma.' Veciana said he attended a few meetings of the group and described the operation as a leaflet-dropping mission over Cuba which involved known soldier of fortune, Frank Fiorini Sturgis." [later of Watergate fame].

The result of Veciana and Bishop re-establishing contact eventually led to Veciana's founding of Alpha 66 which, according to Veciana, was the brainchild of Bishop (whose main thesis was that Cuba had to be liberated by Cubans). "Alpha 66 became one of the most active of the anti-Castro exile groups, buying guns and boats, recruiting and training commandos, and conducting numerous raids on Cuba." "According to Veciana, the man behind all of Alpha 66's strategy was Maurice Bishop. Over the 12-year period of their association, Veciana estimated he met with Bishop more than 100 times . . . Besides contacts with Bishop in Havana and Miami, Veciana also had meetings with him in Dallas, Washington, Las Vegas, and Puerto Rico and in Caracas, Lima, and La Paz in South America." Veciana testified that over the years that he knew Bishop, he had 'at least five meetings with him in Dallas'.

"One of these Dallas meetings, which Veciana believed 'was in late August 1963', took place 'in the lobby of a large office building in the downtown section of the city. [. . .] When Veciana arrived for the meeting, Bishop was there talking with [a young man] . . [The young man] remained with Bishop and Veciana. only for a brief time as they walked toward a nearby coffee shop . . . [The young man] then departed, and Bishop and Veciana continued their meeting alone.

"Veciana testified that he recognized the young man with Bishop as Lee Harvey Oswald after seeing photographs of him following the Kennedy assassination. There was absolutely no doubt in his mind that the man was Oswald, not just someone who resembled him. Veciana pointed out that he had been trained to remember the physical characteristics of people and that if it was not Oswald it was his 'exact' double."

[It is to be noted that notwithstanding the continued "classified" status of relevant material on many aspects of Oswald and other aspects of the JFK Assassination despite the passage of 50 years, bits and pieces of perhaps very meaningful information does get out to the public from time to time through the efforts of persistent people pursuing vehicles such as the Freedom of Information Act. Although such items are not utilized in this book since they are not part of the official documentation of official investigations, it might prove helpful to the reader to know that such material is available. An example of what is slowly becoming available to the public is an item recently disclosed as to a man named George Joannides. It appears that Joannides was the CIA officer who held the role of Chief of Psychological Warfare Operations at the agency's huge Miami station. In such role, Joannides was delivering $51,000 a month to the Cuban Student Directorate, an anti-Castro organization whose members publicized Oswald' pro-Castro activities both before and after JFK was killed. Within hours of JFK's assassination, this CIA sponsored organization was the first to publicly identify and publicly hype Oswald as a Castro supporter. It is rather curious that prior to the assassination the CIA Miami station and this anti-Castro Cuban organization would be publicly proclaiming the pro-Castro credentials of Lee Harvey Oswald, *considering that his actual pro-Castro credentials were self created and totally mythical. The hyping after the assassination would seem to complete that circle. However, there was more. In 1978 as the CIA liaison to the House Select Committee on Assassinations (HSCA), Joannides prevented the HSCA from peeking behind the Oswald pro-Castro façade by concealing the CIA's financial support for this group that had been the first to brand Oswald as a pro-Castro activist. This intentional obstruction of the investigation has since been described as "criminal" by G. Robert Blakey, who served as Chief Counsel to the HSCA.]*

In late September 1963, three men appeared at the Dallas home of Silvia Odio, a member of the Cuban Revolutionary Junta, or JURE, [*an anti-Castro organization*] to ask for help in preparing a fundraising letter for JURE. The House Committee tells us Mrs. Odio stated that "two of the men appeared to be Cubans, although they also had characteristics she associated with Mexicans. The two individuals, she remembered, indicated that their 'war' names were 'Leopoldo' and 'Angelo.' The third man, an American, was introduced to her as 'Leon Oswald,' and she was told that he was very much interested in the anti-Castro Cuban cause.

"Mrs. Odio stated that the men told her that they had just come from New Orleans and that they were about to leave on a trip. The next day, one of the Cubans called her on the telephone and told her that it had been his idea to introduce the American into the underground 'because he is great, he is kind of nuts.' The Cuban also said that the American had been in the Marine Corps and was an excellent shot, and that the American had said that Cubans 'don't have any guts because President Kennedy should have been assassinated after the Bay of Pigs, and some Cubans should have done that, because he was the one that was holding the freedom of Cuba actually.' Mrs. Odio claimed the American was Lee Harvey Oswald.

"Mrs. Odio's sister, who was in the apartment at the time of the visit by the three men and who stated that she saw them briefly in the hallway when answering the door, also believed that the American was Lee Harvey Oswald."

The Warren Commission had concluded that Mrs. Odio was mistaken. They did so, not on the basis that she and her sister were not believable, but because they concluded that other evidence made it impossible for Oswald to have been in Dallas when she said this occurred.

Essentially, they concluded that the event had to have happened on either the 26th or 27th of September: if on the 26th, they asserted they had firm evidence that Oswald was on a bus from Houston to Mexico City; and if on the 27th, Oswald could not have traveled from Dallas and reached Mexico City when they knew he did, unless he had private transportation.

The fact is, as the House Select Committee quoted J. Wesley Liebeler, the Warren Commission assistant counsel, "There really is no evidence at all that Oswald left Houston on that bus."

The House Select Committee stated it "was inclined to believe Silvia Odio. From the evidence provided in the sworn testimony of the witnesses, it appeared that three men did visit her apartment in Dallas prior to the Kennedy assassination and identified themselves as members of an anti-Castro organization. Based on a judgment of the credibility of Silvia and Annie Odio, one of these men at least looked like Lee Harvey Oswald and was introduced to Mrs. Odio as Leon Oswald."

That last sentence is really the important finding, because from at least one aspect of our inquiry, it doesn't matter if Oswald was there or not. Once a determination is made that the Odios are truthful when they say that the man looked like and was introduced as Oswald, the implications become, if anything, more staggering if he was not there: that would mean that less than eight weeks before the assassination, these two men showcased an imposter who looked like and was passed off as Oswald – and the next day one of them called to tell Mrs. Odio that this "Oswald" was an ex-Marine who was an excellent shot and who had talked about killing Kennedy.

In mid September 1963, Lee Harvey Oswald applied for and received a Mexican tourist card. The tourist card immediately preceding his in numerical sequence was issued to William G. Gaudet, a newspaper editor. Two days later, Gaudet departed on a 3 - or 4-week trip to Mexico and other Latin American countries. This happened to coincide with Oswald's visit to Mexico City between 27 September and 3 October 1963. Gaudet, who had once been employed by the CIA, had continued thereafter to serve "as a source of information obtained during his trips abroad" and, in addition, "he occasionally performed errands for the Agency." The Agency's records purport that their contacts with Gaudet ended in 1961, but he testified that they continued through at least 1969, and were never formally terminated. "Gaudet said he could not recall whether his trip to Mexico and other Latin American countries in 1963 involved any intelligence-related activity. He was able to testify, however, that during that trip he did not encounter Oswald, whom he had previously observed on occasion at the New Orleans Trade Mart. . .

Gaudet testified that he had never met Oswald, although he had known of him prior to the assassination because Oswald had distributed literature near his office. 'Gaudet also stated that on one occasion he observed Oswald speaking to Guy Banister on a street corner.'

"While in Mexico City, Oswald visited both the Cuban and Soviet Embassies, representing that he intended to travel to the Soviet Union, and requesting an 'in-transit' Cuban visa to permit him to enter Cuba on September 30 on the way to the Soviet Union.

The evidence is, however, that what he was attempting – or wanted to appear to be attempting – was to use the in-transit visa to get into Cuba legitimately.

When Oswald left Mexico City, he went to Dallas, where he arrived on October 3. On November 9 he sent a letter to the Soviet Embassy in Washington to 'inform [them] of recent events since my meetings with Comrade Kostin in the Embassy of the Soviet Union, Mexico City, Mexico'.

The 'recent events' amounted to a declaration that the FBI was trying to inhibit his activities: "The Federal Bureau of Investigation is not now interested in my activities in the progressive organization 'Fair Play for Cuba Committee' of which I was secretary in New Orleans (state Louisiana) since I no longer reside in that state. However, the FBI has visited us here in Dallas, Texas, on November 1st. Agent James P. Hasty [sic] warned me that if I engaged in FPCC activities in Texas the FBI will again take an 'interest' in me."

The fact is that if Oswald's Mexico trip was on the level, the FBI most certainly should have been aggressively checking up on him. Under the relevant FBI manual provisions then in effect, any contact such as Oswald's with the Soviet Embassy in Mexico City required that immediate investigative action at the appropriate field office be undertaken.

Yet, despite the fact that both the Dallas and New Orleans field offices were aware that Oswald had been in contact with the Soviet Embassy in Mexico City, there is no evidence that either of these field offices intensified their "efforts" to locate and interview Oswald. Most surprisingly, however, is that the "Soviet experts" at FBI headquarters did not intensify their efforts in the Oswald case after being informed that Oswald had met with Vice Consul Kostikov at the Soviet Embassy in Mexico City. Not only were these experts familiar with Soviet activities in general, but they knew that Kostikov was a member of the KGB. Further, the Bureau's Soviet experts had reason to believe he was an agent within the KGB's Department which carries out assassination and sabotage. They were also aware that American citizen contacts with the Soviet Embassy in Mexico City were extremely rare.

CHAPTER 28

"HE IS GOING TO GET HIT"

* * *

September, 1962:

"Trafficante, 'trying to make Aleman realize that he was not saying Kennedy would be defeated in the 1964 election, rather that he would not make it to the election' said, - 'You don't understand me. Kennedy's not going to make it to the election. He is going to get hit.'"

November, 1962:

"Marcello had begun to plan a move. He had ...already thought of using a 'nut' to do the job."

November 3, 1963

Somersett: Well, how in hell do you figure would be the best way to get him?

Milteer: From an office building with a high-powered rifle.

Somersett: They are really going to try to kill him?

Milteer: Oh yeah, it is in the working.

House Select Committee

Milteer: They will pick up someone within hours afterward just to throw the public off"

Senate Select Committee (documents)

The House Select Committee provides us with the following information: On September 11, 1962 at Churchill Farms, his 3,000-acre swampland plantation outside New Orleans, Carlos Marcello and three associates were discussing "the pressure law enforcement agencies were bringing to bear on the Mafia brotherhood as a result of the Kennedy administration." One of those present was Edward Becker, a man with ties to Joseph Sica, the Mafia leader of Los Angeles, and a close friend of Carl Roppolo, reputedly Carlos Marcello's favorite nephew.

In 1969 Ed Reid, a writer on organized crime and a former editor of the *Las Vegas Sun*, published *The Grim Reapers*, which contained what Becker had told him regarding something which had occurred at that Churchill Farms meeting. Becker authenticated so much of Reid's rendition as appears below when he testified before the House Select Committee, from whose work the following excerpts are taken:

"It was then that Carlos' voice lost its softness, and his words were bitten off and spit out when mention was made of US Attorney General Robert Kennedy, who was still on the trail of Marcello:

"'Livarsi na petra di la scarpa!' Carlos shrilled the Mafia cry of revenge: 'take the stone out of my shoe!'

"'Don't worry about that little Bobby son of a bitch,' he shouted. 'He's going to be taken care of!'

"Ever since Robert Kennedy had arranged for his deportation to Guatemala, Carlos had wanted revenge. But as the subsequent conversation . . . showed, he knew that to rid himself of Robert Kennedy he would first have to remove the President. Any killer of the Attorney General would be hunted down by his brother; the death of the President would seal the fate of his Attorney General.

"No one at the meeting had any doubt about Marcello's intentions when he abruptly arose from the table. Marcello did not joke about such things. In any case, the matter had gone beyond mere 'business;' it had become an affair of honor, a Sicilian vendetta. Moreover, the conversation at Churchill Farms also made clear that Marcello had begun to plan a move. He had, for example, already thought of using a 'nut' to do the job.

"Roughly 1 year later President Kennedy was shot in Dallas – 2 months after Attorney General Robert Kennedy had announced to the McClellan Committee that he was going to expand his war on organized crime. And it is perhaps significant that privately, Robert Kennedy had singled out James Hoffa, Sam Giancana, and Carlos Marcello as being among his chief targets."

Becker told the House Committee that "Marcello was very angry and had clearly stated that he was going to arrange to have

President Kennedy murdered in some way;" and that Marcello's statement had been made in a serious tone and sounded as if he had discussed it previously to some extent. Becker commented that Marcello had made some kind of a reference to President Kennedy being a dog and Attorney General Robert Kennedy the dog's tail, and had said, "The dog will keep biting you if you only cut off its tail", but that if the dog's head were cut off, the dog would die.

"Becker stated that Marcello also made some kind of reference to the way in which he allegedly wanted to arrange the President's murder.

"Marcello 'clearly indicated' that his own lieutenants must not be identified as the assassins, and that there would thus be a necessity to have them use or manipulate someone else to carry out the actual crime."

The House Committee specifically noted that "as a consequence of his underworld involvement." Edward Becker "had a questionable reputation for honesty and may not be a credible source of information."

On the other hand, the House Committee commented that Jose Aleman, who testified to a similar event involving Santos Trafficante, "appeared to be a reputable person who did not seek to publicize his allegations, and he was well aware of the potential danger of making such allegations against a leader of La Costa Nostra."

Trafficante, it will be remembered, had such good business ties to the anti-Castro Cuban exile community that the CIA had used him as their contact man for their Castro assassination plots.

Jose Aleman was described by the Committee as "a prominent Cuban exile."

Aleman told the House Committee's investigators that in September 1962, Santos Trafficante met with him relative to financial difficulties Aleman was then experiencing. A relative of Aleman's had helped someone get out of a Cuban jail, and Trafficante in return was offering to arrange a loan from the Teamsters for Aleman. In the course of this meeting, Trafficante was "talking of the many problems in the country and of Kennedy's role in causing problems generally and in particular causing problems for certain individuals." Speaking to a Cuban exile in late 1962, Trafficante may have had good reason to believe that it was sympathetic ears which heard him assert that "a lot of people weren't going to forget the problems Kennedy had caused them, including Hoffa."

Trafficante brought up Jimmy Hoffa's name and said Hoffa would never forgive the Kennedys for what they did to him.

When Trafficante began to talk in specifics, Aleman at first thought Trafficante was talking about knocking Kennedy off in the next election. So Trafficante, "trying to make Aleman realize that he was not saying Kennedy would be defeated in the 1964 election, rather that he would not make it to the election, said: '. . . You don't understand me. Kennedy's not going to make it to the election. He is going to get hit.'"

"Aleman stated that during the course of the discussion, Trafficante had made clear to him that he was not guessing that the President was going to be killed. Rather he did in fact know that such a crime was being planned . . . [and] . . . Trafficante had given him the distinct impression that Hoffa was to be principally involved in the elimination of Kennedy."

The House Committee relates that, "On November 9, 1963 an informant for the Miami police, William Somersett, secretly recorded a conversation with a right-wing extremist named Joseph A. Milteer, who suggested there was a plot in existence to assassinate the President with a high-powered rifle from a tall building. Miami Police intelligence officers met with Secret Service agents on November 12 and provided a transcript of the Somersett recording. It read in part:

"*Somersett*: I think Kennedy is coming here November 18 to make some kind of speech. I don't know what it is, but I imagine it will be on TV.

Milteer: You can bet your bottom dollar he is going to have a lot to say about the Cubans; there are so many of them here.

Somersett: Well, he'll have a thousand bodyguards, don't worry about that.

Milteer: The more bodyguards he has, the easier it is to get him.

Somersett: Well, how in hell do you figure would be the best way to get him?

Milteer: From an office building with a high-powered rifle.

Somersett: They are really going to try to kill him?

Milteer: Oh yeah, it is in the working.

Somersett: Hitting this Kennedy is going to be a hard proposition. I believe you may have figured out a way to get him, the office building and all that. I don't know how them Secret Service agents cover all them office buildings everywhere he is going. Do you know whether they do that or not?

Milteer: Well, if they have any suspicion, they do that, of course. But without suspicion, chances are they wouldn't."

"During the meeting at which the Miami Police Department provided this transcript to the Secret Service, it also advised the Secret Service that Milteer had been involved with persons who professed a dislike for President Kennedy and were suspected of having committed violent acts, including the bombing of a Birmingham, Alabama, church in which four young girls had been killed. They also reported that Milteer was connected with several radical right-wing organizations and traveled extensively throughout the United States in support of their views."

"[T]he information gathered "was furnished [to] the agents making the advance arrangements before the visit of the

President" [to Miami on November 18, 1963]. PRS [Protective Research Section] then closed the case, and copies of its report were sent to the Chief of Secret Service and to field offices in Atlanta, Philadelphia, Indianapolis, Nashville, Washington, and Miami.

"The Milteer threat was ignored by Secret Service personnel in planning the trip to Dallas. PRS Special Agent-in-Charge Bouck, who was notified on November 8 that the President would visit Miami on November 18, told the Committee that relevant PRS information would have been supplied to the agents conducting advance preparations for the scheduled trip to Miami, but no effort was made to relay it to Special Agent Winston G. Lawson, who was responsible for the trip to Dallas, or to Forrest Sorrels, Special Agent-in-Charge of the Dallas office. Nor were Sorrels or any Secret Service agent responsible for intelligence with respect to the Dallas trip informed of the Milteer threat before November 22, 1963."

In the documents of the Senate Select Committee is the information that Milteer in this conversation had further stated that "They will pick up someone within hours afterward just to throw the public off."

[It should be noted that in addition to the above material pointing to plans to assassinate the President in a motorcade in Miami, there are references to a cancelled motorcade in Chicago though the evidence is less than clear that the cancellation was in response to what appears to have been a warning of the threatened attempt. It is also important to keep in mind that Dallas was not the first time anyone would have been aware of the opportunity to shoot Kennedy in the manner done in Dallas. Despite warnings of the danger it presented, JFK was front page news photographed in the same open roofed limousine in numerous cities including Berlin, Naples, Cork, San Diego and Tampa, to mention some of them.]

As part of its examination of the evidence, the House Committee discussed the following fascinating episode. On November 20, 1963, "a woman known as Rose Cheramie, a heroin addict and prostitute with a long history of arrests, was found . . . lying on the road near Eunice, Louisiana, bruised and disoriented. Cheramie was taken to a private hospital in Eunice." The police were called.

Francis Fruge, a lieutenant with the Louisiana State Police, responded. Though the woman needed no further medical care, she appeared to be under the influence of drugs, so Fruge took her to the jail and put her in a cell to sober up. However, as the woman began to display severe symptoms of withdrawal, Fruge called a doctor, who sedated the woman, and Fruge proceeded to transport her to the State hospital in Jackson, Louisiana.

During the trip to Jackson, Fruge asked Cheramie some routine questions. Fruge told the Committee, "She related to me that she was coming from Florida to Dallas with two men who were Italians or resembled Italians. They had stopped at this lounge . . . and they'd had a few drinks and had gotten into an argument or something. The manager of the lounge threw her out and she got on the road and hitchhiked to catch a ride, and this is when she got hit by a vehicle." Fruge said the lounge was a house of prostitution called the Silver Slipper.

"Fruge asked Cheramie what she was going to do in Dallas: 'She said she was going to, number one, pick up some money, pick up her baby, and to kill Kennedy.'

"Fruge claimed during these intervals that Cheramie related the story she appeared to be quite lucid.' He had her admitted to the hospital late on November 20.

"While in the hospital – and before the assassination - Cheramie reportedly told a Dr. Bowers 'that President Kennedy was going to be killed'; and after the assassination she reportedly told a Dr. Weiss that 'she had worked for Jack Ruby', and that while 'she did not have any specific details of a particular assassination plot against Kennedy . . . the "word in the underworld" was that Kennedy would be assassinated."

"On November 22, when he heard the President had been assassinated, Fruge said he immediately called the hospital and told them not to release Cheramie until he had spoken to her. The hospital administrators assented but said Fruge would have to wait until the following Monday before Cheramie would be well enough to speak to anyone. Fruge waited.

"Under questioning, Cheramie told Fruge that the two men traveling with her from Miami were going to Dallas to kill the President. For her part, Cheramie was to obtain $8,000 from an unidentified source in Dallas and proceed to Houston with the two men to complete a drug deal. Cheramie was also supposed to pick up her little boy from friends who had been looking after him.

"Cheramie further supplied detailed accounts off the arrangement for the drug transaction in Houston. She said reservations had been made at the Rice Hotel in Houston. The trio was to meet a seaman who was bringing in 8 kilos of heroin to Galveston by boat. Cheramie had the name of the seaman and the boat he was arriving on. Once the deal was completed, the trio would proceed to Mexico.

"Fruge . . . contacted the chief customs agent in Galveston who reportedly verified the scheduled docking of the boat and the name of the seaman. Fruge believed the customs agent was also able to verify the name of the man in Dallas who was holding Cheramie's son. Fruge recalled that the customs agent had tailed the seaman as he disembarked from the boat, but then lost the man's trail. Customs closed the case. [. . .]

"During a flight from Houston, according to Fruge, Cheramie noticed a newspaper with headlines indicating investigators had not been able to establish a relationship between Jack Ruby and Lee Harvey Oswald. Cheramie laughed at the headline, Fruge said. Cheramie told him she had worked for Ruby, or 'Pinky,' as she knew him, at his nightclub in Dallas and claimed Ruby and Oswald 'had been shacking up for years.' Fruge said he called Captain Will Fritz of the Dallas Police Department with this information. Fritz answered, he wasn't interested. Fritz and the Louisiana State Police dropped the investigation into the matter.

"Four years later, however . . . during the course of the New Orleans DA's investigation . . . Fruge attempted to corroborate the version she had given him [as to how she had ended up by the side of the road, and the number and identity of her companions]. Fruge spoke with the owner of the Silver Slipper Lounge. The bar owner, a Mr. Mac Manual . . . told Fruge that Cheramie had come in with two men who the owner knew as pimps engaged in the business of hauling prostitutes in from Florida. When Cheramie became intoxicated and rowdy, one of the men "slapped her around" and threw her outside.

"Fruge claims he showed the owner of the bar a 'stack' of photographs and mug shots to identify. According to Fruge, the bar-owner chose the photos of a Cuban exile, Sergio Arcacha Smith, and another Cuban Fruge believed to be named Osanto."

In 1961, Arcacha Smith had befriended David Ferrie and both were believed to have ties with Carlos Marcello. Arcacha Smith moved from the New Orleans area in 1962 to go to Miami and later to settle in Houston. The weekend following the assassination, Ferrie took a trip to Houston and *Galveston* for a little 'rest and relaxation.'"

The House Committee informs us that in Chicago, on November 21, 1963, Thomas Mosley, an FBI informant, had a conversation with "a Cuban exile, an outspoken critic of President Kennedy named Homer S. Echevarria." "Mosley 'for some time . . . had been involved in negotiating the sale of illegal arms" with Echevarria. On November 21, "Echevarria had said his group now had 'plenty of money' and that they were prepared to proceed with the purchases "as soon as we [or they] "take care of Kennedy."

". . . Echevarria was a member of the 30th of November (Cuban exile) Movement . . . an associate of his who had also spoken directly with Mosley about the arms sales was Juan Francisco Blanco-

Fernandez, military director for the Cuban Student Revolutionary Directorate (DRE), and that the arms purchases were being financed through Paulino Sierra Martinez, a Cuban exile who had become a Chicago lawyer. Mosley inferred from his conversation with Echevarria and Blanco that Sierra'a financial backers consisted in part of "hoodlum elements" who were "not restricted to Chicago."

"The Committee found that the 30th of November Movement was receiving financial backing through the Junta del Gobierno de Cuba en el Exilio (JGCE), a Chicago-based organization led by Sierra. JGCE was essentially a coalition of predominantly right-wing anti-Castro groups. It had been formed in April 1963 and abolished abruptly in January 1964. During its short life, JGCE apparently acquired enormous financial backing, secured at least in part from organized gambling interests in Las Vegas and Cleveland. JGCE actively used its funds to purchase large quantities of weapons and to support its member groups in conducting military raids on Cuba. The affiliates of JGCE, in addition to the 30th of November Movement, included Alpha 66, led by Antonio Veciana Blanch, and the MIRR, whose leader was the militant anti-Castro terrorist, Orlando Bosch Avila.

"Bosch was interviewed by the Committee in Cuartel San Carlos prison in Venezuela. He is charged with complicity in the October 6, 1975 bombing of a Cuban Airlines plane which resulted in the deaths of 73 people . . . Whether or not Bosch was the principal conspirator in the bombing of the Cuban airliner, it is known that his Cuban Power movement, which merged with other Cuban activists in 1976 to form a Cuban Secret Government, engaged in acts of terrorism. This latter group was linked with numerous recent bombing incidents, an assassination attempt against Henry Kissinger, the assassination of Orlando Letelier in Washington, DC, and the bombing of the Cuban Airlines plane."

CHAPTER 29

THE MOTORCADE

* * *

The question does arise as to why Warren Commission supporters are willing to work on the premise that three days was enough time for Lee Harvey Oswald to put together an assassination, but apparently they believe that three days would not be enough time for folks who have committed dozens if not hundreds of murders in their illustrious careers to do the same.

The Warren Commission stated the following as regards the motorcade: "Although publicity concerning the President's trip to Dallas appeared in Dallas newspapers as early as September 13 1963, the planning of the motorcade route was not started until after November 4 when the Secret Service was first notified of the trip. A final decision as to the route could not have been reached until November 14 when the Trade Mart was selected as the luncheon site. Although news reports on November 15 and November 16 might have led a person to believe that the motorcade would pass the Depository Building, the route was not finally selected until November 18, it was announced in the press on November 19 only 3 days before the President's arrival. Based on the circumstances of Oswald's employment and the planning of the motorcade route, the Commission has concluded that Oswald's employment in the Depository was wholly unrelated to the President's trip to Dallas."

Ever since, the conventional wisdom has been since that Oswald could not have known of the motorcade route onto Elm Street at the time he was hired at the Book Depository, it must follow that the only conclusion must be that there was no conspiracy. In other words, if there was not a plot at the time that Oswald was hired, then necessarily there could not have been a plot in accomplishing the assassination. But, giving full credence and acceptability to the Warren Commission rendition, the most it can be said to establish is the proposition that Oswald did not decide to kill Kennedy until he learned that by "happenstance" that he would be perfectly located to assassinate the President. It in no way proves that Oswald acted alone.

Let's analyze for a moment the premise that it was not until sometime on or after September 19 that anyone could know that the President would be on Elm Street and that Oswald would be in a window above Elm Street. How does that prove in and of itself that Oswald acted alone and with no co-conspirators? Well, if you start with the belief that Oswald acted alone, you might feel so – but all you would really be doing is saying that the conclusion you are electing for justifies the premise you started with.

Instead of starting with the conclusion that Oswald acted alone, suppose we analyze this in the context of the documented facts that a number of people were intent upon assassinating Kennedy, and indeed had discussed doing so with a rifle from a high office building. These people are also documented to believe in a methodology of utilizing someone who is the active culprit (or is fingered as such), and their "MO" is that this culprit will subsequently be killed to cut off any path back to themselves. In this alternative hypothesis, wouldn't such people would be in the same position as claimed for Oswald by the Warren Commission, namely, they could not have known the route until at least November 19.

If the type of people to whom we are referring were intent on killing Kennedy, would they decide not to do it simply because they did not know the route until November 19? Perhaps. But, the question does arise as to why Warren Commission supporters are willing to work on the premise that three days was enough time for Lee Harvey Oswald to put together an assassination, but apparently they believe that three days would not be enough time for folks who have committed dozens if not hundreds of murders in their illustrious careers to do the same.

Lifelong vicious killers are going to give up because they do not know the route until three days before the motorcade? How about what they know before November 19? They would have known for many weeks that the man they wish to kill is coming to Dallas. They would have known that there would likely be a motorcade. Might not such people make plans to try to accomplish their plan allowing for different possible routes? Might they want to line up alternative locations along the most likely routes from which they could accomplish this?

And, if in addition, one considers the documented modality of having such an act performed by some "nut" who would then himself be killed, the logical steps that would be taken would include figuring out how to get such a "nut" into the necessary position.

By what logic do we conclude that an Oswald -or any other potential assassin- would limit himself to the Texas School Book Depository as the only building in Dallas from which to kill John Kennedy?

If one gives an intellectually honest evaluation to the possibility that organized crime, or anti-Castro Cubans, or any combination of reasonably intelligent people set out to kill Kennedy in Dallas, does anyone believe they could not have accomplished this but for the presence of Oswald at the Book Depository? Is the Book Depository the only high building that would be along whatever happened to be the ultimate route of the motorcade? - Was Oswald the only available "nut" in Dallas at that time?

Granted that one possibility is that Oswald woke up on November 19 to learn that he was going to be in a window overlooking the President as he turned through Dealey Plaza. But, why is that possibility any more compelling than the possibility that someone who wanted to assassinate the President woke up on November 19 to learn that Kennedy would be on Elm Street and knew or shortly thereafter ascertained that a "nut" that they knew named Lee Harvey Oswald was employed overlooking Dealey Plaza?

The above discussion is premised on the presumption that the facts set forth by the Warren Commission are accurate and complete. As it turns out, their facts are incomplete and their conclusions were supported only by utilizing a selective set of facts that ignores the complete story as to the motorcade.

The House Committee provides us with the complete facts regarding the planning of the motorcade and the dates that are relevant to a complete understanding of these issues, from which the following is compiled and constructed:

"Governor John B . Connally of Texas indicated that the idea of a Presidential visit to Texas arose first in the Spring of 1962. Vice President Lyndon B .Johnson approached Connally with the information that the President wished to come to Texas for the purpose of fundraising. Connally was not interested at that time in attempting to coordinate such a trip for various reasons." "Connally believed that, for specific reasons, the President wished to come to Texas under Connally's auspices rather than under the auspices of Vice President Johnson or on his own. Since a Governor of a State is the titular head of his party and sets the political tone of his State, neither Kennedy or Johnson would have considered it politically advisable to visit a State without the political support of the Governor."

"The first important meeting between the President and the Governor took place in El Paso, Tex., in June 1963. Kennedy suggested August 27 as a possible date for the visit because that was the Vice President's birthday. The Governor objected since inclement Texas weather at that time of year resulted in the absence of many Texans from the State for vacations. Apart from the President's suggestion that four or five fundraising dinners be held in the major Texas cities, no final decision was reached regarding the date for the trip or the itinerary. Nevertheless, the decision to make the trip was considered final as of this time."

"The Sept. 26 issue of the Dallas Morning News printed an article stating that the President would visit major cities of the state on Nov. 21 and 22".

"In early October the President and Governor Connally met in the Oval Office. Connally told Kennedy that a Presidential visit consisting of four or five consecutive fundraising dinners would be considered by Texans as a financial rape of the State. On the basis of Connally's discussions of the matter with political leaders in the State, the Governor's recommended course of action was that the President meet with moderate and conservative business and political leaders who had not supported him in 1960 and that he attempt to convert them in nonpolitical settings. The President agreed. The specific dates of the trip had been resolved prior to this October meeting.."

"Two luncheon sites had initially been considered : the Women's Building at the fair grounds which was located in the central southern part of the city, and the Dallas Trade Mart, which was located on Stemmons Freeway to the west and north of Dealey Plaza."

"Governor Connally, who was asked by the President to arrange the trip as a means of broadening and strengthening his support among conservatives in Texas, selected the Dallas Trade Mart, a new and attractive convention hall on the Stemmons Freeway, for the luncheon site."

"In the end, President Kennedy's wishes prevailed, and there was a motorcade. Its route was a simple by-product of the decision to hold the luncheon at the Trade Mart."

"The decision to send the motorcade in an eastward or westward direction along Main Street was dependent upon the prior selection of a site for the President's luncheon speech."

The House Committee observed: "An interesting subsidiary issue regarding itinerary planning and motorcade route selection is whether Oswald, when he took the job at the Depository on Oct. 15, 1963, knew President Kennedy planned to visit Dallas and that his motorcade would pass through Dealey Plaza. It is, of course, possible that Oswald could have anticipated well before Oct. 16 that Dallas would be included in the Texas itinerary. The Sept . 26 issue of the Dallas Morning News printed an article stating that the President would visit major cities of the state on Nov. 21 and 22. And it could be inferred that the Presidential motorcade would pass through Dealey Plaza. This is because Dealey Plaza was part of the traditional parade route through Dallas. However, knowledge of an eastward versus westward direction would not have been possible before Oct. 16, since the route was not finalized until Nov.15."

The House Committee also made the following comments that are most relevant to our inquiry here:

"Some question remains concerning the conduct of [Special Agent in Charge] Sorrels and Lawson as to possible violation of the guideline compelling inspection of buildings when a motorcade route has been standard for years. Sorrels stated categorically to the Warren Commission that **Main Street** was the best choice for parades in that it went through the heart of the city**, flanked on either side by tall buildings** which maximized the opportunity for large numbers of people to see the parade. He added that this route was used for a Presidential motorcade in 1936, when President Roosevelt traversed Main Street from east to west, just as Kennedy's motorcade would have done had the Women's Building been selected. [emphasis added]

"If the Women's Building had been selected, the Presidential motorcade would have entered Dealey Plaza on Main Street west of Dealey Plaza and traveled eastward on Main Street, traversing the Plaza briefly, at high speed, without taking any turns in or around the Plaza. **Such a west-to-east route through Dealey Plaza on Main Street would have decreased the probability of the occurrence of**

the assassination for two reasons. First, the Presidential limousine would have presented a more difficult target at which to shoot because it would have been moving more quickly and would have been positioned one block farther away (to the south) from the assassins' locations than it was when the assassination occurred on Elm Street. *[emphasis added]*

Based upon the above, let us consider the following propositions:

1. Either route would have placed the President beneath tall buildings.

2. Apparently none of the tall buildings in Dallas had been inspected.

3. Had the route been west-to east, instead of east-to-west, nonetheless an attempt to shoot Kennedy from the Texas Book Depository could have been attempted.

4. It cannot be said that an attempt from the Book Depository had the route been west-to-east would have been unsuccessful, just that it was less likely to be successful

5. It cannot be said that an attempt from the Book Depository would not have been attempted in the case of either route; after all, even the Warren Commission apologists do not claim that Oswald would not have done what they said he did unless he knew in advance that he would be successful.

6. Unless one starts with the conclusion that Oswald acted alone and without any aid, assistance, persuasion, influence, there is no basis to assume that Oswald or some other nut could not have been placed in one of the other tall buildings, regardless of the route.

7. In fact, if Oswald was going to shoot Kennedy – whether self-motivated or otherwise – why would he limit himself to only the Book Depository? Are we to assume that if Oswald decided to kill the President and the route was west-to east, that he would not have found some other building from which to accomplish his goal?

8. If Oswald would not be so limited by building choice, why would we assume that vicious enemies of Kennedy with long track records for plotting murders would not have equal access to other buildings if they would better serve their means?

Thus, assuming that Oswald could not have known the route of the motorcade when he took the job at the Book Depository, how does that prove that Oswald acted alone?

Why is "happenstance" a legitimate basis supporting one side of that issue, but not an equally legitimate basis for supporting the other? This is possible only by what is called "circular reasoning", where one begins with what one is trying to end up with, and then points to that flawed process to claim "There, I just proved it."

CHAPTER 30

THE ASSASSIN'S ASSASSIN

* * *

"The pattern of contacts did show that individuals who had the motive to kill the President also had knowledge of a man who could be used to get access to Oswald in the custody of the Dallas police. In Ruby, they also had knowledge of a man who exhibited a violent nature and who was in serious financial trouble. The calls, in short, established knowledge and possible availability, if not actual planning."

House Select Committee

At 12:30 p.m., November 22, 1963, as the President's open limousine proceeded at approximately 11 m.p.h. along Elm Street through Dealey Plaza toward the Triple Underpass, shots fired from a rifle mortally wounded President Kennedy. At 1:22 p.m. a rifle was found in the Texas School Book Depository which subsequently was identified as being owned by Lee Harvey Oswald, but by that time Oswald was already in custody. In the interim, Oswald reportedly was involved in what has been described as his escape.

The Warren Report stated: "The possibility that accomplices aided Oswald in connection with his escape was suggested by the testimony of Earlene Roberts, the housekeeper at the 1026 North Beckley rooming house. She testified that at about 1 p.m. on November 22, after Oswald had returned to the rooming house, a Dallas police car drove slowly by the front of the 1026 North Beckley premises and stopped momentarily; she said she heard its horn several times."

Oswald hurriedly left the house, and a few seconds later, shortly after 1 p.m., she saw him standing at a bus stop in front of the house. However, that bus line did not go to where the scene of action now shifted.

About a mile away, at approximately 1:15 p.m., patrolman J. D. Tippit was driving east on 10th Street. About 100 feet past Patton Avenue he stopped his vehicle and spoke to Lee Harvey Oswald, who then approached the car and engaged in some conversation with Tippit. Tippit got out and started to walk around the front of the car. As Tippit reached the left front wheel, Oswald pulled out a revolver and shot Tippit dead. About a half-hour later, Oswald was arrested while sitting in a Texas Theater.

Two days later, as Oswald was being brought through the basement of the Dallas Police Station to be transferred to the county jail, Jack Ruby shot and killed Lee Harvey Oswald.

Ruby would later explain that he had killed Oswald to spare Jackie Kennedy from having to return for Oswald's trial.

Perhaps this mobster's soft-hearted concern for Jackie was the reason he killed Oswald.

However, the question arises as to the troubling possibility that Ruby's role was to shut Oswald's mouth (as we saw in the Joe Colombo assassination and the Victor Reisel blinding, discussed in Chapter 21).

If this second scenario is entertained, two of the questions which immediately follow are:

1- For whom was Ruby acting?

2- Was Ruby the only person who had been given the task of getting rid of Oswald?

The House Select Committee investigated and reported on a number of intriguing relationships of Jack Ruby. Since 14 October, the very same day on which Ruth Payne called Roy Truly at the Texas School Book Depository, Lee Harvey Oswald had been living at Earlene Roberts' home in the Oak Cliff section of Dallas, and maintaining a Post Office box at the terminal annex. Coincidentally enough, Jack Ruby also lived in the Oak Cliff section of Dallas and had a Post Office box at the terminal annex. A fellow boarder at

Oswald's rooming house, John Carter, was friendly with a close friend and employee of Ruby, Wanda Killam. Bertha Cheek, the sister of Oswald's landlady, visited Jack Ruby at his nightclub on November 18,1963.

Jack Ruby's closest friend, was Ralph Paul. Ruby was constantly indebted to Paul for loans to operate his nightclubs, and Paul actually held a half interest in the Carousel until early 1964.

Ruby became friendly with a good friend of Paul's, Austin Cook, a member of the ultra-conservative John Birch Society, and the owner of Austin's Barbeque. For about three years prior to the assassination, Cook had been employing a moonlighting Dallas policeman as a security guard at Austin's Barbeque. The policeman's name was J. D. Tippit.

If the evidence suggests that Oswald was intended to be wiped out, does it become necessary to re-examine the presumed chance encounter of Tippit and Oswald?

As noted earlier, there is evidence that in the summer of 1963, Jack Ruby had placed a call to Chicago to Lenny Patrick, who was said to be "one of the Chicago Mafia's leading assassins, responsible, according to Federal and State law enforcement files, for the murders of over a dozen mob victims." Patrick was not the only unsavory character to whom Ruby spoke. The House Committee undertook an extensive study of Ruby's telephone activity, from which the following excerpts are taken.

"A chronological consolidation of the telephone calls made by [Jack] Ruby from the five separate business and home telephones he used uncovered a significant increase in the number of calls made in October and November 1963. The average number leapt from around 25 to 35 in the months of May through September to approximately 75 in October and approximately 96 during the first 3 -1/2 weeks of November.

"An extensive computer analysis of his telephone toll records for the month prior to the President's assassination revealed that he either placed calls to or received calls from a number of individuals who may be fairly characterized as having been affiliated, directly or indirectly, with organized crime. These included Irwin Weiner, a Chicago bondsman well-known as a front-man for organized crime and the Teamsters Union; Robert "Barney" Barker, a lieutenant of James R. Hoffa and associate of several convicted organized crime executioners; Nofio J. Percora, a lieutenant of Carlos Marcello, the Mafia boss in Louisiana; Harold Tannenbaum, a New Orleans French Quarter nightclub manager who lived in a trailer park owned by Pecora; McWillie, the Havana gambler; and Murray "Dusty" Miller, a Teamster deputy of Hoffa and associate of various underworld figures.

"Between June and August of 1963, Jack Ruby placed seven long distance calls to Lewis J. McWillie . . . In 1959, Ruby had visited Lewis McWillie in Havana, where McWillie was working in an organized crime-controlled casino. Jack Ruby's phone calls to McWillie occurred on June 27, September 2 (two calls), September 4, September 19, September 20 and September 22. The first two calls were placed to McWillie's home number, the remaining five calls were to McWillie's place of business, the Thunderbird Casino in Las Vegas.

"On the afternoon of October 26, 1963, Jack Ruby placed a long distance phone call to Irwin S. Weiner in Chicago, with whom he spoke for 12 minutes. Weiner was and is a prominent bondsman in Chicago, who has been closely linked with such figures as James Hoffa, Santos Trafficante, Sam Giancana, Paul and Allen Dorfman. Weiner, according to Federal and State law enforcement files, is alleged to have served as a key functionary in the longtime relationship between the Chicago Mafia and various corrupt union officials, particularly during Hoffa's reign as President of the Teamsters Union. Additionally, Weiner has been involved in a business relationship with two men long identified as executioners for the Chicago Mafia – Felix "Phil" Alderisio and Albert "Obie" Frabotta.

"At 9:13 p.m., October 30, 1963, 4 days after his call to Irwin Weiner, Jack Ruby placed a call to the Tropical Court Tourist Park, a trailer park in New Orleans. The number Ruby called, 242-5431, was listed as the business office of the Tropical Court, and the duration of the call was one minute. In a partial compilation of numbers called by long distance by Ruby, transmitted to the Warren Commission by the FBI in early 1964, a notation was made indicating that this Ruby call to the Tropical Court went to N. J. Pecora.

"Nofio J. Pecora, alias Joseph O. Pecoraro, was the owner of the Tropical Court Tourist Park. He ran the park from a one-man office located on the premises, the office Ruby had called on October 30. Pecora, a former heroin smuggler, was alleged to be a close associate of Carlos Marcello. The FBI, Justice Department and Metropolitan Crime Commission of New Orleans have identified Pecora as one of Marcello's three most trusted aides. Law enforcement surveillance reports have indicated a particularly close Marcello-Pecora relationship during the early 1960s, with Pecora always close at hand at Marcello's Town and Country Motel headquarters on the outskirts of New Orleans.

"On November 7, 1963 Ruby received a collect call from Robert G. (Barney) Baker of Chicago. The call lasted 17 minutes. Baker is said to have been a top lieutenant and reputed "enforcer" for Teamster President James Hoffa. A former boxer and ex-convict, Baker was perhaps Hoffa's best known assistant during the McClellan Committee investigation of labor racketeering in the late 1950s. The Senate investigation, coordinated by then chief counsel Robert F. Kennedy, had detailed Baker's role as Hoffa's personal liaison to various leading Mafia figures. In his McClellan testimony, Baker recited a long list of Mafia hit men with whom he had been associated. In 1960, Robert F. Kennedy wrote of Baker, 'Sometimes the mere threat of his presence in a room was enough to silence men who would otherwise have opposed Hoffa's reign.'"

"On November 8, 1963, the day after he received the call from Barney Baker, Ruby placed a call to Murray W. (Dusty) Miller at the

Eden Roc Hotel in Miami. The call lasted four minutes. Dusty Miller was another key lieutenant of Teamster President James Hoffa, and as head of the powerful southern conference of the union, he was regarded as a possible successor to Hoffa. Miller, who had been a Teamster leader in Dallas, was associated with numerous underworld figures.

"At 5:22 p.m., November 8, 1963, 31 minutes after he called Dusty Miller, Jack Ruby placed a call to Barney Baker in Chicago. This call lasted 14 minutes.

"The Committee found that the evidence surrounding the calls was generally consistent – at least as to the times of their occurrence – with the explanation that they were for the purpose of seeking assistance in a labor dispute. Ruby, as the operator of two nightclubs, the Carousel and the Vegas, had to deal with the American Guild of Variety Artists (AGVA), an entertainers' union. Ruby did in fact have a history of labor problems involving his striptease performers, and there was an ongoing dispute in the early 1960s regarding amateur performers in Dallas area nightclubs. Testimony to the Committee supported the conclusion that Ruby's phone calls were, by and large, related to his labor troubles. In light of the identity of some of the individuals, however, the possibility of other matters being discussed could not be dismissed.

"In particular, the Committee, was not satisfied with the explanations of three individuals closely associated with organized crime who received telephone calls from Ruby in October or November 1963.

"Weiner, the Chicago bondsman, refused to discuss his call from Ruby on October 26, 1963 with the FBI in 1964, and he told a reporter in 1976 that the call had nothing to do with labor problems. In his executive session testimony before the Committee, however, Weiner stated that he had lied to the reporter, and he claimed that he and Ruby had, in fact, discussed a labor dispute. The Committee was not satisfied with Weiner's explanation of his relationship with

Ruby. Weiner suggested Ruby was seeking a bond necessary to obtain an injunction in his labor troubles, yet the Committee could find no other creditable indication that Ruby contemplated seeking court relief, nor any other explanation for his having to go to Chicago for such a bond.

"Barney Baker told the FBI in 1964 that he had received only one telephone call from Ruby (on November 7, 1963) during which he had curtly dismissed Ruby's plea for assistance in a nightclub labor dispute. The Committee established, however, that Baker received a second lengthy call from Ruby on November 8. The Committee found it hard to believe that Baker, who denied the conversation ever took place, could have forgotten it.

"The Committee was also dissatisfied with the explanation of a call Ruby made on October 30, 1963, to the New Orleans trailer park office of Nofio J. Pecora, the long-time Marcello lieutenant. Pecora told the Committee that only he would have answered his phone and that he never spoke with Ruby or took a message from him. The Committee considered the possibility that the call was actually for Harold Tannenbaum, a mutual friend of Ruby and Pecora who lived in this trailer park, although Pecora denied he would have relayed such a message.

"Additionally, the Committee found it difficult to dismiss certain Ruby associations with the explanation that they were solely related to his labor problems. For example, James Henry Dolan, a Dallas AGVA representative, was reportedly an acquaintance of both Carlos Marcello and Santos Trafficante. While Dolan worked with Ruby on labor matters, they were also allegedly associated in other dealings, including a strong-arm attempt to appropriate the proceeds of a one-night performance of a stage review at the Adolphus Hotel in Dallas called *Bottoms Up.* The FBI, moreover, has identified Dolan as an associate of Nofio Pecora. The Committee noted further that reported links between AGVA and organized crime figures have been the subject of Federal and State investigations that have been underway for years. The Committee's difficulties in separating Ruby's AGVA contacts from his organized crime connections was, in large degree, based on the dual roles that many of his associates played.

"According to FBI records, AGVA has been used frequently by members of organized crime as a front for criminal activities.

"In assessing the significance of these Ruby contacts, the Committee noted, first of all, that they should have been more thoroughly explored in 1964 when memories were clearer and related records (including, but not limited to, additional telephone toll records) were available.

"Further, while there may be persuasive arguments against the likelihood that the attack on Oswald would have been planned in advance on the telephone with an individual like Ruby, the pattern of contacts did show that individuals who had the motive to kill the President also had knowledge of a man who could be used to get access to Oswald in the custody of the Dallas police.

"In Ruby, they also had knowledge of a man who exhibited a violent nature and who was in serious financial trouble. The calls, in short, established knowledge and possible availability, if not actual planning."

The House Committee reported that it had "also investigated the relationship between Ruby and the Dallas Police Department to determine whether members of the department might have helped Ruby get access to Oswald for the purpose of shooting him. Ruby had a friendly and somewhat unusual relationship with the Dallas Police Department, both collectively and with individual officers, but the Committee found little evidence of any significant influence by Ruby within the force that permitted him to engage in illicit activities. Nevertheless, Ruby's close relationship with one or more members of the police force may have been a factor in his entry to the police basement on November 24, 1963.

"Both the Warren Commission and a Dallas Police Department investigative unit concluded that Ruby entered the police basement on November 24, 1963, between 11:17 a.m. when he apparently sent a telegram, and 11:21, when he shot Oswald, via the building's Main Street ramp as a police vehicle was exiting, thereby fortuitously creating a momentary distraction. The Committee, however, found that Ruby probably did not come down the ramp, and that his most likely route was an alleyway located next to the Dallas Municipal Building and a stairway leading to the basement garage of police headquarters.

"The conclusion reached by the Warren Commission that Ruby entered the police basement via the ramp was refuted by the eyewitness testimony of every witness in the relevant area, only Ruby himself excepted. It was also difficult for the Committee to reconcile the ramp route with the 55-second interval (derived from viewings of the video tapes of the Oswald murder) from the moment the police vehicle started up the ramp and the moment Ruby shot Oswald. Ruby would have had to come down the ramp after the vehicle went up, leaving him less than 55 seconds to get down the ramp and kill Oswald. Even though the Warren Commission and the Dallas police investigative unit were aware of substantial testimony contradicting the ramp theory, they arrived at their respective conclusions by relying heavily on Ruby's own assertion and what they perceived to be the absence of a plausible alternative route.

"The Committee's conclusion that Ruby entered from the alley was supported by the fact that it was much less conspicuous than the alternatives, by the lack of security in the garage area and along the entire route, and by the testimony concerning the security of the doors along the alley and stairway route. This route would also have accommodated the 4-minute interval from Ruby's departure from a Western Union office near police headquarters at 11:17 a.m. to the moment of the shooting at 11:21."

The House Committee declared that, "Based on a review of the evidence, albeit circumstantial, the Committee believed that Ruby's shooting of Oswald was not a spontaneous act, in that it involved at least some premeditation. Similarly, the Committee believed that it was less likely that Ruby entered the police basement without assistance, even though the assistance may have been provided with no knowledge of Ruby's intentions. The assistance may have been in the form of information about plans for Oswald's transfer or aid in entering the building or both.

"The Committee found several circumstances significant in its evaluation of Ruby's conduct. It considered in particular the selectively recalled and self-serving statements in Ruby's narration of the events of the entire November 22-24 weekend in arriving at its conclusions. It also considered certain conditions and events.

"The Committee was troubled by the apparently unlocked doors along the stairway route and the removal of security guards from the area of the garage nearest the stairway shortly before the shooting; by a Saturday night telephone call from Ruby to his closest friend, Ralph Paul, in which Paul responded to something Ruby said by asking him if he was crazy; and by the actions and statements of several Dallas police officers, particularly those present when Ruby was initially interrogated about the shooting of Oswald.

"There is also evidence that the Dallas Police Department withheld relevant information from the Warren Commission concerning Ruby's entry to the scene of the Oswald transfer. For example, the fact that a polygraph test had been given to Sergeant Patrick Dean in 1964 was never revealed to the Commission, even though Dean was responsible for basement security and was the first person to whom Ruby explained how he had entered the basement. Dean indicated to the Committee that he had "failed" the test, but the Committee was unable to locate a copy of the actual questions, responses and results.

"The Committee noted that other Ruby activities and movements during the period immediately following the assassination – on November 22 and 23 – raised disturbing questions. For example, Ruby's first encounter with Oswald occurred over 36 hours before he shot him. Ruby was standing within a few feet of Oswald as he was being moved from one part of police headquarters to another just before midnight on November 22. Ruby testified that he had no trouble entering the building, and the Committee found no evidence contradicting his story. The Committee was disturbed, however, by Ruby's easy access to headquarters and by his inconsistent accounts of his carrying a pistol. In an FBI interview on December 25, 1963, he said he had the pistol during the encounter with Oswald later in the evening of November 22. But when questioned about it by the Warren Commission, Ruby replied, "I will be honest with you. I lied about it. It isn't so. I didn't have a gun."

"Finally, the Committee was troubled by reported sightings of Ruby on Saturday, November 23, at Dallas police headquarters and at the county jail at a time when Oswald's transfer to the county facility had originally been scheduled. These sightings, along with one on Friday night, could indicate that Ruby was pursuing Oswald's movements throughout the weekend.

The Committee also questioned Ruby's self-professed motive for killing Oswald, his story to the Warren Commission and other authorities that he did it out of sorrow over the assassination and sympathy for the President's widow and children. Ruby consistently claimed that there had been no other motive and that no one had influenced his act.

"A handwritten note by Ruby, disclosed in 1967, however, exposed Ruby's explanation for the Oswald slaying as a fabricated legal ploy. Addressed to his attorney, Joseph Tonahill, it told of advice Ruby had received from his first lawyer, Tom Howard, in 1963:

'Joe, you should know this. Tom Howard told me to say that I shot Oswald so Caroline and Mrs. Kennedy wouldn't have to come to Dallas to testify. OK?'"

"The Committee examined a report that Ruby was at Parkland Hospital shortly after the fatally wounded President had been brought there on November 22, 1963. Seth Kantor, a newsman then employed by Scripps-Howard who had known Ruby, later testified to the Warren Commission that he had run into him at Parkland and spoken with him shortly before the President's death was announced. While the Warren Commission concluded that Kantor was mistaken, the Committee was impressed by the opinion of Burt W. Griffin, the Warren Commission counsel who directed the Ruby investigation and wrote the Ruby section of the Warren report. Griffin told the Committee he had come to believe, in light of evidence subsequently brought out, that the Commission's conclusion about Kantor's testimony was wrong."

Subsequent to Ruby's apprehension, he was given a polygraph examination. There is general agreement by everyone who has reviewed the test (Warren Commission, FBI, House Committee) that it was unsatisfactorily administered. However, while unable to interpret the test as an overall piece, the panel retained by the House Committee did observe – contrary to what had been concluded in 1964 – that, because it produced the largest valid GSR reaction together with a constant suppression, Ruby was possibly lying when he answered 'No' to the question 'Did you assist Oswald in the assassination?'

The Committee noted several other areas of telephone contact or relationship of probative interest. Of note is the fact that they are not likely to be explainable on the basis of Ruby's labor problems.

"The Committee found that Barney Baker had placed a telephone call to another onetime associate of Jack Ruby on the evening of November 21, 1963. The person Baker called was David Yaras of Miami. Yaras was a close friend and partner of Lenny Patrick. He had also been acquainted with Ruby during their early years in Chicago. Like Lenny Patrick, Dave Yaras has served, it is alleged, as a key lieutenant of Chicago Mafia leader Sam Giancana, reputedly as an executioner.'

The Committee also found that shortly before midnight on November 21, 1963 Jack Ruby had drinks at the Cabana Motel with Jean Aase West, and a mutual friend, Lawrence Meyers. The Committee further found that, while in Chicago on September 24, 1963, Miss West had received a 15-minuter telephone call from an 'investigator' working for New Orleans Mafia boss, Carlos Marcello. The man who placed that call to Chicago, to this person who was with Jack Ruby on the eve of the assassination, was the staunch anti-Communist, anti-Castro activist who had once been Oswald's CAP squadron leader, the man who only weeks before this call had been with Oswald in Clinton, Louisiana – David Ferrie.

CHAPTER 31
THE ROSETTA STONE

* * *

*Once we know that "protect Jackie" was not his motive for
killing Oswald, our search for his Ruby's motive must at least
consider his mob background and associates. If Ruby was
acting for others, those others had to have a reason to want
Oswald eliminated. As, for example, in the Joe Colombo
assassination and the Victor Reisel blinding - specifically
chosen to be identified and then eliminated.*

The overwhelming and conclusive evidence is that President
John F. Kennedy had at least two sets of bitter enemies within the
US, each of which had the means, motive and opportunity to
assassinate him; and each of which had an unbroken history
demonstrating absolutely no reluctance to the use of force. The
evidence is inescapable that these two groups –organized crime and
anti-Castro Cuba exiles– owed their very existence to their continued
use of violence.

That is not to say that all members of organized crime or all
anti-Castro Cuban exiles were involved in the Kennedy
assassination. No such finding is warranted – or necessary.
However, the proof is that important elements from each group
were involved in very specific planning to murder the President.

Importantly, those very same elements had a common bond,
having been united (to provide their unique services) by the CIA,
some of whose agents secretly continued to encourage their projects
long after being ordered to stop them.

The evidence is, to say the least, abundant that the CIA, and
indeed all of the American intelligence community including the
FBI, routinely utilized what can only be described as a motley group
of people to perform various services for them.

Here in our own little story we find that Congressional investigations have identified the following people to have been involved with American intelligence: Yuri Nosenko, a KGB officer; Richard E. Snyder, consular officer in the US Embassy in Moscow; Dr. Alexis H. Davidson, US Embassy physician in Moscow; George de Mohrenschildt, friend of Oswald; John Rosselli, Mafia; Sam Giancana, Mafia; Santos Trafficante, Mafia; Guy Banister, anti-Castro activist; Sergio Arcacha Smith, anti-Castro activist; amongst others.

Even if one rejects the implication that Oswald was himself an American intelligence agent, it seems unarguable that he was not the loner he has been made out to be, and that he was associated with people who were, at the least, involved on the periphery of American intelligence.

As the Kennedy years proceeded, the Mafia and the anti-Castro activists – who might be forgiven for believing that their CIA activities had earned them the right to be ignored – instead found themselves more and more the primary targets of relentless and unmerciful campaigns instigated and prosecuted by the Kennedy administration.

Given the fact that these were people who truly existed both by and for violence, it should not be surprising that certain elements of these deadly enemies of the President might see assassination as the answer to their problems.

Those who challenge the official findings by questioning whether Oswald pulled the trigger are probably missing the central issue, for even if he did, the more important point is that the evidence also rather strongly indicates that he may have been the designated 'nut', specifically chosen to be identified and then eliminated.

If we eliminate Jack Ruby's alleged reason for killing Oswald (the lawyer-inspired 'protect Jackie'), we are left in our search for his motive with the evidence of Ruby's mob background and associates – that, and our common sense.

Indeed, the question of Ruby's motive may well be the "Rosetta Stone" of the Kennedy assassination, for if Ruby was acting for others, those others had to have a reason to want Oswald eliminated.

SOURCES

SOURCES

Abbreviation

WARREN COMMISSION:

"Warren"   *"Warren" Report of the President's Commission on the Assassination of President John F. Kennedy*, published by the US Government Printing Office (1964).

SENATE SELECT COMMITTEE:

"Interim"   *"Interim" Alleged Assassination Plots Involving Foreign Leaders*, conducted by the Select Committee to Study Governmental Operations with respect to Intelligence Activities, United States Senate, published by the US Government Printing Office (1975).

"JFK"   *"JFK" Investigation of the Assassination of President John F. Kennedy*, conducted by the Senate Select Committee to Study Governmental Operations with Respect to Intelligence Activities, United States Senate, published by the US Government Printing Office (1976).

HOUSE SELECT COMMITTEE:

"HSCA"   *Investigation of the Assassination of President John F. Kennedy*, conducted by the Select Committee on Assassinations of the US House of Representatives, published by the US Government Printing Office (1979).

RECORD REVIEW BOARD:

"ARRB"   *Final Report of the Assassination Records Review Board* (1998) as mandated by the President John F. Kennedy Records Collection Act of 1992, 44 U.S.C. Section 2107 (Supp. V 1994)

NOTES

NOTES

Quotes by Government Officials:
  see: http://www.maryferrell.org/wiki/index.php/
  JFK_Assassination_Quotes_by_Government_Officials

Chapter 1 The Family

  Exchange Alley's character
  HSCA: Vol. IX, pp. 93-94.

  Early life, Marguerite, New York City
  Warren: pp.377-383, 669-679.

Chapter 2 Another Kind of "Family"

  HSCA: Vol. IX, pp. 95-103, 115-17.

Chapter 3 Svengali

  David Ferrie, Civil Air Patrol
  *HSCA:*Vol. IX, pp. 103-15;
        Vol. X pp. 105-8.

  Enlisting in Marines
  Warren: p.384.

Chapter 4 The Chameleon

  Communist Literature, possible motives
  Warren: p.385.

  Civil Air Patrol, David Ferrie Connection
  HSCA: Vol. X, pp. 103-115.

Communist fears
Interim: p. XIII.

Cointelpro
JFK: Book III, pp. 3-19.

I Led Three Lives
*Marguerite Oswald testimony, before
the Warren Commission, Vol. I, p.200.*

Letter to YPSL
Warren: p. 681.

Chapter 5 The Unique Marine

Warren: pp.681-689.
HSCA: Report, pp. 235-237.

Chapter 6 Destination Golub

Defection
Warren: pp. 689-690.
HSCA: Report, pp. 211-12.

Passport
Warren: Vol. XVIII pp.160-171
        (Exhibit # CE 946).

Hotel Torni
Warren: Vol. XXVI p.32
        (Exhibit # CE 2676, 2677).

Chapter 7 Russia

Warren: pp.390-400,655-8, 689-712, 746-7.

KGB surveillance
ARRB: Report p 141, 209.

Chapter 8 The Diary that Wasn't

Oswald's "Historic Diary"
HSCA: Vol. II, pp.372-397;
            Vol. VIII, pp. 223-7, 232-247.

Chapter 9 Yuri Nosenko, KGB Defector

HSCA: Vol. II, pp. 436-87;
            Vol. XII, pp. 475-527.

Chapter 10 Pick Your Polygraph

HSCA: Vol. VIII, p. 187-96.

Chapter 11 Not Worthy of Belief

Mr. D. C.
HSCA: Vol. XII, pp. 571-644.

John Hart
HSCA: Vol. II, pp. 487-536.

Richard Helms.
HSCA: Vol. IV, pp. 1-250.

Chapter 12 A Disinformation Mission?

HSCA, Vol. II, pp. 436-87;
            Vol. XII, pp. 475-527.

Prior Ongoing relationship
HSCA: Vol. IV, p 36-39.

Telegram a fake
HSCA: Vol. II, p 444.

Conclusion that Nosenko lied
and speculation as to why
HSCA: pp. 101-2.

Chapter 13 Who Sent Nosenko?

HSCA, Vol. XII, pp. 475-644.

Harold J. Osborn
HSCA: Vol. IV, p36-39.

Chairman Stokes / Richard Helms.
HSCA: Vol. IV, p. 96.

David Murphy
HSCA: Vol. XII, p.533.

Chapter 14 The Agency

HSCA: Report, p. 196-215.

Minsk plant
HSCA: Report, p.208-209.

Fake U-2 manuals
ARRB: p.113.

Chapter 15 The Aristocratic Spy

Oswald's return
Warren: pp. 713-730.

George de Mohrenschildt
House Select, Vol. XII, pp. 47-69.

Chapter 16 Covert Operations

Covert Action
Interim: pp. xiii, 9-10.

Lumumba
Interim: pp. 13-69.

Trujillo
Interim: pp. 191-215.

Chapter 17 Strange Bedfellows

CIA / Mafia / Cuban Exile plots against Castro
Interim: pp. 71-180;
HSCA: Vol. X, pp. 147-95.

Chapter 18 Castro Retaliation?

CIA Plots Against Castro
HSCA: Vol. X, p. 147-197.

Attorney Edward Morgan
JFK: Vol. V, pp. 80-6.

Joseph Langosch
HSCA: Report, p. 112.

Debut of the Retaliation Theory
HSCA: Vol. X, p.154.

Chapter 19 Anti-Castro Cubans

HSCA: Vol. X, pp. 5-15.

Chapter 20 Kennedy Had Enemies

HSCA: Report, pp. 24-35.

Chapter 21 Enemy #1, The Mob

Organized crime
HSCA: Report pp. 33-34;
    Vol. IX, pp. 6-60.

Hoffa plot
HSCA: Report, pp. 176-7.

Carlos Marcello
HSCA: Vol. IX, pp. 61-92

Chapter 22 Jack Ruby, Mobster

Warren: Appendix XVI, p.802;
HSCA: Report, p. 149-153;
    Vol. IX, p. 802-5.

Chapter 23 Curious Activities

Writing to communist organizations
Warren: 289, 400, 411, 722.

Chapter 24 The FBI and Oswald

Targeting Fair Play for Cuba
JFK: Book III, p. 466-467.

Hoover Report
JFK: Vol. III, p.465-466.

Contacts, FBI / Oswald
HSCA: Report pp.190-196.

Hosty note
*HSCA:*Report, p.195.

Chapter 25 Fact or Fiction

Background for the Warren Commission Investigation: Cuba
and the Intelligence Agencies
JFK: Book V: p.9 - 22.

Carlos Bringuier
Warren: p.728-729.

Bringuier testimony (excerpts):

Warren: Vol. X, p.34-38.

Quigley visit

Warren: p.194;
HSCA: Report, p.191.

Alba
HSCA: Report, pp. 193-194.

"False Flags" / Operation Northwoods / Operation Mongoose
ARRB:

Agency: Army
Record Number: 198-10004-10020
Califano Papers, Box 6, Folder 7. Package of \ proposed actions
to be used against Cuban \ regime to oust Castro and potential
reaction to \ US involvement.

Agency: JCS
Record Number: 202-10002-10104
U.S. Military Intervention in Cuba;
Contingency Planning, Cuba; Operation
Mongoose; Uprising in Cuba; Covert Operations, Cuba; Soviet
Base in Cuba; Caribbean Security; Patrol Posts; Invasion of
Cuba; Justification for U.S. Military Intervention.

Chapter 26 The Return of Svengali

David Ferrie
HSCA: Vol. X, pp. 105-22.

544 Camp Street
HSCA: Vol. X, p123-127.

Clinton sightings
HSCA: Report pp. 142-143.

FBI / voting rights
JFK: Hearings Nov-Dec 1975;
    Vol. 6, pp. 888, 906, 954-955.

"Racial Matters"
JFK: Hearings Nov-Dec 1975;
    Vol. 6, p. 697 (exhibit 64-3).

Library card
HSCA: Vol. X, p. 113-114.

Chapter 27 Closet Anti-Communist?

Veciana
HSCA: Vol. X, pp. 37-56,
ARRB: p.103.

Odio
HSCA: Vol. X, p. 19-35.

Gaudet
HSCA: Vol. X, p. 218-219.

Chapter 28 He Is Going To Get Hit

Marcello
HSCA: Report, p. 171-172;
　　　Vol. IX, pp. 75-6.

Aleman
HSCA: Report, p. 173-174.

Milteer / Somersett
HSCA: Report, p. 232-233;
　　　Vol. III, p. 450;
See also:
Church Committee,
　　　Boxed Files p. 106.

Echevarria
HSCA: Report, p. 236-237.

Bosch
HSCA: Vol. X, pp. 89-91.

Rose Cheramie
HSCA: Vol. X, p. 197-205.

Chapter 29 The Motorcade

Warren: p.28-46;
HSCA: Vol. XI, p. 505-537.

Chapter 30 The Assassin's Assassin

Oswald / Tippit
Warren: p. 165, 253.

Ruby and Oswald
HSCA: Report, pp. 148-9.

Ruby / Cook / Tippit
HSCA: Vol. XII, pp. 41-2.

Ruby polygraph
HSCA: Vol. VIII, pp. 217-8.

Ruby's telephone calls
HSCA: Vol. IX, pp. 188-96.

Police headquarters
HSCA: Vol. IX, p.127-32.

About The Author
JAMES R DUFFY

* * *

One of the preeminent trial attorneys in the nation, James R. Duffy is the senior trial partner at Duffy & Duffy. Recognized by both The Best Lawyers in America and Who's Who in America, Mr. Duffy is extremely active in championing the rights of injured persons and advancing their cause. He is a Founding Member of the New York Academy of Trial Lawyers and is a member of The American Trial Lawyers Association. Mr. Duffy has lectured and been interviewed throughout the United States and Great Britain as an expert on the mysterious and largely unknown background of Lee Harvey Oswald.

You can contact Mr. Duffy via email at xxexam@aol.com, or visit him on the web at http://www.ahitwaitingtohappen.com